Corporate Social Responsibility, Entrepreneurship, and Innovation

Routledge Studies in Business Ethics

Corporate Social Responsibility, Entrepreneurship, and Innovation

Kenneth Amaeshi, Paul Nnodim, and Onyeka Osuji

Routledge
Taylor & Francis Group

NEW YORK AND LONDON

First published 2013
by Routledge
711 Third Avenue, New York, NY 10017

Simultaneously published in the UK
by Routledge
2 Park Square, Milton Park, Abingdon, Oxon OX14 4RN

*Routledge is an imprint of the Taylor & Francis Group,
an informa business*

Library of Congress Cataloging-in-Publication Data

Amaeshi, Kenneth.
Corporate social responsibility, entrepreneurship, and innovation / by Kenneth
    Amaeshi, Paul Nnodim, and Onyeka Osuji.
        p. cm. — (Routledge studies in business ethics ; 6)
    Includes bibliographical references and index.
    1. Social responsibility of business.   2. Corporate governance.
3. Entrepreneurship.   I. Nnodim, Paul.   II. Osuji, Onyeka.   III. Title.
    HD60.A399   2012
    658.4'08—dc23
    2012018742

ISBN: 978-0-415-88079-4 (hbk)
ISBN: 978-0-203-08194-5 (ebk)

Typeset in Sabon
by Apex CoVantage, LLC

For Iheoma, Amanda, and Jeffrey—K.A.
For Nelson Chinonye—P.N.
For Nkiruka and Onyeka—O.O.

Contents

Acknowledgments

We are grateful to the following colleagues at Massachusetts College of Liberal Arts for their critical reviews and comments: Dr. Matthew Silliman, Dr. David K. Johnson, Dr. Graziana Ramsden, Dr. Stan Yake, and Dr. Rita Nnodim. Our gratitude also goes to Dr. Austin Okigbo of Williams College. We are equally thankful to Bryan Acton (TA) for helping organize the bibliography in the proper order.

Introduction

Corporate social responsibility (hereafter, CSR) often features in some business-related discourses as the investigation of the role of business in society. This exploration includes issues such as response to present or anticipated climate change challenges, fair trade, corporate governance, and responsible investment. Despite the popularity of CSR in both business theory and practice, recent developments in the early part of the 21st century continue to challenge the role of business in society and question the efficiency and effectiveness of markets to deliver fair and just societies in the United States and around the world. Prominent among these are the Great Recession of 2008, the Supreme Court's campaign finance ruling (January 2010), the British Petroleum (BP) oil spill in the Gulf of Mexico (April 2010), and the Occupy Wall Street movement (September 2011).

Since 2008, the financial and economic crisis that battered the United States and the world cost millions of people their homes, jobs, and savings. The Great Recession, as it is now commonly referred to, officially ended in 2009, yet the widespread unemployment, fear, and financial insecurity it spawned continue to create pessimism about economic recovery in the United States and to beleaguer international markets. It was by any measure the worst economic and financial downturn in the United States since the Great Depression of the 1930s.

There seems to be some consensus among liberal and conservative economists on the fundamental causes of the Great Recession. The conservative American jurist and economist Richard A. Posner blames excessive deregulation for the crisis: "The movement to deregulate the financial industry went too far by exaggerating the resilience—the self-healing powers—of laissez-faire capitalism" (Posner 2009: xii). However, he does not think that the government alone was responsible for the crisis. He gives the market some degree of culpability by insisting that while the government's "myopia, passivity, and blunders" (Posner 2009: xii) were major players in the crisis, these factors are not enough to "extenuate the market's failure" (Posner 2009: 248). On the liberal side of the analysis, Joseph Stiglitz in *Freefall* (2010) attributes market failures to neoliberal interpretations of the classical economic theories of Adam Smith, David

Ricardo, and others, which eschew regulation while placing undue faith in the self-correcting capacity of unfettered markets and globalization in a time of economic crisis. Stiglitz argues that the financial and economic crisis "has shattered the illusion" of sustained, unregulated economic growth along with accompanying mantras such as "The best government is a small government, and regulation only impedes innovation" (Stiglizt 2010: xi–xii). Paul Krugman, in a *New York Times* article titled "Inflation and Economic Hooliganism," locates the source of the crisis in a widespread and irresponsible "complacency whose main financial manifestation was ever-growing leverage. Bankers and households alike piled on levels of debt that would have been sustainable only if nothing ever went wrong" (Krugman 2011: MM11).

Although corporations induced the financial crisis of 2008, its effects were, nevertheless, borne by society in the form of negative, corporate externalities (see chapter 1 and chapter 4). These externalities include not only deaths and loss of jobs, homes, and livelihood, but also, as in the case of the United States, the government's use of the taxpayers' money to bail out "too big to fail" corporations.

The second illustrative event relevant for our purpose is the US Supreme Court's ruling of January 2010, which barred the government from restricting corporations and unions from spending their general funds in support of, or in opposition to, the candidacy of an individual seeking political office. Justice Kennedy, representing the conservative wing of the Supreme Court, argued that the existing law censored corporations and violated the First Amendment. In his judgment, since for-profit business organizations are "persons" who share the same right to freedom of expression as individual citizens, the state has no business regulating the political "speech" of corporations (Liptak 2010: A1).This ruling, which gives corporations and unions enormous power to finance US elections, especially through their surrogates or the so-called Super PACs (political action committees), could very possibly be the dominant influence with regard to the outcome of the 2012 US presidential election. The Supreme Court's campaign finance ruling could lead to an overreaching of corporate power. For this reason, Justice Stevens argued dissentingly that the Supreme Court's ruling "threatens to undermine the integrity of elected institutions across the nation" (Vogel 2010: 1).

President Obama, for his part, denounced the ruling in strong terms as "a major victory for big oil, Wall Street Banks, health insurance companies and the other powerful interests that marshal their power every day in Washington to drown out the voices of everyday Americans" (Vogel 2010: 1) The ruling invalidated two previous decisions by the court—namely, a 1990 law that allowed the government to hinder corporations and unions from spending general treasury funds on advertisements in support of or against a candidate's election, and the McCain-Feingold act of 2003, which upheld restrictions on independent corporate expenditures (Vogel 2010: 1).

In spite of this ruling, it is important to note that the trade unions, unlike corporations, have been severely weakened in the United States in recent times in the context of global market liberalization, outsourcing, and the race to the bottom. Underlying the discontent over the Supreme Court's campaign finance ruling is the discourse about the proper role of the modern corporation in society and its responsibility toward stakeholders, especially in a globalized world fraught with the challenges of the transnational governance void. Chapters 2 and 4 discuss corporations from both the perspectives of conventional, neoclassical economics and the stakeholder theory.

A third occasion for serious reflection is the BP oil spill in the Gulf of Mexico, which resulted from the explosion of the Deepwater Horizon oil rig, operating on the Macondo exploration well for BP on April 20, 2010. The spill released an estimated 206 million gallons (4.9 million barrels) of oil into the environment between April 20 and July of 2010 (Burdeau 2011: 1). Surpassing the Exxon Valdez oil spill of 1989 in Alaska by about 20 times, BP's Deepwater Horizon disaster is by far the worst maritime oil spill in the history of the United States. The explosion of the oil rig claimed 11 lives, destroyed marine and wild life, and seriously disrupted people's livelihoods in the tourist and fishing communities of the Gulf States—Alabama, Florida, Louisiana, and Mississippi. President Obama marshaled the Coast Guard to contain and clean up the mess with the help of BP.

At the end, the US Interior Department cited BP and two of its partners—Transocean (the Swiss owner and operator of the oil rig) and Halliburton (a US energy services firm) for having failed to operate the Deepwater Horizon rig in a safe and responsible manner, for endangering the lives of their workers, and for failing to follow proper control procedures and maintain safety (Broder 2011: A18). BP in turn traded blame with its contractors Halliburton and Transocean for the spill. It accused Halliburton of destroying evidence that could prove the firm operated fraudulently by using a thin "foamy cement slurry" that ultimately failed to cap the deepwater well properly. Halliburton denied the accusation (Burdeau 2011: 1). On January 2, 2012, BP announced that it would be seeking at least $20 billion in damages from Halliburton and Transocean for the cost of the spill and the cleanup. BP eventually filed a suit with the US district court in New Orleans against Halliburton. Halliburton for its part sued BP (Bergin and Roumeliotis 2012: 1).

This blame game among BP, Halliburton, and Transocean points to the difficulty of assigning accountability not only in relation to the supply chains and services of multinational corporations, but also to the problem of accountability in the context of global networks of production (see chapter 7). With some of these events as the backdrop, this text examines the responsible use of power in the supply chains of larger and more powerful corporations, which leads to issues of accountability and liability in supply chains management. In the capitalist world order, multinational corporations struggle to deal with the challenges posed by the global reach of their supply chains and the possible irresponsible practices that take place within the companies on these supply chains. Pressure is then exerted on these multinational corporations to protect their brands, even if doing so entails that these large corporations assume responsibility for the practices of their suppliers. However, we also recognize the fact that multinational corporations sometimes apply enormous negative pressure on small- and medium-sized firms on their supply chain to meet the demand of consumers, thus reducing the profit margins of these companies. As a result, manufacturers or enterprises on the supply chains of large corporations tend to violate labor rights and safety regulations and exploit the low-waged labor force. Moral appeals in some of these cases from multinational corporations become mere public image campaigns, rather than the practice of CSR principles.

Notwithstanding its popularity, CSR remains largely vague. Drawing from the examples here, we argue that CSR is essentially a self-governance mechanism. By considering CSR as a self-governance mechanism, this book examines the intricate relationship between powerful corporations and smaller firms on their supply chains. It investigates the moral and legal underpinnings of the concept of responsibility. We identify the use of power as a critical factor to be considered in allocating responsibility in firm–supplier relationships. We suggest that the more powerful party in the firm–supplier relationship has the responsibility to exert some moral influence on the weaker party. We highlight the use of codes of conduct, corporate culture, personnel training, and value reorientation as possible sources of wielding positive moral influence along the supply chains.

Furthermore, multinational corporations in developing countries, such as Shell in Nigeria or Texaco in Ecuador, occasionally pollute the natural environment of their host countries, though usually too little attention is given to such incidents when compared to the dramatic public exposure with which the US and international media spotlighted the Gulf of Mexico oil spill of 2010. For instance, as recently as December 20, 2011, Shell spilled about 40,000 barrels of oil in the Niger Delta. The spill, considered by environmentalist groups as one of the worst off the coast of Nigeria in 10 years, happened just four months after the United Nations Environment Programme issued a report (UNEP 2011) indicting Shell for contributing to 50 years of environmental degradation and pollution in the region of the Niger Delta. According to the UN report, a cleanup in Ogoniland, which constitutes one small part of the Niger Delta region, could take 30 years and cost $1 billion (Vidal 2011: 1). The Shell incident in the Niger Delta raises questions about the business practices of multinational corporations in both developed and developing countries—questions that this study considers (see chapters 3 and 6).

Exploring the roles and purposes of corporations in the global world order is one of the theoretical and practical challenges that business scholars face, especially given the governance void at the transnational level. This governance void is so apparent, especially in developing countries, that sometimes corporations assume the roles of the state in order to fulfill minimum international standards of operation. Multinational corporations obviously face some tough moral challenges when they operate in societies with different ethical, political, and economic expectations. How CSR shapes the business practices of multinational corporations in the developed economies of the West, in contrast to the activities of the same transnational firms in developing countries, is one of the core issues this book examines.

The fourth key event that helped shape our approach to the study of CSR is the ongoing grassroots movement known as Occupy Wall Street (OWS). It is a protest movement that began on September 2011. The OWS movement has no centralized theme, no leader, no well-set-out agenda. It is made up of heterogeneous groups of individuals and organizations. However, it has a potent slogan—"We are the 99%"—which draws attention to the steep economic disparity between the wealthiest 1% of Americans and the 99% others. The symbolism of 99% is powerful, though the figure may be inaccurate and misleading. The group, which began to occupy Zuccotti Park in New York City's Wall Street district with dozens of people on September 17, 2011, has seen the number of its adherents burgeoning across the United States, Canada, and other regions of the world. Most of the protesters want the government and society as a whole to curb corporate interest in politics and to reduce or eliminate corporate greed. Some want jobs. Others protest the huge income gap between the rich few and the rest of the citizens and greed on Wall Street. OWS is not aligned with any political party, as demonstrated by episodes of civil disobedience against both President Obama, a Democrat, in New Hampshire (November 22, 2011), and Republican presidential candidate Michelle Bachman in South Carolina (November 10, 2011). The emergence of the OWS movement seems to indicate a change in people's expectations about the role of corporations in society, which bears on certain questions of social justice. As a result, this text also studies the philosophical foundations of CSR as a form of social justice (see chapter 8). It reinforces the perspective that corporations are both social institutions and economic actors. From the positioning of firms as social institutions, the book establishes CSR as a form of justice. In this sense, adherence to CSR principles or guidelines by corporations will become the legitimate expectation of citizens of any well-ordered society, rather than a mere act of charity. To realize this goal, we employ a contractarian approach in our study of justice. This will enable us to demonstrate that corporations and economic markets are socially shared institutions operating within the conceptual framework of a society that might then be increasingly seen as a fair system of cooperation over generations. In such a developed human society, members engage in the process of reciprocity of perspectives by granting one another a fair share in the distribution of the benefits and burdens of social and economic cooperation.

By appropriating a neo-Kantian, contractarian conception of justice, as modeled by John Rawls, we explore conditions under which rational individuals would obligate themselves to upholding cooperative institutions that are mutually advantageous to all members of their society and thus find a moral basis for the public justification of their social, political, and economic institutions. In so doing, we favor a deontological understanding of moral responsibility over teleological or consequentialist variations. We reject the teleological notion of responsibility found in utilitarian conceptions of justice because, we believe, it serves as the foundational principle employed by anti-CSR proponents to vindicate social, economic, and institutional inequalities inherent in present-day capitalism.

As the private governance of corporate externalities, we view CSR as a change-management project (albeit at the scale of system transformation) with far-reaching implications for markets, business practice, and entrepreneurship (chapter 5). Moreover, we hope this conception of CSR provides a new paradigm for translating knowledge into action and offering reflective managers an alternative philosophical framework in which to express their corporate strategies and decisions. The long-term goal of the CSR movement, as we see it in this book, is to reform capitalism from within by encouraging and providing examples of new approaches to business, where the maximization of profit by corporations does not automatically override other ethical and social obligations.

1 Corporate Social Responsibility
Definitions and Meanings

Corporate social responsibility (CSR) has become a global phenomenon in both private and public sectors. In spite of its growing popularity in recent times, CSR remains a multifaceted and contested concept. At conferences on CSR, participants often take its meaning for granted. They freely talk about *it*, as if *it* had a homogenous significance. There are nearly as many definitions of CSR as there are writers in the field, leaving the construct nebulous (van Marrewijk 2003; Gobbels 2002; and Henderson 2001) and open to conflicting interpretations (Windsor 2001). This makes one wonder how actors in this field cope with such diversity of meanings and interpretations. Some scholars prefer to call it "corporate responsibility," others "corporate citizenship." It also figures under the names "corporate sustainability," "corporate sustainability and responsibility," and so forth. Nonetheless, "corporate social responsibility" is the term predominantly employed by most business scholars and professionals (see Table 1.1).

Amidst these different ideas, the European Union (EU) offers what appears to be a leading definition of CSR, which is "a concept whereby companies integrate social and environmental concerns in their business operations and in their interaction with their stakeholders on a voluntary basis as they are increasingly aware that responsible behavior leads to sustainable business success" (European Commission 2002).[1] When articulated from a managerial standpoint, this definition calls for corporations to be ethical and promote the virtues of good corporate citizenship, as well as obey the law while striving to make profit (Carroll 1991: 42).

As the CSR movement broadens its appeal among ordinary citizens in capitalist society, CSR also transcends its original definitional boundaries as corporate philanthropy and assumes the form of justice. Consequently, capitalist market structures tend to challenge the meaning of CSR as a distinct economic philosophy while undermining its significance as a business practice. Nonetheless, we see CSR as an integral part of the capitalist system and, as such, consider the governance of corporate externalities (i.e., positive and negative effects of corporations on society and the environment) as the central theme of the CSR discourse and practice. In this sense, CSR becomes the active and voluntary participation of firms in the governance of

Table 1.1   Multiple Interpretations of CSR

Interpretations	Authors
Business ethics and morality	Stark 1993; Fulop, Hisrich, and Szegedi 2000; Freeman 1994; Bowie 1998; Phillips 1997, 2003; Phillips and Margolis 1999
Corporate accountability	Owen, Swift, Humphrey, and Bowerman 2000; O'Dwyer 2005
Corporate citizenship	Carroll 2004; Matten and Crane 2005; Andriof and Waddock 2002
Corporate giving and philanthropy	Carroll 1991, 2004
Corporate greening and green marketing	Hussain 1999; Saha and Darnton 2005; Crane 2000
Diversity management	Kamp and Hagedorn-Rasmussen 2004
Environmental responsibility	DesJardins 1998; Rugman and Verbeke 1998
Human rights	Cassel 2001; Welford 2002
Responsible buying and supply chain management	Drumwright 1994; Emmelhainz and Adams 1999; Graafland 2002; Spekman, Werhane, and Boyd 2005; Amaeshi 2004
Social responsible investment	Warhurst 2001; Jayne and Skerratt 2003; Synnestvedt and Aslaksen 2003; McLaren 2004
Stakeholder engagement	Freeman 1984, 1994; Andriof et al. 2002; Donaldson and Preston 1995
Sustainability	Bansal 2005; Amaeshi and Crane 2006; Korhonen 2002

Source: Culled from Amaeshi and Adi (2007).

corporate-induced externalities—a field that until now only the state regulated with oftentimes coercive machinery. The involvement of corporations in the governance of corporate externalities opens a new discursive space that previously was either nonexistent or suppressed. At first glance, this view of CSR may appear to run roughshod over the foundational principles of neoclassical economics and its conceptualization of the firm within the marketplace, which makes it all the more difficult for the conventional economist to articulate CSR within the existing theoretical frameworks.

CSR defined as a form of organizational behavior (among other definitions) in contemporary society signals the constant collision of the private and public spheres in the governance of corporate externalities. CSR, thus, presents an arena for contestations. Corporations enter the private governance space with different motives in the background. Some enter this space willingly or are coerced into it by social or economic factors, while others "sleep-walk" into the space in the form of institutional mimicry and isomorphism (DiMaggio and Powell 1983). Corporations that enter the private governance space readily may articulate their actions from the standpoint of diverse normative or instrumental reasons. Some firms voluntarily engage in self-governance because they sincerely believe that it is the right thing to do, while others enter the space for some instrumental or strategic reasons. Such strategic reasons may include reputational gains, sustainable innovation, risk minimization, employee or customer attraction and retention, and other advantages or incentives that CSR practice may offer to the bottom line. For some corporations, however, coercion from local communities and nongovernmental organizations (NGOs), pressure mounted by competitors, or even threats from local or international regulators may be the compelling reason to engage in the private governance of externalities. For these entrants, it is all about meeting the minimum requirements to assuage the demands of pressure groups and to remain competitive.

CSR puzzles many business scholars and political economists because it appears to run contrary to the idea of the firm as an entity built for the satisfaction of private interests and the maximization of profit. However, this dominant view of the firm is beginning to abate in today's society where many citizens see corporations (especially large corporations) as part of the basic structure of the society. Accordingly, corporations are no longer exclusively for-private organizations, but function also inclusively as social institutions. The question of social responsibility in relation to firms is, therefore, at the root of the new theory of corporate citizenship, according to which corporate citizens share the burdens and benefits of social cooperation (Crane, Matten, and Moon 2008).

Thus, the CSR movement necessitates a recast of the traditional theory of the firm. The emergent theory of the firm will draw from established disciplines such as economics, sociology, psychology, anthropology, philosophy, political science, and law to address the realities of the increasingly interdependent world, as well as to come to terms with the demands of contemporary society—a society that many citizens now consider as a system of cooperation over generations.

At the very heart of modern firms lies entrepreneurship—that is, the ability to identify and enact business opportunities primarily for private benefits in the form of profit maximization or the maximization of certain utilities. This particular notion of entrepreneurship gained legitimacy over time through a narrow interpretation of some neoclassical economic maxims, such as that of Adam Smith (1976)—"It is not from the benevolence of the butcher, the brewer, or the baker that we expect our dinner, but from their regard to their own self-interest"—and a more radical position attributed to Milton Friedman (1962): the "business of business is business."

Although the positions of Smith and Friedman on entrepreneurship seem prima facie reasonable, their in-depth analysis reveals some underlying distortions. In the case of Adam Smith, the butcher maxim reflects his defense of the free market and the presumed positive externalities that accrue to society in a free market economy, as well as the motive for profit in business rooted in self-interest. The essence of Smith's maxim is that the pursuit of self-interest in a free market economy has some substantial benefits to the larger society. For example, in order to maximize his or her own interest, the butcher must contribute to the welfare (interests) of his or her customers, who are members of the society. The butcher can do this by perfecting the art of butchery, as well as by providing quality products and services to his/ her customers. In this way, specialization engendered by self-interest maximizes the overall good of society. For Smith, there is an "invisible hand" in the free market that directs self-interest toward the common good (Donaldson 1982: 62–65).

However, the history of domestic and global economic activities over a quarter century demonstrates that the cliché[2] based on Smith's metaphor of the invisible hand is fundamentally flawed. In a piece published by the *New Statesman* in 2008, Joseph Stiglitz, discussing the global economic crisis, describes Adam Smith's invisible hand as an illusion:

> This crisis is a turning point, not only in the economy, but in our thinking about economics. Adam Smith, the father of modern economists, argued that the pursuit of self-interest (profit-making by competitive firms) would lead, as if by an invisible hand, to general well-being. But for over a quarter of a century, we have known that Smith's conclusions do not hold when there is imperfect information—and all markets, especially financial markets, are characterised by information imperfections. The reason the invisible hand often seems invisible is that it is not there. The pursuit of self-interest by Enron and WorldCom did not lead to societal well-being; and the pursuit of self-interest by those in the financial industry has brought our economy to the brink of the abyss. No modern economy can function well without the government playing an important role. Even free marketers are now turning to the government. But would it not have been better to have taken action to prevent this meltdown? This is a new kind of public-private partnership—the financial sector walked off with the profits, the public was left with the losses. We need a new balance between market and government. (Stiglitz 2008: 1)

Friedman's more radical approach to entrepreneurship, which is an offshoot of Adam Smith's position, limits the scope of corporate affairs. Corporations exist primarily for the sake of doing business, and every business should be geared toward profit maximization. In line with Smith, Friedman assumes that when corporations pursue profit maximization through specialization and the development of efficient business strategies, there is a trickle-down effect on the larger society in the form of social benefits. For Friedman, corporations are ill equipped to take on social roles because social responsibility is not within the special scope of businessmen and businesswomen:

> It shows a fundamental misconception of the character and nature of a free economy. In such an economy, there is one and only one social responsibility of business—to use its resources and engage in activities designed to increase its profits so long as it stays within the rules of the game, which is to say, engages in open and free competition, without deception or fraud. (Friedman 1962: 133; Donaldson 1982: 68)

According to this view, when corporations begin to practice social responsibility, they step outside their field of specialization into the domain reserved for the government or other public agencies. Friedman considers such a behavior an infringement on the economic freedom of citizens to pursue profit: to buy and sell freely (Donaldson 1982: 69). Such an unnecessary infringement produces a disastrous business environment for firms. Therefore, Friedman argues that corporations should engage only in what they do best: the pursuit of self-interests and the attendant profit maximization, while leaving social responsibility issues to the government or other public agencies: "Are corporate officials . . . good judges of what the social interest is? They are not, and they should not be. Understanding social welfare lies beyond their specialized area of competence and should be left to those whose specialty it is: government officials" (Donaldson 1982: 69).

The underlying assumption behind Friedman's position is the existence of a robust institutional context, that is, an enabling economic environment that prompts the effective and efficient use of available tools to align corporate, private benefits to social benefits (Heal 2005). But Friedman's assertion does not necessarily factor in situations where such institutional mechanisms are either not in place or are weak. This implies that some corporations may not fully internalize the costs associated with their entrepreneurial activities in society.

In the business literature, entrepreneurial costs of production include private costs, such as inventories, price of raw materials, labor, capital, and other input factors borne by the entrepreneur, and external costs, such as pollution arising from the entrepreneur's production process, public health hazards, and human rights infringements arising in the course of enacting entrepreneurship, which are borne by the society. The external costs are often neglected in the measurement of an entrepreneur's performance. Focusing only on the private costs in accounting for entrepreneurial profitability not only distorts the true cost of entrepreneurship in the market, but may as well give rise to free riding.[3] While this approach to accounting may suggest the efficient use of private resources, it tends to undermine social efficiency. We see today's firm as a means of economic coordination, which ought to embody a mechanism for enhancing both market efficiency and overall social efficiency when properly managed. In this sense, CSR is compatible with the modern understanding of entrepreneurship. The CSR movement is not antiprofit, but rather insists that the maximization of profit by firms must not override the basic obligations they owe society.

CSR, as we know it, is still struggling to become an economic theory in isolation from the traditional disciplines that ground the understanding of firms and their behaviors in good theories. Many CSR proponents, regrettably, offer emotive arguments in favor of the concept in an attempt to build a religion out of the movement, instead of presenting valid and sound arguments that could aid ongoing, legitimate efforts to position CSR as a viable business practice. The CSR agenda ought to emphasize the need for organizations to enhance their positive impacts on society, even as they reduce their negative impacts. Although the CSR movement is a new movement in nomenclature, some of its aspirations are not quite new. While the role of business in society is an old debate, the vigor, intensity, and prevalence of CSR discourse in the contemporary scheme of things are new, especially in the face of the recent global financial crisis. One of the early effects of this crisis, which is yet to run its full course with hard-to-forecast consequences, is the redirection of attention to capitalism as an economic system. Is capitalism destroying itself from within? Ought economic policies to be measured independent of their effects on the well-being of the community?

These questions draw attention to welfare economics, a branch of economics marginalized by the capitalist system. Welfare economics poses deep philosophical questions about the outcomes of economic thoughts and methods, as well as the nature of equity and equality embedded in the principles of economic efficiency. It also raises red flags about issues of marginalization, class differences, and social costs and benefits that could arise in the course of the pursuit of economic efficiency. In other words, the realization of economic efficiency does not necessarily guarantee or maximize social welfare. The quest for economic efficiency comes with social costs and benefits: negative and positive externalities. The overall welfare of society is a good in itself that the forebears of modern economics sought to achieve. Today, this good does not figure among the top interests of most business practitioners, who in their seemingly unbridled quest for self-interest and private gains employ *privatized morality*. The goal of welfare economics is to enhance positive externalities and minimize negative externalities.

CSR as the private governance of externalities is the quintessential moral core of economics. It redefines and advances economics as a discipline by drawing it back to its ethical root. Neoclassical economics accords priority to the mathematization of the real and the measurable, while relegating ethical matters to the background. Although mathematics is a useful analytical tool, it is easily susceptible to the hubris of intellectualism and the amoralization of reason interpreted as rational self-interest. This approach to economics undermines the pursuit of the common good because the amoral individual is unreasonable: "The amoral man, however rational he may be (in agent-centered terms), is unreasonable just because he is not convinced or moved by any considerations except those that best promote his antecedent ends" (Freeman 2007: 25).

The capitalist paradigm of profit maximization, deregulation, and moral disinterest in the free market, which according to many economists brings about a favorable outcome to the larger society, has, rather, led to major market failures, namely widespread class struggles, inequality, poverty, trade imbalances, and so forth. CSR as an economic philosophy encourages responsible business practices among firms from a self-regulatory or private dimension. In so doing, it reforms capitalism from within. This understanding of CSR as a metacapitalist approach to business makes it a grand-scale, change project with features that often run parallel to the flawed capitalist system it seeks to transform. We highlight some of these differences in Table 1.2.

As the table portrays, CSR presents a new economic paradigm that alters corporate design and structure so as to enable corporations to promote moral behavior from the inside, rather than merely obeying rules established by "alien" authorities. Corporate behavior, we argue, is not only determined by market structures and market forces, but also by changes in organizational structure and design.[4]

Table 1.2 Different Underpinning Philosophical Paradigms between Conventional Capitalism and the CSR Agenda

	Capitalism	CSR Agenda
Motivation/drive	Self-interest	Collective/communal interests
Goal orientation	Profit	Social welfare
Process	Efficiency	Equity/fairness
Guide	Rationality (logic)	Empathic rationality
Performance criterion	Shareholder value	Externalities (impacts)
Nature of firms	Private institutions	Social institutions
Governance of firms	Contractual (legal entity concept)	Networked governance
Dominant strategy	Competing with strife	Competing responsibly
Dominant operational time horizon	Short-term	Long-term

Though CSR is a movement that seeks to address shortfalls in the runaway capitalist system, it is, nevertheless, not unitary in nature. On the contrary, one can rightly call CSR a very broad church. Within this church, there are *iconoclasts* (those who would prefer to dismantle the current capitalist system); *reformers* (those who want to drive change from within the current capitalist system); *revelers* (those who celebrate the movement as an aspiration and a satisfaction in itself, even if it doesn't change anything in the end); and *critics* (those who believe that it is a distraction, after all).

Over the years, the CSR movement has leveraged strife and antagonism to sustain itself. Although pulled in different directions by the different interest groups and actors, it has gained currency and relevance anyway. It is also able to sustain itself through its fluidity. The understanding of CSR as responsible business practices gives it the leeway to appropriate and reconstitute its content as it journeys into the future. This is a very powerful attribute of CSR, which may not be readily available to other management fads and fashions of the same scale and contemporariness. For example, the CSR agenda now includes climate change, binge drinking, and obesity debates.

While the fluidity of CSR confers on it some sort of strength and resilience, it nonetheless carries with it some managerial challenges. Quite often, managers struggle to fit the requirements of the CSR agenda into the conventional capitalist paradigm mainly because its foundational principles or underpinning philosophies are not clear and distinct yet. Hence, many business managers often look for a CSR business case that provides some competitive advantage to their organization or search for the link between their CSR agenda and corporate performance (Orlitzky, Schmidt, and Rynes 2003). Sometimes business managers do not get the answers they seek; at other times, they rationalize their findings with the hope that the answers they are searching for lie in the long-term sustainability of the business. While accepting the possible truism in the long-term rationalization rhetoric, business managers often miss a crucial point about the CSR movement: that it can draw its support from certain philosophical principles that may be antithetical to the current capitalist system.

CSR, as a change project, needs to win the hearts and minds of its target actors and interest groups, who may be already versed and neck-deep in the current system. One way to do this is through education and training, which, we hope, will prepare the ground for sowing the seeds of economic reformation. A reformed capitalist system will require a new or modified paradigm. If not, the CSR movement runs the risk, in a figurative sense, of filling old jars with new wine.

In summary, fostering CSR culture in organizations, therefore, entails an understanding of the divergent philosophical principles underlying the current capitalist system and the new mode of economic coordination propagated by the CSR movement. It needs to take these differences seriously and explore the implications they would have for such important things as leadership, organizational success and performance, corporate governance, organizational structure, vision and strategy, business operations in different localities, and so on, if CSR as a business practice in organizations is to be fully realized. The main goal of the CSR movement, as we present it in this book, is to reform capitalism from within by envisioning a new approach to business, where the maximization of profit by corporations takes into account social and moral obligations firms have toward the larger society.

2 Corporate Social Responsibility as Stakeholder Orientation to Management

It would not be inappropriate for someone to claim that the contemporary corporate social responsibility movement is essentially a "stakeholder movement" because the stakeholder approach is central to both CSR discourse and practice. In fact, it is CSR-related questions that animate the discourse on the stakeholder ethos as they continuously draw attention to multiple actors and nexuses of relational networks that accentuate the complex nature of the modern firm or corporation. The complex network of relations that a business organization could subscribe to is not limited to customers, employees, local communities, investors, the media, competition, pressure groups, and the society at large, but rather has come to encompass inanimate entities such as the natural environment and ecology. The argument is that these networks could affect or be affected by the activities of the firm (Rowley 1997). On this account, CSR is an organization's commitment to operate in an economically and environmentally sustainable manner while recognizing the interests of its stakeholders.[1]

The stakeholder view of organizing and managing firms is one of the major management paradigm shifts in the late last century. The theory, in its present form, is attributed to Freeman (1984: 246), who defines stakeholders as "those groups and individuals who can affect, or are affected by the achievement of an organization's purpose." In addition, Freeman offers a more instrumental definition of stakeholders in a more recent publication. He sees them as "those groups who are vital to the survival and success of the corporation" (Freeman 2004: 58). The use of the term *stakeholder* in an economic sense can be traced to the works of the Stanford Research Institute (now SRI) in the 1960s (Freeman 1984; Slinger 1999; Freeman and McVea 2001). It was then used as a metaphor to encourage an inclusive management approach, which had to take into consideration the many diverse issues in the turbulent business environments. From the start, the stakeholder approach grew out of management practice (Freeman and McVea 2001: 190) to such areas as corporate planning, systems theory, organizational theory, and eventually CSR. In the early 1980s, Edward Freeman—in his classic, *Strategic Management: A Stakeholder Approach*—articulated the stakeholder approach as a framework for strategic management (Freeman and McVea 2001). And, since then, the concept assumed a conventional status in management scholarship and in managerial practice (Mitchell, Agle, and Wood 1997).

Nonetheless, the term *stakeholder* lends itself easily to multiple applications in support of "fashionable constructs" within the general trend of economic thought or Zeitgeist. For example, it features in such combinations as stakeholder society (Ackerman and Alstott 1999), stakeholder capitalism (Kelly, Kelly, and Gamble 1997; Jones 1999), stakeholder corporation (Kay 1997), and so forth, which makes any attempt to provide a succinct definition of stakeholding problematic. On the other hand, many business scholars tend to circumvent this problem by defining stakeholders in ways they consider most relevant to the term itself—namely, by the nature of the "stakes" stakeholders "hold" (for details see Mitchell, Agle, and Wood 1997: 858).

The meaning of the term *stakeholder* in management literature ranges from broad (inclusive definitions) to narrow views of the firm's environment. Carroll (1993: 22) notes that the narrow view of stakeholding refers to those "individuals or groups with which business interacts who have a 'stake,' or vested interest, in the firm." These may include employees, shareholders, management, government, society, and so forth, as long as they have explicit stakes or vested interests in the firm. The broad view of stakeholding goes beyond the narrow view to comprise those stakeholders who could affect or be affected by the activities of the firm (Starik 1994, 1995). Starik (1994: 92), for instance, suggests that these stakeholders could be "any naturally occurring entity which affects or is affected by organizational performance." Hence, the broad view of stakeholding goes beyond the interests of humans and takes into consideration animals, the natural environment, and ecology. By extension, the broad view, as some scholars express in sustainable development discourse, may encompass futuristic groups such as "unborn generations" (Friedman and Miles 2006).

Furthermore, the stakes and vested interests associated with stakeholding can be categorized into primary and secondary stakeholding. Primary stakeholding involves fiduciary obligations from the firm, while secondary stakeholding does not involve such obligations. In this regard, examples of primary stakeholders will include shareholders, employees, and managers, while those of secondary stakeholders might be local communities, environmental groups, suppliers, and so on. This notion of fiduciary and nonfiduciary stakeholding underpins most of the existing corporate governance frameworks and typologies (Aguilera 2005; Aguilera and Jackson 2003; Slinger 1999). Commenting on this from a comparative governance perspective, Aguilera and Jackson (2003: 454) wrote:

> The corporate governance literature largely neglects employees.... This omission partly reflects weak employee participation in the United States relative to that in economies such as Germany or Japan, where labor

participation is politically important and often a source of competitive advantage. . . . In addition, a major assumption of agency theorists is that shareholders are the only bearers of ex post residual risk, and, thus, employee interests are treated only as an exogenous parameter.

In addition, the understanding that stakeholders have intrinsic value and that managers have a moral duty to be responsible to a variety of stakeholders (Donaldson and Preston 1995; Evan and Freeman 1988; Freeman and Evan 1990) is the basis for some inclusive definitions of stakeholding. More narrow, strategic, or instrumental perspectives (Donaldson and Preston 1995), on the other hand, define stakeholders as those groups or individuals who are in a mutually dependent, risk-based, or exchange relationship with a firm (e.g., Clarkson 1995; Mitchell et al. 1997). This alternation between the narrow and broad interpretations often leads to multiple views and practices of stakeholding in management literature—especially as highlighted by Donaldson and Preston (1995). One of Donaldson and Preston's major contributions to the stakeholder theory in management studies is identifying that in the business literature, scholars largely theorize the stakeholder concept from three main perspectives: (a) descriptive, (b) instrumental, and (c) normative.

The descriptive aspect of the stakeholder theory, as the name suggests, merely describes what the corporation is—"a constellation of co-operative and competitive interests possessing intrinsic value" (Donaldson and Preston 1995: 66)—as well as who the possible stakeholders are. This aspect also highlights the interaction between firms and their stakeholders with the aim of contributing to knowledge, theory, and practice. Its goal is to show that theory corresponds to observed reality. It is neither judgmental nor prescriptive. However, it is difficult to claim that it is value neutral, as research and researchers are often and even inadvertently value laden and value driven (Darke, Shanks, and Broadbent 1998; Appadurai 1999; Hardy, Phillips, and Clegg 2001; Ritchie and Lewis 2003; Johnson and Onwuegbuzie 2004).

The instrumentalist perspective of stakeholding examines the consequences of corporate stakeholding. It is based on the view that meeting stakeholder needs could be driven by some strategic goals and objectives (Jones, Felps, and Bigley 2007). According to Jones and colleagues, "instrumentalist firms place preeminent value on the pursuit of corporate self-interest with *guile*. Other terms used to convey this orientation are *enlightened self-interest, pragmatic morality,* and *strategic morality*" (2007: 152). The instrumentalist form of stakeholder relationship does not necessarily give voice to stakeholders; it is usually characterized by a one-way communication and unequal balance of power (Crane and Livesey 2003). A more critical view suggests that it is not genuine. It is selfish, and firms engage in it because "it makes good business sense . . . [and] . . . helps companies to mitigate risk, protect corporate brand, and gain competitive advantage" (Deloitte Touche Tohmatsu 2002: 2, cited in Brown and Fraser 2006). From a neutral stance, it resonates with the language of contemporary capitalism more than most other perspectives (Amaeshi and Adi 2007).

Stakeholder theory, one may argue, is fundamentally and originally rooted in norms and mores. The normative perspective to stakeholding is largely prescriptive of who ought to be considered as stakeholders and what is right or wrong to do in relation to stakeholders. It draws its legitimacy from existing moral standards. As Donaldson and Preston (1995: 72) put it: "A normative theory attempts to interpret the function of, and offer guidance about, the investor-owned corporation on the basis of some underlying moral or philosophical principles." In other words, morality in this case could be seen as not merely a matter of rules, but also of principles—general standards for evaluating conduct, standards that we apply to all behaviors and rules. Normative can refer to:

- The norms or standard practices of society as it exists
- The way one would live in an ideal, good society
- What we ought to do, either in order to achieve a good society or unconnected with any notion of the good (Freeman and Miles 2006: 36)

It could be reasonably conjectured, therefore, that firms with high moral standards will undertake genuine stakeholder engagement characterized by genuine intentions, dialogue, engagement, trust, and fairness (Phillips 1997; Swift 2001). Conversely, "moralist firms have a genuine concern for stakeholder interests, making legitimacy the *primary* driver of salience for their managers" (Jones et al. 2007: 152).

Firms adhering to the normative perspective in stakeholding do so for some underlying intrinsic value associated with this engagement—namely, because they know that this approach to stakeholding is good in itself. For Donaldson and Preston (1995: 67), the fundamental basis of the stakeholder theory is normative and entails a commitment to the following ideas:

a. Stakeholders are persons or groups with legitimate interests in procedural and/or substantive aspects of corporate activity. Stakeholders are identified by their interests in the corporation whether the corporation has any corresponding functional interest in them or not.
b. The interests of all stakeholders are of intrinsic value. That is, each group of stakeholders merits consideration for its own sake and not merely because of its ability to further the interests of some other group, such as the shareholders.

Leveraging on these ideas, Phillips (2003) makes a distinction between normative and derivative stakeholder legitimacy. On the one hand, he classifies normative stakeholders as those stakeholders to whom the organization has a moral obligation and for whom it must provide an answer to the seminal stakeholder question: "For whose benefit . . . should the firm be managed?" (Freeman 1984). On the other hand, Phillips (2003) sees derivative stakeholders as "those groups whose actions and claims must be accounted for by managers due to their potential effects upon the organization and its normative stakeholders."

While these stakeholding paradigms have been presented as if they are independent of each other, Donaldson and Preston (1995: 66) conclude that the three approaches to stakeholder theory—descriptive, instrumental, and normative—"are mutually supportive and that the *normative* base serves as the critical underpinning for the theory in all its forms." They argue that the different aspects of the stakeholder theory are rather nested:

> The external shell of the theory is its descriptive aspect; the theory presents and explains relationships that are observed in the external world. The theory's descriptive accuracy is supported, at the second level, by its instrumental and predictive value; *if* certain practices are carried out, *then* certain results will be obtained. The central core of the theory is, however, normative. The descriptive accuracy of the theory presumes that managers and other agents act as *if* all stakeholders' interests have intrinsic value. In turn, recognition of these ultimate moral values and obligations gives stakeholder management its fundamental normative base. (Donaldson and Preston 1995: 74)

Despite the stakeholding paradigms highlighted by Donaldson and Preston (1995), there are pressures on corporations to manage their stakeholders effectively, even where there are no institutional rights on the part of the stakeholders to warrant doing so (Andriof and Waddock 2002). As such, corporations should consider the interests of their stakeholders, whether for ethical reasons (Evan and Freeman 1998; Donaldson and Preston 1995) or for the achievement of strategic and economic objectives (Maignan, Ferrell, and Hult 1999—all cited in Crane and Livesey 2003). In this light, Andriof and colleagues (2002: 9) write:

> In today's societies successful companies are those that recognise that they have responsibilities to a range of stakeholders that go beyond mere compliance with the law or meeting the fiduciary responsibility inherent in the phrase "maximising returns to shareholders." If in the past the focus was on enhancing shareholder value, now it is on engaging stakeholders for long-term value creation. This does not mean that shareholders are not important, or that profitability is not vital to business success, but that in order to survive and be profitable a company must engage with a range of stakeholders whose views on the company's success may vary greatly.

Furthermore, the business world has moved from a trust-based culture where stakeholders placed implicit and explicit faith on the belief that corporations would act in their best interests to an evidence-based culture in which stakeholders want to be reassured that organizations will do what is morally right (Swift 2001). Today, the business world continues to move toward a new paradigm, which we may call a participation-based culture in which stakeholders legitimately expect to work in partnership with organizations (Cumming 2001). It is in this partnership model that the essence of stakeholder engagement, corporate social responsibility, and accountability ought to be grounded.

As a management practice, corporate stakeholding involves identifying and prioritizing stakeholder issues based on managerial perceptions of stakeholder salience (Mitchell et al. 1997). Mitchell and colleagues identify these stakeholder salience variables as power, legitimacy, and urgency. The stakeholder has power when it can impose its will on the firm. Legitimacy implies that stakeholder demands comply with prevailing norms and beliefs. In other words, power accrues to those who control resources needed by the firm (Pfeffer 1981), and legitimacy is achieved when patterns of organizational practice are in congruence with the wider social system (Scott and Meyer 1983; Scott 1987, 1995; Powell and DiMaggio 1991). However, power and legitimacy can appear together, giving authority to those who have both, but they can also appear independently. Finally, the concept of urgency in relation to stakeholding is predicated on two factors: (1) the importance stakeholders accord their own demands; and (2) their sensitivity to how long it takes managers to deal with their demands (Gago and Antolin 2004). These salient variables according to Mitchell and colleagues will determine how managers respond to stakeholders.

Drawing from social cognition theory (Fiske and Taylor 1984), Agle and colleagues (1999: 509) explain that "as the stakeholder attributes of power, legitimacy, and urgency cumulate in the mind of a manager, selectivity is enhanced, intensity is increased, and higher salience of the stakeholder group is the likely result." Relying on the findings of Mitchell and colleagues (1997), Agle and colleagues (1999: 151) assert that "in the minds of CEOs, the stakeholder attributes of power, legitimacy, and urgency are individually . . . and cumulatively . . . related to stakeholder salience across all groups; [which] . . . suggests that these stakeholder attributes (of power, legitimacy and urgency) do affect the degree to which top managers give priority to competing stakeholders."

While the stakeholder approach to management is no doubt a knowledge structure, which helps determine how managers selectively perceive, evaluate, and interpret attributes of the environment (Wolfe and Putler 2002: 65), some have criticized the stakeholder theory of management on the grounds that it provides unscrupulous managers with a ready excuse to act in their own self-interest, thus resurrecting the agency problem that the shareholder's wealth maximization imperative was designed to overcome (Phillips et al. 2004). Opportunistic managers can easily act in their own self-interest by claiming that the action actually benefits some stakeholder group or another (Jensen 2000; Marcoux 2000; Stenberg 2000). In this regard, Marcoux (2000: 97) notes: "All but the most egregious self-serving managerial behavior will doubtless serve the interests of some stakeholder constituencies and work against the interests of others." In the same trend, Sternberg (2000: 51f) argues that stakeholder theory "effectively destroys business accountability . . . because a business that is accountable to all, is actually accountable to none."

In response to the criticism of opportunistic self-interest on the part of managers, Phillips and colleagues (2003) argue that no small measure of managerial opportunism has occurred in the name of shareholder wealth maximization as well. While this sounds like a *tu quoque* (and you too) fallacy, Phillips and colleagues simply describe this criticism as a version of the evil genie argument—"one that is no more (or less) problematic for any one theory or idea than any of the extant alternatives" (2003: 482). Though Phillips and colleagues consider managerial opportunism a problem, they nonetheless think that it is not more of a problem for stakeholder theory than the alternatives. On the criticism of multiple master service (i.e., accountability to all), Phillips and colleagues, citing examples from Hill and Jones's (1992) stakeholder-agency theory, argue that managers' interest in organizational growth runs contrary not only to the interests of stockholders, but also contrary to the interests of stakeholders. Although the claims of different groups may conflict, yet each group can be seen as having a stake in the continued existence of the firm on a more general level (Hill and Jones 1992: 145). Stakeholder theory, therefore, does not advocate for the service of two masters. Rather, "managers serve the interest of one master: the organization" (Phillips et al. 2003: 484).

However, in fulfilling their managerial obligations to their organizations, Jawahar and McLaughlin (2001: 401) argue that "managers do not have unbridled strategic choice . . . but must make strategic choices within constraints." One of these constraints includes the stage of an organization in its life-cycle development—in other words, where it is in one of the four phases of development: start-up, emerging growth, maturity, and revival (2001: 404). As an organization struggles to survive, it is likely to gravitate toward those stakeholders that provide essential resources to its survival and sustenance.

> Organizations in start-up or decline/revival stages are likely to favor certain stakeholders . . . , depending on the extent to which they are dependent on those stakeholders for resources critical to organizational survival.
>
> Organizations are unlikely to fulfill all the responsibilities they have toward each primary stakeholder group. Instead, they are likely to fulfill economic and all noneconomic responsibilities of some primary stakeholders but not others and, over time, to fulfill responsibilities relative to each stakeholder to varying extents. This variation is how

organizations deal with different stakeholders, simultaneously and over time, i.e., across life cycle stages. (Jawahar and McLaughlin 2001: 397)

The dependency on specific resourceful stakeholders is the source of power over the firm on the part of the stakeholders (Mitchell et al. 1997). Jawahar and McLaughlin (2001: 405) in their study confirm that:

1. At any given organizational life cycle stage, certain stakeholders, because of their potential to satisfy critical organizational needs, will be more important than others.
2. Specific stakeholders are likely to become more or less important as an organization evolves from one stage to the next.
3. The strategy an organization uses to deal with each stakeholder will depend on the importance of that stakeholder to the organization relative to other stakeholders.

Each of the four phases of development identified by Jawahar and McLaughlin (2001) and their implications for corporate stakeholding are outlined and further explored here:

Start-up phase: In this phase, the organization is desperate to survive and hence requires access to both finance and market. Given these required resources, the organization is more likely disposed to the interests of stakeholder groups, seen as shareholders and creditors (for finance), and to customers (for access to market share). Jawahar and McLaughlin argue that the other stakeholder groups, such as government, employees, and suppliers, would only be considered if they were thought to be critical to the survival of the organization at this stage.

Emerging growth stage: This stage is mainly characterized by the need to build quality brand, workforce, and products, and to obtain resources to accommodate rapid growth in expansion (Jawahar and McLaughlin 2001: 408). Employees and suppliers are considered very important at this stage because they provide the quality of workforce and material inputs to production development needed to sustain the organization.

Mature stage: This stage is often characterized by "tempered overconfidence" of success and followed by strong cash flows without particularly attractive investment opportunities (Jawahar and McLaughlin 2001: 408). The organization is likely to deal with all primary stakeholders in a proactive manner at this stage. Jahawar and McLaughlin (2001) in this case borrow Clarkson's perspective on primary stakeholders as groups, which typically comprises shareholders and investors, employees, customers, and suppliers, together with the public stakeholder group. The public stakeholder group includes the government, communities that provide infrastructures, and markers, whose laws and regulations must be obeyed and to whom taxes and other obligations may be due (Clarkson 1995: 106).

Decline/transition stage: At this stage, the organization is likely to experience dwindling patronage and loss of market share and may make efforts to build new markets or rebuild existing market share. Main stakeholder focus will be customers and creditors. Unless government, community, trade associations, and so on are essential for survival, the organization is very likely to adopt defensive strategies toward these latter groups (see Table 2.1).

One of the limitations of this framework, among others, is that it does not explicitly address differences in stakeholder salience arising from the industry of the organization. For instance, most firms in such sectors as chemical and or oil/gas might be constrained by government policies or environmental pressures to take on environmental and community issues earlier in their life cycle (for details on industry-driven differences in corporate

Table 2.1   Stakeholder Salience and Organizational Life Cycle

Phases	Pressing needs	Important stakeholders
Start-up	Access to finance, market share	Shareholders, creditors, customers
Emerging growth	Need to build a quality workforce and products and obtain resources to accommodate rapid growth and expansion	Suppliers, employees
Mature stage	Often characterized by "tempered overconfidence" of success and attended by strong cash flows, without particularly attractive investment opportunities	Likely to deal with all primary stakeholders in a proactive manner
Decline/transition stage	Dwindling patronage, loss of market share, and or efforts to build a new market or rebuild market share	Main stakeholder focus will be customers and creditors. Unless government, community, trade associations, and so on are essential for survival, the organization is very likely to adopt defensive strategies toward these latter groups.

stakeholding, see Jones 1999; Beliveau, Cottrill, and O'Neill 1994; Greening and Gray 1994; Baucus and Near 1991). However, several scholars suggest that an organization can adopt different approaches to deal with its stakeholders, including pro-action, accommodation, defense, and reaction (Carroll 1979; Clarkson 1995; Gatewood and Carroll 1981; Wartick and Cochran 1985).

Notwithstanding, one of the popular propositions of the stakeholder theory is the view that firms exist at the nexus of a series of interdependent relationships with groups that can affect or are affected by them (Crane and Livesey 2003). Given the infinite network of relationships a firm could be entangled with, it is often difficult for managers to comprehensively identify their various stakeholders and effectively manage these relationships, which often come with conflicting interests and goals.

Although stakeholder salience is a precursor to stakeholder accountability, both terms nonetheless exist independent of each other. Roberts and Scapens (1985: 447) define accountability as "the giving and demanding of reasons for conduct." It is an art of "making the invisible visible" (Munro 1996: 5) through the "provision of information." Traditionally, under the principal-agent dispensation, firms have limited their accountability to shareholders as economic and legal owners of the firm. Friedman (1962) reinforces this form of accountability by stating that the primary responsibility of firms is to pursue profits within the limits of the law. The economic logic of accountability leans heavily on what Korhonen (2002) calls the "dominant social paradigm" (DSP) of profit maximization for the owners of the firm. DSP emphasizes such issues as competitive advantage, cost minimization, equilibrium, market efficiency, optimal returns on investments (including labor), and market dominance. Shareholder accountability is the bedrock of modern capitalism. Stakeholder accountability emerged recently as a complement to shareholder accountability (Gray, Owen, and Maunders 1988; Gray 2002; Owen et al. 2000).

Swift (2001: 17) broadly describes accountability as "the requirement or duty to provide an account or justification for one's actions to whomever one is answerable" and narrowly as "being pertinent to contractual arrangements only . . . where accountability is not contractually bound there can be no act of accountability." Borrowing from a later work of Gray and colleagues (1997), Swift notes that "essentially accountability is about the provision of information between two parties where the one is accountable, explains or justifies actions to the one to whom the account is owed." This form of accountability can easily be glimpsed from that characteristic of principal-agent relationship, which is central to the firm as an economic and legal entity. But no matter the side taken, and however defined, one factor that is central to the notion of accountability is the *duty to account,* which connotes the institution of rights (Owen et al. 2000). In the same line of thought, Gray and colleagues (1988) claim that the firm's accountability to the wider society is inherent in a social contract between society and the business organization—the idea that business derives its existence from the society. This accountability inherent in the form of social contract is enforced through market forces that punish or reward corporate behavior (Swift 2001; Donaldson and Preston 1995). Korten (2004) argues that the market by necessity needs information to be effective. Hence, corporations ought to produce the information needed by the market to punish or reward any one person or organization. This will constitute accountability to the market, which cannot be achieved through self-regulation. Accountability, therefore, connotes some level of transparency, and transparency carries with it some risks of disclosure that could hurt an organization or an agent (Gray 2002; Owen et al. 2000).

Stakeholder accountability seems to be driving the current surge of interests in social reports. Interest in and demand for stakeholder accountability has been on the increase. The 1970s enjoyed a boom in social accounting, which disappeared in the 1980s but has reappeared since the 1990s. In addition, the accounting and governance travesties of firms such as Enron and WorldCom in the United States, and Parmalat in Italy, to mention but a few, make such demands for corporate accountability and social reports even more pertinent. Within these social reports, firms aim to signal accountability toward, and willingness to be held accountable by, their different stakeholder groups on such issues as their environmental footprints, poverty reduction, labor and employment conditions, gender and equality, community and consumer welfare, corporate governance and ethics—the very issues that lie at the very heart of the contemporary CSR movement.

In this chapter, we explored the link between CSR and the stakeholder theory of the firm, as well as its connection to the stakeholder accountability agenda. In the next chapter, we extend our analysis to CSR in the context of a globalized world order and global governance void.

3 Corporate Social Responsibility, Globalization, and the Global Governance Void

Like the terms *corporate social responsibility* and *stakeholding*, the term *globalization* is easily and commonly understood, but difficult to encapsulate in a definition. According to Van Der Bly (2005: 875), the difficulty in defining the concept of globalization is rooted in three dialectics: globalization as a process versus globalization as a condition; globalization as reality versus globalization as futurology, and one-dimensional globalization versus multi-dimensional globalization. For example, Held and colleagues (1999:16) define globalization as "a process, which embodies a transformation in the spatial organization of social relations and transactions . . . generating transcontinental or interregional flows and networks of activity," while Clark and Knowles (2003: 368) define it as "the extent to which the economic, political, cultural, social, and other relevant systems of nations are actually integrated into World Systems." A critical view of globalization suggests that it "has become part of a powerful political-economic ideology through which capital–labor relationships and relative class power positions are shifted in profound ways" (Swyngedouw 2004: 28). Notwithstanding the opacity of its definition, globalization has had profound effects on governance, corporate social responsibility, and their conceptual and practical reach, particularly the role of multinational enterprises.

Globalization and multinational enterprises are interlinked as the latter's evolutionary process may reveal. Individual multinational firms usually go through an evolutionary process as an autonomous subsidiary, international division, and global division (Muchlinski 2007a: 45–51; Rapakko 1997: 95). A picture has now emerged that shows that globalization has constituted multinational enterprises as the "dominant form" (Vernon 1992: 18, 36) of business structure and organization with significant domestic and global socioeconomic influence. In some instances, multinational enterprises and not national governments provide "the direct source" (Anderson 2005: 28) of decisions affecting the lives of individuals and groups. This, as Stopford (1994: 267) observes, has emphasized the roles of multinational enterprises that used to be dismissed as "a footnote . . . [but] are now appearing in the main text." The trend indicates that rather than diminishing the power of multinational enterprises, globalization foreshadows a growing influence of multinational enterprises and increasingly transboundary implications of their activities. In international law, for example, globalization has highlighted the position of multinational enterprises as direct subjects of international law with recognized rights and obligations, a clear departure from classical international law, which has been directed toward states only. Previously, as Oppenheim (1905: 341) submitted, international law used to govern only states, which constituted the exclusive subjects of international law. International law has now moved from the state-only focus and appears to recognize nonstate entities including multinational enterprises and other corporations as the subjects of rights and obligations (MacLeod 2008). This refocalization probably provided the platform for the current international human rights law that applies to nonstate actors. The 1999 United Nations General Assembly declaration,[1] for instance, affirmed that "all members of the international community shall fulfill, jointly and separately, their solemn obligation to promote and encourage respect for human rights and fundamental freedoms." Articles 16 and 18 of the declaration specifically identify some human rights obligations of nonstate entities such as individuals, groups, institutions, and nongovernmental organizations. Consequently, article 3 of the United Nations Sub-Commission on the Promotion and Protection of Human Rights' code (2002)[2] asserts that multinational enterprises and other corporations "shall not engage in nor benefit" from human rights violations. The language of "shall not engage in nor benefit" indicates that violations of human rights standards by multinational enterprises can arise from the direct action or omission of the business organization or its agents, such as private security forces. The language also suggests that violations of human rights by multinational enterprises can be indirect—for example, by providing support for host repressive regimes that commit human rights abuses (Jägers 2002: 53; Leader 2006: 657; Human Rights Watch 1999).

As Weissbrodt and Kruger (2003) demonstrate, there are several international instruments that specifically identify human rights norms applicable to multinational enterprises. Multinational enterprises and other corporations are expected to observe a range of human rights norms (Clapham 2000: 190; Kaufman 2007: 155–241; MacLeod 2008: 65–76), a tentative list of which has been identified in academic commentary (Joseph 2000; Jägers 2002: 51–73; Muchlinski 2007a: 518–24; Muchlinski 2007b: 440–47; Tófalo 2006; Deva 2003; Stephens 2000; Ramasastry 2002: 108). Although some authors appear to make suggestions to the contrary (Muchlinski 2007a: 514–18; Ratner 2001: 443; Clapham 2006: chap. 6; Muchlinski 2001: 35–44; Clapham and Jebri 2001: 339), corporate human rights obligations can be summarized as obligations to respect, protect, and fulfill human rights (Jägers 2002: 78). The obligation to protect human rights applies to the acts and omissions of the business organization and those of its business partners and does not depend on the location of the business activity. It is instructive that business partners of multinational enterprises have been highlighted as being one of the "major sources" of human rights violations in several countries, particularly the developing nations (Jägers 2002: 83). In relation to the obligation to fulfill human rights, the pressure to comply is more likely to apply to large corporations, particularly multinational enterprises, since this obligation appears to depend on the size and resources of the business organization (Jägers 2002: 83).

The human rights obligations of corporations, including multinational enterprises, seem to include the duty "not to cooperate" with, or refrain from being complicit in, human violations by host state agencies or business partners (Jägers 2002: 78, 92–93). In *Doe v. Unocal Corp*[3] (1997) the court held that multinational enterprises that accepted forced labor from state agencies in their host country could be violating human rights. Similarly, in *Wiwa v. Shell*[4] (2000), Shell's alleged complicity in the execution of certain Nigerian human and environmental rights activists by a Nigerian military regime could constitute a violation of the human rights of the victims and their families. Consequently, Judge Paez held in *National Coalition Government of the Union of Burma v. Unocal, Inc*[5] (1997: 349) that a multinational enterprise could be in breach of human rights where it is a "willful participant in joint action with the State or its agents" (Jägers 2002: 232). A United States' court in *The Presbyterian Church of Sudan v. Talisman Energy and the Republic of Sudan* (2005)[6] confirmed this principle, a decision that suggests that the principle is not constrained by the national boundaries of the location of the business organization or its activity.

Clearly, globalization has constituted human rights as a reputational issue for multinational enterprises and other corporations (Williams 1999: 63), leading to the suggestion by Campbell (2007: 529) for the classification of human rights as the center of corporate social responsibility. However, when it is twined with the emergence of multinational enterprises as global business operations, globalization challenges the authority of the state in at least seven different ways. First, it reveals a discrepancy between traditional notions of state power over its residents and the reality of an increasingly interlinked global economy. As Kline (1993) notes, the reality is that multinational enterprises could be "directly subject to each nation's authority where they operated, yet appeared fully controllable by no single political sovereign [while] [m]ultinationally located and transnationally integrated operations yield resources and options unavailable to solely national firms, giving [multinational enterprises] more independence from a local government's policy direction." Multinational enterprises make investment decisions based on factors of competitive advantage in which states provide the conditions for the existence and sustenance of business and investment. It is for this reason that many states may not be "in a position to screen and control potential investors" (Michalet 1994: 16).

Governments, particularly of developed countries, are concerned with the establishment of "conditions for *increased* economic activity in the interests of the companies themselves rather than with control of the social and environmental impact" of corporate activities (Gray, Owens, and Adams 1996:

129). States in various stages of development now compete for inward investments and, unlike in the 1970s, the control of corporations is no more a priority to national governments (Anderson 2006: 28; Held et al. 1999: 259; Ratner 2001: 454–58). A government may have no overriding reason to enact regulations to protect interests located beyond its national boundaries or to enter into agreements that conflict with the national (including corporate) self-interest.

The second challenge posed by globalization is the difficulty of geographically situating the multinational enterprises, a topic of debate among scholars. Some scholars distinguish between "international" corporations and "global" corporations (Anderson 2005: 23). International corporations have stronger national ties, while global corporations apply "global strategies of operations" (Sklair 2001: 48). Held and colleagues (1999: 3–10) argue that multinational enterprises are national entities with international and not global influence. However, Hirst and Thompson (1996: 98) insist that the state maintains its power of regulation over multinational enterprises notwithstanding that corporate power may have increased. This controversy has significant implications for corporate behavior and control because geographical location ordinarily indicates the source of regulatory or other type of external state control over corporations.

Locating the legal domicile of multinational enterprises may appear "arbitrary," particularly when such enterprises practically attempt to be "good corporate citizens" and "adapt to the political realities" of different host countries (Bowman 1996: 289). However, with relative ease, multinational enterprises can pool together, distribute or exploit production methods, processes, costs, resources, research, management and technical knowledge, and funding across different countries and jurisdictions. This advantage has resulted in the growth and expansion of multinational enterprises: a result that is significantly encouraged by developments in science, technology, transport, communications, production methods, international trade, and financing. These developments that facilitate globalization are exploited by multinational enterprises as both users and primary agents. It is for this reason that globalization may be regarded as the "accelerating interdependence" of states with multinational enterprises as the "primary agent" (Ostry 1992).

One of the major assumptions of globalization is that the world is being overrun by a super-ideologue that seeks to harmonize practices across national borders. This harmonization permeates all facets of life and society—including the behaviors and performances of firms. Notwithstanding, the literature on globalization is simultaneously challenged by contradictory pressures of exclusion and inclusion, divergence and convergence, localization and transnationalization—or centralization and decentralization—(Jones and Fleming 2003). Some also see it as a fusion of the global and the local in form of "glocalization" without one running over the other, so to speak—what Swyngedouw describes as a "twin process whereby, firstly, institutional/regulatory arrangements shift from the national scale both upwards to supra-national or global scales and downwards to the scale of the individual body or to local, urban or regional configurations and, secondly, economic activities and inter-firm networks are becoming simultaneously more localised/regionalised and transnational" (Swyngedouw 2004: 25).

The literature, therefore, appears to assume the existence of a homogeneity of markets and regulations when, in fact, corporations largely operate in a transnational and global arena that lacks an overarching regulatory structure for multinational enterprises (Kysar 2004: 599; Yosifon 2011: 1246). However, the transnational scope of corporate power shows that it may simply be "misleading" to analyze such power only nationally (Bowman 1996: 141). Multinational enterprises, increasingly strong national political actors that can influence the shape and direction of regulations (Cutler, Haufler, and Porter 1999; Kobrin 2009; Wettestein 2009), may not always guarantee the recognition and protection of stakeholder interests and even universally accepted standards in multiple places of operation. Internationally, corporations, particularly multinational enterprises, have also been seen as "political actors" (Grant 1993: 85). Such enterprises are active participants in the global public domain through various overt and indirect public policy interventions such as the formulation and design of formal rules (Scherer, Palazzo, and Baumann 2006: 506) and self-regulation (Haufler 2001). As the regulatory capture theory shows, regulations can in fact benefit corporations to the detriment of other interested persons and stakeholders because of the extent of corporate power and its influence over regulations and regulators (Dal Bó, 2006).

Consequently, the third challenge of globalization relates to the shareholder primacy approach to corporate governance, which is the traditional and prevalent model in the Anglo-American systems. Rather than insisting on a sole focus on shareholders and profit maximization, globalization has induced external direct and covert pressures that urge a shift from the traditional view to the recognition of a range of multistakeholder interests affected by the operations of multinational enterprises in both developing and developing countries. As Clarke (2004: 23) argues, the shift from sole shareholder concern to the inclusion of other stakeholder interests assumes that "social capital [involves] an evaluation of a deeper and more complex set of social relationships of the corporation." In contrast, the shareholder primacy model accepts that state agencies can intervene with regulations to deal with exploitative conduct against nonshareholder interests. One example is the use of consumer protection legislation (Bainbridge 2008: 28–30; Jensen 2001: 301; Jensen 2010: 38). This view, however, assumes that external regulations can curb corporate excesses and that host state agencies exist and are able to regulate effectively.

The second tenuous assumption is that nonshareholders are more likely than multinational enterprises and other corporations to influence regulations by state agencies (Bainbridge 2008: 71–72) when evidence suggests to the contrary. Yosifon (2011: 1202–12) has found that multinational enterprises and other corporations often strongly desire to control external regulations to the extent that a significant corporate activity is influencing regulators and combating the development, administration, and implementation of regulations in domestic and foreign locations.

Also, the public choice theory recognizes the relative strength and advantage of corporations over other interest groups in the competition for favorable regulation. As Macey (1988: 46) argues, the public choice theory "implies not only that certain sorts of groups are more effective in obtaining desirable legislation, but also that certain sorts of issues will be most attractive to entrepreneurial politicians." The position of multinational enterprises is profoundly stronger than that of other corporations. For instance, states may be unable to guarantee compliance by multinational enterprises with internationally accepted standards, even though the enterprises themselves are "not always willing" to follow such standards, particularly in countries with weak institutions (Rieth 2004: 181). Globalization has created a power shift in which corporations are equals or even stronger negotiating partners of governments, particularly those of developing countries (Reed 2002). The weak bargaining position of developing countries has been amplified by globalization with significant fallouts for regulatory and enforcement actions. While developed countries may lack the motivations to act in favor of the interests of developing countries, the latter generally lack the ability and opportunity to effect changes in the substantive provisions of relevant international law to respond to their concerns and interests (Reichman and Dreyfuss 2007). Therefore, public choice problems can manifest at national and global levels, particularly in developing countries.

This then triggers the fourth challenge from globalization—the possible production of a "reconfigured state" (Anderson 2006: 17) and the elevation of multinational enterprises as major global political actors. Evidence of corporate power in this regard could be seen from corporate influence on political processes, the performance of governance roles by corporations, and their role in the global economy (Anderson 2006: 26). It is apparent that globalization continually blurs the roles of states and large multinational enterprises (Servais 2005: 102; Boiral 2003; Hepple 1999). This has consequently expanded the breadth of corporate power (Anderson 2006: 18; Held et al. 1999: 281; Sklair 2001: 54). However, a good number of multinational enterprises are often looked upon by their host countries with great suspicion. They are perceived as economic raiders, mainly interested in repatriating wealth to their home countries while doing very little to empower the citizens of their host countries (Meyer 2004; Oetzel and Doh 2009). In addition, multinational enterprises are frequently accused of exerting negative influences on local politics (Rodriguez et al. 2006; Frynas, Mellahi, and Pigman 2006) and stifling competition (De Backer and Sleuwagen 2003). Some of these negative perceptions, which are, unfortunately, supported by research evidence, tend to overshadow the fact that multinational enterprises are equally great sources of economic opportunities: they create jobs (Ramamurti 2004), transfer technologies (Teece 1977; Günther 2002), and create wealth (Prahalad and Hammond 2002). The negative views associated with multinational enterprises, especially in developing economies, generate tensions between them and their host countries and thus challenge their quest for legitimacy. In addition to these tensions, there is a transnational governance void (Djelic and Quack 2008) that unsettles most familiar socioeconomic institutional arrangements. For example, the neat divide between the responsibilities of firms, markets, and nation states in both politics and economics has been blurred by the globalization process and its consequent discontents (Stiglitz 2002).

Nevertheless, the fifth challenge of globalization is governance and relates to the perception that multinational enterprises are not willing to voluntarily apply or implement "high" international standards of conduct especially in respect to their operations in the less developed countries (Rieth 2004: 181; Brühl and Rittberger 2001: 22; Kaul, Grunberg, and Stern: 1999: xxvi). Multinational enterprises from developed countries are often involved in major industrial accidents and environmental pollution (Francioni 1991: 275) and sometimes ignore international best practices in health and safety and labor standards (Frank 1985: 84; Clinard 1990: 91–92, 141; Mokhiber 1988; Mills 1987; Servais 2005: 31–32). This is often the case in several developing countries. For example, the 1984 Bhopal gas leak incident in India (Clinard 1990: 137–59) was arguably a case of an attempt by a multinational enterprise to avoid liability for its recklessness despite having prior knowledge of the danger of its operations conducted via a subsidiary in the host developing country. It is probably true that developing countries' competitive desire to attract investments usually results in low regulatory standards for multinational enterprises (Redmond 2003: 80). Also, developing countries may not have adequate institutional support and stakeholder pressure for improved corporate behavior (Stovall et al. 2009: 119–26). For example, a 2011 environmental assessment report by the United Nations Environment Program (UNEP 2011) revealed that multinational oil companies operating in Nigeria's Ogoniland disregarded industry best practices, international standards, and even weak national regulations. About 10 years earlier, the African Commission on Human and Peoples' Rights (ACHPR) found that "pollution and environmental degradation to a level humanly unacceptable has made living in Ogoniland a nightmare" and that the multinational oil companies colluded with the Nigerian government to ignore "internationally established principles."[7]

It may be true that globalization has brought about a growth in the size and importance of "transnational regulation" (Djelic and Sahlin-Andersson 2006: 251). In some cases, states have attempted to regulate activities with transboundary implications. However, without taking relevant transnational and global developments into consideration, rules may be ineffective or counterproductive if they are formulated "solely in terms of national entities" (Martiny 2001: 136). Consequently, several initiatives have proved inadequate for controlling multinational enterprises, perhaps because the current international legal system largely supports domestic regulation only. This exclusive domestic regulation of multinational enterprises has not been satisfactory, and there are doubts about its effectiveness (Zia-Zarifi 1999: 84–86). The present international legal framework suggests that the globalization of regulations has not emerged in the same way as nor has accompanied the globalization of corporate operations. In fact, globalization of regulations does not exist in binding rules for the conduct of multinational enterprises, and several attempts have failed due to lack of interstate cooperation. As Gray, Owen, and Adams (1996: 128) have observed, "the need for international cooperation and regulation on corporate activity has never been greater; but, similarly, the difficulties of introducing such global agreement have never seemed insuperable."

What globalization appears to have achieved is the preponderance of nonbinding initiatives from international governmental organizations (Raustiala 2002). These initiatives may present a more realistic (Vogelaar 1980: 129) approach to international issues because of the difficulties in achieving a sufficient level of interstate cooperation. For example in 1999, the European Parliament recommended the adoption of a model code on human rights, environment, and labor standards for European enterprises operating in developing countries.[8] Such voluntary international corporate social responsibility–related initiatives are numerous and can be useful (Baines 2009; Organization for Economic Cooperation and Development 2008). As Metcalf (2010: 155, 192, 199) argues, depending on the effectiveness of voluntary commitments, corporate social responsibility can provide a "complementary" and "potentially important mechanism for the transmission of public law norms in the global sphere, particularly as norm setting in the realm of public international law often has relatively weak implementation or enforcement mechanisms."

Nevertheless, such instruments are meant to be nonmandatory and not legally enforceable. They may represent only statements of policy or principles that, although they may be important in some respects, are similar to "expressing a political message [with] no legal value" (Servais 2005: 318). This is, for instance, confirmed by the history and negotiation of the Organization for Economic Cooperation and Development Guidelines for multinational enterprises (Vogelaar 1980: 135). A major reason for recourse to these "soft international law" nonbinding international mechanisms (Shelton, 2000) is the real or potential lack of willingness to subject policies to formal ratification processes, even where agreements on such policies exist (Cohen 2005: 1091). Zerk (2006), for example, doubts the likelihood of a binding general corporate social responsibility treaty and therefore proposes using soft law to regulate multinational enterprises. The expectation is that nonbinding principles can evolve into binding treaties and customary international law at some point (Zerk 2006; Kuschnik 2008). Even then, international efforts in different forms for regulating multinational enterprises have not always been successful. Within the World Trade Organization (WTO), for example, developing countries oppose discussions on labor standards (Singh and Zammitt 2004: 1). Also, some commentators argue against compulsory enforcement of labor standards for developing countries (Singh and Zammitt 2004: 1). The draft UN Code on Code of Conduct for Transnational Corporations was aborted as a consequence of disagreements on the content, nature, and legal form of the code (Jägers 2002: 119–22). The result is that despite the recognition of certain obligations of multinational enterprises, their liabilities for violating international standards of conduct are few or even nonexistent (Kamminga and Zia-Zarifi 2000: 1; Vagts 1970: 739).

Therefore, globalization may have created a void in governance and in the regulation of multinational enterprises, which other nonstate regulatory actors want to occupy. As a result, global firms appear to be directly or indirectly compelled by some external actors (e.g., nongovernmental organizations [NGOs], international organizations, and pressure groups) to fill in the transnational governance gap for nation states, especially in developing economies with weak and fragile institutions that are incapable of regulating the activities of multinational enterprises. Multinational enterprises are, therefore, encouraged to be more socially responsible and transparent in their practices. This subtle compulsion often reveals itself in the growing trend of corporate social responsibility as self-regulation (Graham and Woods 2006; Brown and Woods 2007; Vogel 2008; Mattli and Woods 2009) and the private governance of corporate externalities (Crouch 2006).

Consequently, this sets the stage for the sixth challenge of globalization, where it questions the idea of the state as the "exclusive or even primary source of law" (Anderson 2006: 17). According to Morss (1991: 55), "the era in which nations rule the world is over . . . [since] three groups have joined nations as important global players: transnational corporations, international organizations, and special interest groups." The reasons for the expanding role of private regulation include deregulation, privatization, and delegation of regulatory power to private organizations, business associations, or agencies (Cutler 2002: 1). It is instructive that deregulation, for example, may be defined as "the reduction of economic, political and social restrictions on the behavior of social actors" (Jordana and Levi-Faur 2004: 6). Therefore, globalization has created "regulatory arenas [that] go beyond governments" (Radaelli and De Francesco 2007: 16). Apart from large corporations and multinational enterprises, other nonstate actors and institutions engage in private regulation. Civil society and interest groups at local, national, and international levels are increasingly influential regulatory actors (Engwall 2006: 165). In addition to this private regulation, the freedom of modern corporations is limited by threats of civil litigation and pressures from the media, public opinion, and stakeholders (Smith and Walter 2006: 48). These global issues and pressures, coupled with growing concerns about poverty, corruption, inequalities, and sustainable development in most developing economies, challenge the role and purpose of transnational corporations in the global world order.

The seventh challenge from globalization is therefore its relationship to corporate social responsibility. Globalization increasingly connects corporate social responsibility issues to modern corporations and expands the relevance of such matters to multinational enterprises in particular. The key to this relationship is probably the role of globalization in the generation and spread of ideas. This is globalization in the sense of "the transnational extension and habituation of local ideas and practices" (Anderson 2006: 19), which confirms that the domestic field does not exist in isolation. Globalization therefore increases the awareness of corporate social responsibility issues by placing them "at the centre of public policy debates" (Sullivan 2006: 183). One reason is the transboundary implications of corporate social responsibility issues. For example, "competitive erosion of labor standards" (Singh and Zammitt 2004: 6) may result from globalization since multinational enterprises can outsource workforce and supply chains to countries with weak labor standards. As previously discussed, human rights constitute another reputational issue for multinational enterprises. The defects in the global governance system have instigated the current anticapitalism movement and antiglobalization protests, which "illustrate a growing public demand for greater transparency, representation and regulation under the conditions of globalization" (Lipschutz and Fogel 2002: 115). These movements demonstrate that corporate social responsibility is as relevant to international business as it is to the domestic operations of multinational enterprises (Cerne 2011) and may justify the assertion that "transnational influences can and do condition relations of power, conventions, and shared cultural constructions in the domestic sphere" (McNichol 2006: 370).

The influence of globalization on corporate social responsibility can also be seen in the link between the relative size of particular multinational enterprises and their professed (or public) support for corporate social responsibility. This is in line with business practices that suggest the existence of a connection between company size and the level of embrace of corporate social responsibility (Barnard, Deakin, and Hobbs 2004: 33, 34). Evidence suggests that small companies are less conscious of corporate image or positive reputation, including social performance and compliance with sustainability principles (McLeay 2006: 236–37; Barnard et al. 2004: 33–35). High-profile business organizations are often organized transnationally, which makes the corporate image the sum of corporate operations across different national boundaries. These business organizations are more likely to appreciate the link between their conduct and "practical social values" and "public expectations" often expressed in the news media and by pressure groups (Smith and Walter 2006: 234). Although both small and large companies often focus on profit making, the large ones may prefer longer term planning and position (Berle 1965: 29), resulting in different approaches to determining corporate responses to social and sustainability issues. The larger the size of the company the more likely "size extends business decisions from the purely economic into fields of social movement" (Berle 1965: 30). It is often the case that large companies and dealers in consumer goods are more likely to be affected by public interest in social issues than small companies or producers of unbranded goods (Parkinson 2006: 9). Also, large companies tend to adopt codes of labor standards since they are more sensitive to criticisms of poor working conditions and practices (Servais 2005: 94, para. 199). It is therefore instructive that a significant number of corporate codes of conduct directly concern the operations of multinational enterprises (Sauvant and Aranda 1994: 86–87). As Kline (1993: 312) has illustrated, in some cases multinational enterprises are even concurrently affected by several codes from different countries and international bodies.

It may be true that globalization demonstrates that multinational enterprises exist in a "global public domain" where they are supposed to recognize shared values and expectations (Hofferberth 2011: 216; Ruggie 2007: 519–21). This is evident from article 2(2) of the United Nations General Assembly "Declaration on the Right to Development" (1986), which attempts to impose responsibility on all, including states, multinational enterprises, and other corporations. Multinational enterprises and other corporations are increasingly compelled to acknowledge "that the legal boundaries of their firm are no longer a safe haven" (Flanagan and Whiteman 2007; Smith 2003: 16–17). This approach is reflected in some international initiatives such as the European Parliament "Resolution on EU Standards for European Enterprises Operating in Developing Countries" (1999)[9] and the United Nations "Norms on the Responsibilities of Transnational Corporations and Other Business Enterprises with Regard to Human Rights" (2003),[10] which concern the application of international best practices in the transnational operations of multinational enterprises. Another illustration is the United Nations Global Compact. As its history (Jägers 2002: 128–30) indicates, the Global Compact was initiated by a United Nations secretary-general as a cooperative venture between the United Nations and some large corporations (mainly multinational enterprises) for the promotion of 10 principles in business operations.

Corporations voluntarily agree to apply certain principles derived from the areas of human rights, labor standards, protection of the environment, and anticorruption in their global operations. Critics argue that enterprises that subscribe to the Global Compact usually act contrary to those principles (Jägers 2002: 129–30) and in the United States are often subjected to regulatory and enforcement actions for abuses of rules (Clinard 1990: 163). Nevertheless, the principles of the Global Compact and transnational reporting initiatives such as the Global Reporting Initiative and the Accountability Initiative demonstrate that universalism of standards for the operations of multinational enterprises is not only possible but also desirable (Chiu 2010).

However, values and expectations alone may not be enough as positive changes in corporate behavior are adopted either voluntarily or through the coercive process of laws and regulations (Rivoli and Waddock 2011: 94–97). Surveys, for instance, revealed a "minimal" connection between codes of conduct and the elimination of corporate abuses, while such codes have been described as "not [being] real evidence of self-regulation or of [even corporate social responsibility]" (Clinard 1990: 163). At the global level are the relative power of multinational enterprises, regulatory and enforcement gaps in international law, and public choice problems that prevent effective regulation, particularly in developing countries.

Despite the global diffusion of corporate social responsibility and corporate self-regulation, available evidence suggests that corporate social responsibility does not follow a uniform pattern of operation in all countries (Newell 2005: 556). Graham and Woods (2006), for instance, question the effectiveness of the current practices of corporate self-regulation in transnational social spaces (Morgan 2006) with little or no equivalent transnational governance mechanisms (Djelic and Quack 2008). Graham and Woods (2006: 868) argue that to make such voluntary governance mechanisms more effective, "government action—in the North and South—remains vital to effective regulation, by setting social goals and upholding the freedom of civil society actors to organize and mobilize. International organizations and legal instruments may be able to assist developing country governments in fulfilling these roles." This suggestion fits in perfectly into what Midttun (2008) aptly describes as partnered governance. According to Midttun, most current global issues (e.g., climate change, human rights, and corruption) are no longer able to be governed by a single governance institution (e.g., markets, firms, or the state), especially as global economic entities continue to transverse territories with weak and fragile governance institutions. Therefore, he suggests a constructive, but complementary, mixture of public, market, voluntary, and civil regulatory mechanisms.

What is clear is that although in relation to multinational enterprises, the concept of "international corporate social responsibility" has emerged (Muchlinski 2007a: v, 101–4), the traditional voluntary model of corporate social responsibility may be defective in this area. This voluntary model (Voiculescu 2007: 365–97) enjoys widespread support. This view, however, disguises the complex nature of the corporate social responsibility–law relationship and the normative links between corporate social responsibility and law (Osuji 2011; Shum and Yam 2011). The traditional model does not seem to recognize that the legal environment may clarify the scope of corporate responsibilities. It may exclude legal compliance as part of corporate social responsibility, particularly in developing countries (Buhmann 2011: 150). This is notwithstanding that responsibility not propped by law may have a neutral impact on corporate behavior if corporations, including multinational enterprises, choose to avoid a proactive stance toward social responsibility. As the stakeholder theory (Kassinis and Vafeas 2006; King 2007; Reynolds, Shultz, and Hekman 2006) and the institutional theory, which supports using regulations to improve corporate behavior (Aguilera et al 2007; Campbell 2007; Marquis, Glynn, and Davis 2007; Richter 2011), explain, external stimulus can increase the likelihood of social considerations in the corporate agenda (Lee 2011).

A different approach to the traditional voluntary model of regulation may regard corporate social responsibility as questioning the kind of legal environment particular multinational enterprises operate in. This will recognize the three alternative passive, restrictive, and opportunistic legal domains Schwartz and Carroll (2003) have identified as the legal contexts of corporate activity. Corporations in the passive domain act without specific consideration of legal provisions and may just happen to be acting within the rules. The restrictive domain may compel corporations to consider legal requirements and compliance, while the opportunistic domains usually contain weak standards and loopholes corporations may exploit. As Vogel (2005) observes, there may exist spaces in the market for both socially responsible and irresponsible corporations. In view of the alternative legal environments, there is the possibility that multinational enterprises may choose to adopt one of four corporate social responsibility strategies: obstructionist, defensive, accommodative, and proactive (Fisher 2004; Lee 2011).

An obstructionist strategy is the exclusive pursuit of economic goals and the rejection of ethical responsibility. A defensive strategy means passive compliance with legal requirements and the rejection of ethical responsibility, while an accommodative attitude complies with legal requirements and minimalist and passive ethical responsibility. A proactive corporate social responsibility strategy is the active recognition of ethical and social responsibility. Nevertheless, several multinational enterprises adopt obstructionist strategies in developing countries where the legal and institutional environment is weak (Lee 2011; Li et al. 2010). This could mean that corporate social responsibility may not be separated from the regulatory, cultural, and other contexts of the operations of multinational enterprises, including the host country's legal system (Gainet 2011; Matten and Moon 2008). The public choice theory demonstrates that if coercion is unlikely to improve corporate behavior, another mechanism may be required to prevail on multinational enterprises and other corporations to adopt a multistakeholder approach in economic decisions (Yosifon 2009). This therefore creates room for corporate social responsibility's recognition of stakeholders (Freeman 1984: 46; Zadek 2007: 131–47), multiple constituencies, and the nonexclusivity of profit maximization even for multinational enterprises with global operations.

For example, the Global Economic Ethic manifesto 2009, with subscribers including the United Nations Global Compact Office, intergovernmental and nongovernmental organizations, businesses, and individuals, attempts to fill gaps created by the failures of the markets, institutions, and moral virtues in the global capitalist system (Hemphill and Lillevik 2011: 214; Küng, 2009), which are the three types of failure identified in Dunning's (2001) work on globalization.

In the next chapter, we articulate and explore corporate social responsibility as a private governance mechanism for addressing market failure–led externalities.

4 Corporate Social Responsibility as the Private Governance of Externalities

In this chapter, we aim to offer a unifying interpretation of CSR as an economic philosophy of entrepreneurship and innovation with a distinct theoretical course. We argue that CSR, whether as a management idea or a management innovation, is implicated in various forms of governance of corporate actions, which are largely private. CSR deals with the reduction (internalization) of negative externalities and the promotion of positive externalities by an organization. It is worthwhile to note that *externalities* here is not used in the strict sense of the term, but as a shorthand metaphor for the impacts firms have on both society and the environment. Thus, we envision CSR as a self-regulatory mechanism adopted or to be adopted by corporations in the governance of these positive or negative impacts. This is in line with the new definition of CSR offered by the European Commission (2011): "firms taking responsibilities of their impacts on the society." This way of viewing CSR also limits the profusion of often incongruous meanings and interpretations associated with the term, while making a case for a different way of doing business.

Our goal in positioning CSR as the private governance of corporate externalities is not to undermine the role of the government or other public governance modes in regulating corporate externalities. Rather, we argue for a plurality of governance modes, where CSR complements the existing public and informal governance modes. This, we believe, creates a better chance that both the public and private governance modes will compensate for each other's weaknesses in the governance of corporate externalities. In other words, CSR becomes a private initiative or voluntary effort by firms to address governance voids or to complement existing governance modes within specific institutional configurations (Kang and Moon 2009).

The governance of corporate externalities is not a new science. However, what is new about it is the private dimension of such governance, which features in CSR as an economic philosophy. As already mentioned, CSR is a firm's voluntary participation in the governance of positive and negative externalities. A firm engages in CSR practices when it brings some private initiatives to the governance of externalities—an arena often dominated by the state, the market, and the civil society in developed economies, and by informal groups (e.g., clans and communities) in weak institutions (Portes and Haller 2005). However, the incursion of the private into the public domain is not always a seamless process. Hence, the CSR movement often signals the constant collision of the private and public spheres in the governance of corporate-induced externalities, which fashions the controversies around the concept. Indeed, CSR itself, as a form of organizational behavior, is one of the effects produced by this collision of ideas and, ipso facto, operates in a domain characterized by power relations and contestations. The participation of firms in the governance of corporate externalities opens a new discursive space, which until now was either nonexistent or suppressed. But does this role not undermine the original ideas for the existence of the firm?

Several economic theories give different but related reasons for a firm's existence. The neoclassical model of the firm sees profit maximization as the main reason for a firm's existence, while other views range from an increase in sales (Baumol 1967) and a maximization of managerial utility (Baumol 1967) to the efficient allocation of scarce resources and the firm as a legal nexus of contracts (Williamson 1996). Beyond these mainstream reasons lies the understanding of a firm as a social entity constituted to facilitate a "just and fair" society (Fligstein 1996). Unfortunately, in most free and perfectly competitive markets,[1] this goal of facilitating a just and fair society is not often attained because the supply curves of producing firms rarely internalize the full social costs and benefits[2] associated with the production of goods and services in society. The inability of markets to reflect the full social costs or benefits of a good, service, or state of the world is technically referred to as market failure.[3] In this regard, markets fail to ensure the most efficient or beneficial allocation of resources.

The inefficiency exhibited by firms in their relation to the larger society often results in some sort of intervention from the government, markets, the civil society, consumer groups, and other relevant constituencies, and in some cases self-regulation exercised by the firms themselves. Such intervention aims to restore the socially optimal equilibrium in production and to enable firms to internalize the externalities resulting from their production activities. The government, for instance, uses various policy instruments, such as taxes, subsidies, quotas, and tradable permits, to achieve the required social optimal level in production. The graph in Figure 4.1 illustrates market failure and government intervention.

To ensure that these external costs are internalized by firms, the government intervenes with economic policy instruments that incorporate the external costs into the supply curve (MPC + MEC), and B becomes the new equilibrium. In keeping with the law of demand and supply, an exogenously driven price rise (P to P') produces a decline in demand and consequently a decrease in the production quantity or supply. It is worthwhile to point out that such interventions come with the redistribution of losses and surpluses between the producer and the consumer.

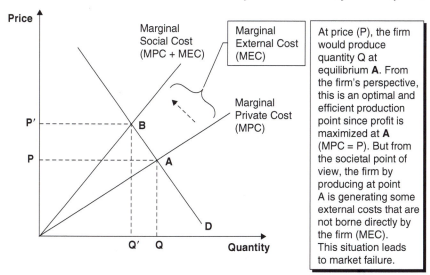

Figure 4.1 Illustrating market failure and government intervention.

The idea of externality is a complex and contentious one since what constitutes an externality is a central area of debate. If the notion of externality poses some theoretical difficulties, then the governance of externalities is an all-the-more daunting task. There is no one route to governing externalities. Different mechanisms have been employed to this effect by different governance modes, depending on whether positive externalities are to be maximized or negative externalities minimized.

Traditionally speaking, corporate externalities for the most part have been positioned in the public space, and the burden of governing them has always been borne by the state. Externalities are the costs borne by an uninvolved third party as a result of a corporate transaction. This could be at the production, sale, or consumption point. A good example of a negative externality is the pollution arising from a production plant, which causes some health hazards to residents not involved in the business transaction. Another negative externality could be the impacts of binge drinking on the society, which is not factored into the production cost of alcohols. In such instances, the social costs are borne by the society. In order to curtail such negative externalities, the state often uses governance mechanisms such as taxation and regulation. Externalities in both neoclassical economics and political economy are quite often articulated from a negative dimension (i.e., negative externalities), which are also known as "market failures."

However, corporate externalities can also be positive, such as the salaries of employees, which directly or indirectly have a positive impact on the local economy (i.e., multiplier effects). It could also be the extra cost voluntarily incurred by a producer to go beyond the minimum expected by regulation or the provision of education and other social infrastructure by firms through philanthropic or other citizenship activities. These forms of externalities have traditionally also been governed by the state through the provision of subsidies as incentives for private businesses to be involved in the production of such goods and services. These incentives today could be offered by other relevant publics: customers through loyalty, employees through commitment and retention, the local community through provision of conducive environment and license to operate, and financial markets through reward for brand equity and enhanced reputation.

CSR as the private governance of externalities is illustrated in Figure 4.2.

In any case, whether positive or negative, the issue of free riding is pertinent to the governance of corporate externalities. Free riding promotes self-interest at the expense of another's interest. The quest for self-interest by firms in the governance of externalities expressed through free riding gives rise to a lack of trust at the individual or personal level. In such instances, institutional trust expressed through formal rules and regulations is preferred well and above personal trust. Accordingly, the market and its actors, including firms, become formalized trust systems (Beckert 2009; Möllering 2006). This understanding of the market and the firm is at the root of the conventional theory of the firm in economics and political economy, where business transactions are often seen as impersonal and amoral.

The public regulation of firms often comes with implementation costs borne by firms and enforcement costs borne by regulators, both of which contribute to an increase in the overall social costs.[4] This has led to the call for smarter regulation. Here, CSR positions itself as a smarter, more efficient, and less costly complementary or alternative mode to the hitherto existing governance mechanisms of corporate externalities. But for the CSR project to be successful as a complementary, private governance mode to government interventional mechanisms, the larger society has to provide the enabling environment for self-regulation to thrive.

In other words, the success or failure of CSR as a self-regulatory mechanism is dependent on the existence of complementary governance mechanisms. For example, if a firm tries to reduce negative externalities, this effort can only be sustained under certain conditions—namely, customers paying more for products, NGOs helping make standards visible, and governments having disclosure rules that affect competitors. In such an enabling environment, CSR affords firms and managers the opportunity to adjust their means of production in a way that gives them competitive advantage and enhances their long-term sustainability. These adjustments are expected to enhance social benefits and reduce social costs simultaneously. CSR in this sense becomes a strategic force for successful business through the creation of entrepreneurial opportunities. This idea is supported by some data from the Canadian Centre for Social Performance and Ethics at the University of Toronto and similar findings elsewhere, which indicate that over a longer

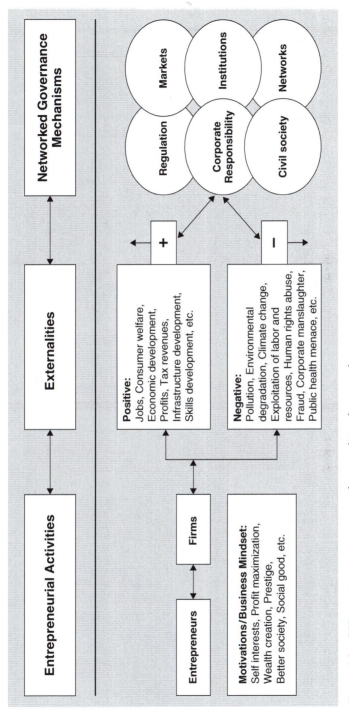

Figure 4.2 CSR as private governance of externalities framework.

term, companies that do well on ethics and CSR are also profitable (Orlitzky et al. 2003; Zairi and Peters 2002).

But do firms always enter the private governance space for the sake of making profit in the long term? Research has shown that firms enter the private governance space for diverse reasons. DiMaggio and Powell (1983), in what has become a classic text, outline three major motivations for the adoption of management ideas: coercive, mimetic, and normative motivations. An example of a coercive motivation is a situation where there is a regulation for firms to behave in specific ways and with strong penalties for any deviations from the expected regulation. Mimetic motivation occurs when a firm simply adopts practices that have worked for competitors or leaders in the same or related sectors, instead of reinventing the wheel. Normative motivations for firms to adopt certain practices are often driven by their engagements with such intermediaries as professional associations and consultancies. In so doing, these intermediaries pass on to firms some "received wisdoms" in the form of "good management practices," and in some cases, these so-called good practices are cocreated by the firms and the intermediaries (Handley et al. 2007).

Any of these motivations can equally apply to the adoption of CSR as private governance of corporate externalities. Some firms may choose to practice CSR on their own accord, motivated by nothing else other than their background culture. Such background culture may include values or the foundational principles of the firm or orientation—a history of successive, organizational activities that are now viewed as important traditions of the firm. Other firms may be coerced to become socially responsible by external factors within the public/political culture of the larger society. Such factors may include fear of public outrage, boycotts, loss of reputation, or potential lawsuits.

CSR as a management idea gives rise to several management innovations. Birkinshaw, Harnel, and Mol (2008) make a subtle distinction between management ideas and management innovations. While management ideas are often macro and generic as "fairly stable bodies of knowledge about what managers ought to do . . . a system of assumptions, accepted principles and rules of procedure" (Kramer 1975), management innovations are management ideas put into practice at the operational level: "The invention and implementation of a management practice, process, structure, or technique that is new to the state of the art and is intended to further organizational goals" (Birkinshaw, Harnel, and Mol 2008: 10). Thus, innovative business practices such as fair trade, accounting for sustainability, corporate governance, responsible investments, and philanthropy can be seen as management innovations arising from CSR as a management idea. Nevertheless, the conception of CSR as a management idea expressed through management innovations is not common. In fact, it has been at the center of contentious debates among scholars. For example, as it has evolved, the CSR concept has undergone some rebranding and remodeling, resulting in the proliferation of terms such as *corporate responsibility*, *corporate citizenship*, *corporate social performance*, and *sustainability*. However, what is often missing in these characterizations of CSR is the common philosophical foundation they share, in spite of their lexical differences.

We argue that CSR is an economic philosophy of entrepreneurship and innovation with a distinct logic. Whether as a management idea or a management innovation, CSR is implicated in various forms of governance of corporate actions, which are largely private. CSR deals with the reduction of negative externalities and the promotion of positive externalities by management. It acts as an antidote to market failure by assisting the market to internalize its externalities.

As already demonstrated, governance can be private or public. We have positioned CSR as a private governance mechanism. In the following section, we will explore the implications of positioning CSR as a complementary private governance mechanism for public governance. We will draw attention to the fact that this view of CSR is largely marginalized in the extent management literature and encourage further research in this area.

CORPORATE SOCIAL RESPONSIBILITY AS A PRIVATE GOVERNANCE MECHANISM: IMPLICATIONS FOR PUBLIC POLICY AND GOVERNANCE

> For all the increasing importance of CSR, public policy remains the most important vehicle by which private business purposes and broader social objectives can be reconciled.
>
> —Moon and Vogel 2009: 318

Firms and markets may fail when they are unable to meet the public interest test or when they give rise to negative impacts borne by third parties. The scale of the 2010 BP oil spillage disaster in the Gulf of Mexico, coming on the heels of the near collapse of the global financial system in 2007–08, for instance, highlighted the colossal and far-reaching impacts of corporate activities on society. The negative impacts of the BP oil disaster were borne by wildlife, small businesses, and people's livelihoods, among others. The brunt of the global financial crisis, engineered by banks in the advanced capitalist economies, was mainly borne by the taxpayers who bailed out the banks, depositors and investors who lost their money, and politicians and administrators who failed to regulate the banks appropriately. In both cases, there were negative spill-over effects mainly borne by people who did not cause the problems in the first instance.

Traditionally, markets have been governed through such fiscal mechanisms as taxation, subsidies, quotas, and incentives, as well as by hard law—for example, an outright ban of a market practice in order to avoid such third-party costs. More recently, self-regulation is gradually being recognized as an equally effective mechanism to govern the market through light-touch and nonprescriptive regulation.

CSR is a form of self-regulation (Vogel 2008). However, the choice and mix of market governance mechanisms have always been a challenge for policy makers. First, the case examples cited here arguably raise concerns about market failure—because of the third-party costs they generate—and second, they creatively draw attention to the contemporary complexities of market governance compounded by globalization and the heightened interest in CSR as a form of corporate regulation because of the proliferation and preference of CSR, as self-regulation, to hard regulation. Third, they raise further questions on how far hard regulation should go without stifling the market for innovation, and fourth, they challenge the role of CSR, currently positioned in mainstream management literature as a profit-promotion mechanism, in governing economic actors who are mainly driven by the pursuit of private interests.

Given its inclination toward appropriating CSR from its profit-promoting perspective, management scholarship appears to inadvertently marginalize and occlude the view of CSR as primarily a market governance mechanism. On the contrary, the public policy and market governance view of CSR conceptualizes it, not necessarily as a profit-promoting mechanism, but rather as a form of corporate self-regulation (Graham and Woods 2006; Brown and Woods 2007; Vogel 2008; Midttun 2008; Mattli and Woods 2009), especially with regards to the private governance of corporate externalities (Vogel 2005; Crouch 2006; Marques and Utting 2009) often necessitated by market failures within capitalist political economies. It seeks to understand private firms and their actions in the broader context of society and the pursuit of public interests (Moon and Vogel 2009). From this perspective, it articulates the role of firms not only as private political actors (Scherer and Palazzo 2007, 2011) or corporate citizens (Crane, Matten, and Moon 2008), but also as a complementary and relevant market governance mechanism, especially where conventional public policy market governance mechanisms (e.g., taxation, quotas, incentives, sanctions, and/or outright bans) are not entirely sufficient. Windsor (2006) describes this as the "expansive public policy" role of CSR, which is important in shaping CSR discourses and practices but is often marginalized in management literature.

This section, therefore, is a theoretical attempt and a discursive project (Phillips, Lawrence, and Hardy 2004) to draw attention to and emphasize the public policy role of CSR (Vogel 2005; Crouch 2006; Marques and Utting 2009), in the form of a market governance mechanism, before it disappears from the management scholarship radar. In line with Crouch (2006: 1534) we accept the view that CSR is a "behavior by firms that voluntarily takes account of the externalities produced by their market behavior" and, thus, explores CSR as a public policy instrument from a market governance perspective. It starts with an overview of the concepts of public governance and regulation in order to provide a background for market governance and the role of CSR, as self-regulation, in capitalist political economies. We finally explore the implications of this view for the emergent literature on comparative CSR, especially with regards to CSR discourse and practice in weak and emergent capitalist political economies.

CSR, PUBLIC GOVERNANCE, AND REGULATORY INSTITUTIONS

Peters (1997: 51–52) articulates public governance as "a more general term for providing direction to the society." It is a generic form of control or coordination that goes beyond those provided by the government, as "the conventional institutions and processes of the public sector" (Peters 1997: 51), to include both formal and informal control or coordination from other sources, actors, and institutions in the society—for example, markets, business networks, communities, families, civil society, and so on. This approach to public governance is not equivalent to governance by public authorities but refers to the governance of the public space involving an "interdependence between organizations," broader than government and including nonstate actors (Rhodes 2007). In other words, public governance is a spatial concept that accepts the existence of "multiple authorities that are not necessarily public" (Morth 2006: 123); and while government is exclusively state and a function of public institutions of the state, public governance encompasses governmental institutions and nongovernmental mechanisms, persons, and organizations (Rosenau 1992: 4–5). This understanding of public governance underpins the new governance movement (Moon 2002), which recognizes the existence and role of private authorities in formulating, influencing, shaping, and driving public policy. It also brings to the fore the subtle distinction between public and private spaces of governance.

The public space of governance, in the main, refers to issues, decisions, and actions relating to, concerning, or affecting the whole of the people or area of a state or nation or a section of either as a political entity. Public space occupiers include government agencies and elected and appointed officials exercising political authority as well as other persons and bodies that perform functions and services of a governmental character. Private space of governance, in contrast, refers to issues, decisions, and actions confined exclusively to particular persons, groups, or areas lacking the constitutive element of the state, nation, or a section of either political entity. Private governance is an arena occupied by nongovernmental social and economic actors and groups. These actors share a common identity of nonstate actors (Lipschutz and Fogel 2002: 116–17) but vary in scope, influence, effect, and functional responsibility.

The emphasis on functional responsibility demonstrates that governance rather than government suggests an affinity with regulation. A broad definition of regulation indicates "principles or rules which aim to govern the behavior of entities or individuals that are subject to them" (Ferran 2001: 384), while a narrow approach argues that regulation is concerned with "valued activities" (Ogus 1994: 1). Both the broad and narrow views of regulation implicitly recognize a regulating role for private actors and groups; whichever approach is taken, private regulation implies a functional role usually but not necessarily exclusively occupied by state actors or public institutions as there are spaces for private actors and groups. Although regulation is obviously understood in the public institutional context of legislative mandate, administrative agency, and judicial interpretation of rules, diverse private forms of regulatory authority exist and are still emerging (Lipschutz and Fogel 2002: 125; Cutler, Haufler, and Porter 1999). As a result, one can define regulation as a deliberately defined control of valued activity by a public agency or a private body.

When apparently private social or economic actors move from passive participation in public affairs to active involvement in public policy, a functional role in governance and regulation exists as either or both part of the process and consequences. This functional responsibility is not restricted to its source. Targets of private regulatory authorities can extend from private actors to public institutions in the bid to promote desired local and international rules and ensure compliance with them (Lipschutz and Fogel 2002: 116–17). This is, at the least, a tacit acknowledgment that regulation is not an exclusive public institution role while private regulatory authorities can and do exist. Regulation certainly includes public laws enforced by a state or government agency, but it may also include private arrangements and even social norms, principles, and customs (Lipschutz and Fogel 2002: 118). The critical factor is not the nature of the actor but rather the fact that the process and result of such private arrangements, norms, principles, and customs are directed at and attract public policy implications. A definition of regulation "in the context of a public agency" (McGee 1999: 145) as "sustained and focused control exercised by a public agency over activities that are valued by a community" (Selznick 1985: 363) is, therefore, too narrow and cannot convey an appropriate scope of the concept of regulation.

Whether public or private, regulation within the governance structure is essentially purposive and targeted at implementing collective goals. Nevertheless, governance has a dual component structure and requires both regulation and enforcement to complete the picture. While regulation sets standards and rules of conduct, the enforcement regime translates those rules and standards into social reality (Yeung 2004: 3). The implication is that the effectiveness of a governance structure is measured by reference to the regulation and enforcement components. Effective enforcement is, therefore, critical to the success of regulatory regimes.

"Rules" establishment is the first stage in regulation. Public economic governance relies on rules established and enforceable by state and governmental authorities. A state actor or public institution can make use of legally binding and soft rules. Soft rules occupy a middle position between "general policy statements and legislation" within regulation (Morth 2006: 120). Although lacking legal force, such rules have "practical effects" (Snyder 1993: 198; Morth 2006: 120). Nevertheless, rules, whether or not legally enforceable, ordinarily relate to the three key elements of regulation, which are "standard-setting, behavior modification and information gathering" (Lodge 2004: 127). Authority for regulation in the sense of these three elements is not necessarily associated with state actors or government institutions (Friedman 1990: 64). The implication is that the state can no longer be assumed as the sole source of regulation; in some cases, it may be clear that the state may not even be the principal regulator (Hall and Biersteker 2002: 5; Ogus 1994: 1–3).

Private actors and groups can also set standards, establish rules, and gather information to ensure understanding and adherence. Just like state actors and public institutions, they can establish and enforce legally binding rules primarily using private contracts. For example, clauses relating to social matters such as relationships with employees and host communities are increasingly included in supply chain contracts, and parties are now more inclined to enforce such clauses (McBarnet and Kurkchiyan 2007: 77–83). Contractual undertakings can be enforced by recourse to litigation and alternative dispute resolution mechanisms where there is appropriate agreement by the parties. Nonstate regulatory actors can also make use of soft rules in a manner similar but not identical to public instruments. Within private regulation, soft rules are simply "non-hierarchical rules that are not legally binding" (Djelic and Sahlin-Andersson 2006: 248). They may be largely but not necessarily or exclusively dependent on reciprocity. As a reciprocal arrangement, however, soft rules usually constitute elements of self-regulation and coregulation and may include voluntary and sanctions-lacking standards, codes of conduct, recommendations, and guidelines (Djelic and Sahlin-Andersson 2006: 247). Tacit norms, conventions, and cultural beliefs are other examples of private regulation in economic governance (McNichol 2006: 351).

Notwithstanding that the obvious understanding of regulation seems to, naturally, point to some form of governmental intervention at the least, evidence of "authoritative decision making" by private actors and groups is increasing (Cutler, Haufler, and Porter 1999: 16) in diverse areas. Economic governance is one such area. Within the sphere of economic governance, regulatory activity may be interpreted in three ways. First, in a narrow sense, regulation may be regarded as "the promulgation of an authoritative set of rules, accompanied by some mechanism, typically a public agency, for monitoring and promoting compliance with these rules" (Jordana and Levi-Faur 2004: 3–4). Second, regulation may refer to "all the efforts of state agencies to steer the economy" (Jordana and Levi-Faur 2004: 4). In this broader middle-ground approach, regulation includes both rule making and measures such as taxes, subsidies, public ownership, and redistribution of property. In the third and broadest sense, regulation covers "all mechanisms of social control, including unintentional and non-state processes" (Jordana and Levi-Faur 2004: 4). This broad approach extends the scope of regulation to "anything producing effects on behavior [even] without mechanisms for monitoring and enforcement" (Baldwin, Scott, and Hood 1998: 4). In contrast to the first and second approaches, this model of regulation implicitly recognizes spaces for private actors and groups in economic governance.

This model has been corroborated by evidence and practice that demonstrate that regulation is not the exclusive preserve of state actors and public institutions. Evident in several areas is the "fluidization of regulatory space" (Lipschutz and Fogel 2002: 122). Historical accounts demonstrate varying degrees of private public policy involvement in economic governance (Braithwaite and Drahos 2000; Murphy 1994). Public and private regulators have existed in different areas of economic activity although the regulatory agenda may be diverse and dynamic. Several historical examples abound of activities "governed by customs, laws, and contracts among and between individuals and groups, often but not always with the approval or support of the state" (Lipschutz and Fogel 2002: 121).

Whether in setting agendas, rules, or monitoring mechanisms, private economic governance roles are apparently increasing. Modern economic governance proves, as a fact, that "regulatory arenas go beyond governments" (Radaelli and De Francesco 2007: 16). Reasons for the emergence and expanding role of private regulation include deregulation, privatization, and delegation of regulatory power to private organizations, business associations, or agencies (Cutler 2002). As Morss (1991: 55) rightly observes, "the era in which nations rule the world is over . . . [since] three groups have joined nations as important global players: transnational corporations, international organizations, and special interest groups." Civil society and interest groups at the local, national, and international levels are increasingly influential actors in economic governance (Engwall 2006: 165). In addition to regulation from state and public institutions, the freedom of modern firms is also limited by threats of civil litigation and pressures from the media, public opinion, and other external stakeholders (Smith and Walter 2006: 48).

CAPITALIST POLITICAL ECONOMIES AND MARKET GOVERNANCE

It is a culture of economic coordination that places significant emphasis on individual freedom and the free pursuit of self-interests for profit accumulation (Swedberg 2003). Although all economies involve production, distribution, and consumption, Swedberg (2003: 58) argues that "what distinguishes capitalism from other economic systems is primarily the way in which distribution is organized: as exchange in the market and not as reciprocity or redistribution . . . [and] . . . the continuous reinvestment of profit into production." The neoclassical version of capitalism takes the centrality of markets seriously and places an excessive emphasis on the virtue of markets as free and perfect social exchange spaces and institutions.

As social exchange spaces and institutions, the market in itself can constitute a private governance arena made up of actors, such as firms, investors, shareholders, and consumers, that are capable of exercising some form of control over corporate activities. Reputation management and control, for instance, illustrates the reality and potency of private regulation in the market governance arena. Reputation as a component of such regulation is connected, for example, to the influence of brand in attracting or discouraging custom. Reputation may create and build brands, and the strength of brands may be connected to consumer expectations and perception of the consistency of performance of the firm concerned. In this sense, individuals and groups of consumers can play a regulating role in an economic governance structure with a firm–consumer interface. For example, the fair-trade movement has flourished on account of consumer expectation of the observation of fair-trade principles by firms, leading to demands for ethical products. The movement has emerged as a critical consumer control mechanism and addresses the seller–buyer power imbalance due to its inspection and monitoring systems (Dine and Shields 2008; Nicholls and Opal 2005). The movement uses certification, labeling, monitoring, and inspection as part of its regulatory methods.

Despite the emphasis on markets, the capitalist system, as discussed earlier, is also made up of a range of other institutions, which include "the firms as institutions of production, and the state as the creator and regulator of the institutions governing their relationships (while itself being a political institution), as well as other informal institutions such as social convention" (Chang 2003: 8). The primary purpose of these institutions is to coordinate and allocate resources in a way that ensures societal stability, progress, and development and, thus, could be narrowed down to what Streeck and Shmitter (1985) described as the three ideal-typical principles of coordination and allocation: "dispersed competition" (market), "hierarchical control" (the state, as well as the firm), and "spontaneous solidarity" (community).

However, there could be debates and tensions as to how these institutions should be configured and operate in any society—in other words, debates over how free the market should be without the interventions of the state and community and to what extent the market should internalize its externalities on both the state and the community (Chang 2003). In some cases, the primacy of markets over the other institutions is advocated for, and in some instances others argue for the supremacy of the state over the other institutions as the main source of governance in the form of law and order necessary for the functioning of both markets and communities (Streeck and Shmitter 1985). The possibility of combining and recombining these institutions with different degrees of calibration has given rise to different capitalist political economies. The practice of capitalism in different societies and economies, therefore, becomes a function of national history, culture, philosophy, and ideological tastes. In other words, despite the fact that capitalist political economies exhibit some similar characteristics, they are not necessarily homogeneous.

There is an already established literature on comparative capitalism that explores the institutional configurations of different varieties of capitalism and national business systems (for example see: Whitley 1999; Hall and Soskice 2001; Dore 2000; Amable 2003; Fiss and Zajac 2004; Crouch 2005; Hancké, Rhodes, and Thatcher 2007). The central theme of the varieties of capitalism model, for instance, is the macroeconomic dichotomization of institutional contexts in which firms operate, based on such indices as legal and governance systems, sources of finance and skills, and other sociolegal indices like degree of labor unionization and incursions of regulatory authorities. It is not uncommon in comparative capitalism literature to stylize coordinated market economies (CMEs) as stakeholder oriented and liberal market economies (LMEs) as shareholder oriented (Dore 2000). The CME is society oriented, and firms within it focus on meeting a broad range of stakeholders' needs (e.g., employees, suppliers, shareholders, etc.), whereas the LME is market oriented and focuses more on meeting shareholders needs than those of any other stakeholder groups (Dore 2000; Amable 2003; Hall and Soskice 2001; Fiss and Zajac 2004; Jackson 2005; Hancké et al. 2007). Japan and Germany are prime examples of CME whereas the United Kingdom and the United States are prime examples of LME. In this regard, proponents of the varieties of capitalism theoretical view argue that different national and institutional contexts provide some sort of comparative advantages to firms within them. This theoretical framework has been applied to the study of capitalist political economies outside the Anglo-Saxon world—for example, Latin America (Schneider 2009), Africa (Wood and Frynas 2007)—and the role of business in the society (Amaeshi and Amao 2009; Amaeshi 2007; Matten and Moon 2008).

Notwithstanding these subtle differences, most advanced capitalist economies are characterized by: (a) strong rule of law; (b) a functioning state; (c) strong market institutions; and (d) freedom of speech and association (see Table 4.1).

In summary, these basic elements of the capitalist political economy could be described as a collective apparatus of institutional accountability. They work in tandem and reinforce one another. The markets provide or deny finance to the state, and the state in turn regulates the markets. Essential societal services that could not be provided through the market, due to market failure, are complemented by the state and/or the civil society. And the civil society in turn is free to hold the state and the market to account whenever necessary. All these interactions among and between the different elements are founded on and bounded by the rule of law embodied in free and fair

Table 4.1 Key characteristics of advanced capitalist economies

Elements	Descriptions
Rule of law/property rights	The rule of law, the delineation of rights, and the right to own properties are central to the functioning of capitalism as an economic mode of coordination. The rule of law and the consequent rights enable entrepreneurs to invest in and exchange goods and services through contracts.
A functioning state	It is the role of the state to protect lives and properties upon which the rule of law and property rights are founded. According to Swedberg (2003: 158), "the very existence of modern economic actors and economic institutions presuppose, among other things, that the issue of violence has been solved and removed from the arena of the economy; that when conflicts emerge in the economy, solutions can be reached and enforced; and that decisions can be taken about the role of economic and non-economic activities in society as a whole. All of these factors point to the crucial existence of separate political authorities, and to politics, as a way to influence these authorities." The World Bank Anti-Corruption and Governance Index is based on six broad measures of good governance: (1) Voice and Accountability, (2) Political Stability, (3) Government Effectiveness, (4) Regulatory Quality, (5) Rule of Law, and (6) Control of Corruption (Kaufmann, Kraay, and Mastruzzi 2008).
Strong market institutions	The construction of markets as exchange mechanisms is fundamentally predicated on the neoliberal conception of democratic politics and its antecedent institutional arrangements, wherein agents are free and have the rights to exercise and exert their property rights within legitimate institutional boundaries.
Freedom of speech and association	The right to freedom of speech and association contributes to strong capitalist political economies. This is particularly necessary for the emergence of strong media, business networks, organized labor unions, NGOs, and other civil society networks.

legal institutions. The combinatory strength of each of these elements constitutes the distinguishing hallmark of the advanced capitalist economies. Weak capitalist political economies usually arise where one or more of the collective apparatus of institutional accountability does not exist or is undermined (Wood and Frynas 2006).

On the practice level, therefore, the conceptualization of CSR as a market governance and public policy mechanism offers a complementary lens to the ethical (normative) and strategic (instrumental) positioning of CSR in the mainstream management literature. It both challenges and encourages firms and managers to appreciate their engagements in CSR as a participation in public governance for a progressive society. In other words, one of the advantages of framing CSR as a market governance mechanism of the capitalist political economy is that it extends the language project of CSR as a neutral management practice (Amaeshi and Adi 2007). It also saves it from the debates in the literature on normative and instrumental CSR practices, which appear to stand in the way of advancing scholarship in this field and are likely to generate new meanings and foster new ways of engaging with the practice other than for-profit motives only.

However, a possible explanation for the marginalization of the public policy role of CSR in management literature could, arguably, be as a result of the narrow focus of business schools on micro-organizational efficiency and performance, which currently inform management scholarship (Stern and Barley 1996). In addition, most of the conversations on the political role of CSR currently take place in such disciplines as law (e.g., Rogowski and Wilthagen 1994; Hess 1999; Branson 2001), political science (e.g., Lowi 1964; Vogel 2008), public administration (e.g., Moon 1998), and international relations and development (e.g., Knil and Lehmkuhl 2002; Newell 2002, 2005; Blowfield and Frynas 2005; Graham and Woods 2006). The few attempts to migrate this thinking to management literature (e.g., Crane, Matten, and Moon 2008; Scherer and Palazzo 2011; Moon and Vogel 2008; Moon, Kang, and Gond 2010) have to a large extent mirrored the basic social sciences disciplines (especially those of political science and international relations) underlying them. Fewer attempts (e.g., Crouch 2006; Campbell 2007; Midtunn 2008) have been made to develop a public policy role for CSR from such disciplines as economic sociology and/ or institutional political economy, which are gaining significant traction in other areas of management scholarship. Moreover, these latter disciplinary perspectives hold significant potential for enhancing our understanding of the global CSR movement, especially since CSR loses its essence outside the frameworks of the capitalist political economy.

One of the reasons often advanced by CSR critics is that managers are inept with regards to public policy decisions and issues. While recognizing the merit of this criticism, it does imply the need to change management education in such a way that it enhances the public policy competences of managers. The new generation of managers will need public policy skills—especially partnering skills—to navigate the complex interpenetration of public and private interests in the globalized contemporary world of business. This will place significant emphasis on business schools in shaping managerial practices and diffusing fads and fashions (Patriotta and Starkey 2008; Starkey and Tempest 2005; Ghoshal 2005). And herein lie new challenges for business schools and management educators, as well as management consultants and other producers of management education, as we gradually drift into another turn in the evolution of capitalism.

The craving for a turn in capitalism lies at the heart of the growing uptake of responsible investment practice in different markets. In the next two chapters, we explore the implications of articulating CSR as a private governance mechanism, first for the market for responsible investments, and second for CSR in different institutional contexts. The latter is particularly important since capitalism is said to be a function of institutional contexts and configurations (Hall and Soskice 2001), and CSR is a product of institutional path dependency (Matten and Moon 2008).

5 Corporate Social Responsibility as a Private Governance Mechanism
Implications for Markets

> Not everything worth measuring is measurable; not everything measurable is worth measuring.
>
> —Albert Einstein

Does the corporate social responsibility governance logic resonate with the dominant financial market logic of calculation and singularization? There is interest in business scholarship to render CSR calculable and to show a connection between it and corporate financial performance (e.g., Mackey, Mackey, and Barney 2007; Hull and Rothenberg 2008; Baron 2009). While some of these studies report a positive relationship between CSR and corporate financial performance, a rigorous meta-analysis of these studies conclude that, at best, the relationship between CSR and corporate financial performance is neutral—with a negligible or marginal positive impact (Orlitzky, Schmidt, and Rynes 2003). CSR, in this regard, comes across as a corporate hygiene factor—in other words, the absence of it hurts, but the presence does not have a significant impact on the fortune of the firm. Whilst these studies are laudable, they often tend to assume the automatic absorption of CSR into the conventional financial market space, as if the former is susceptible to the logic of calculation and singularization of the latter. These studies often take the market performativity of CSR for granted. First of all, they do not easily recognize the possibilities of the existence of different markets for different goods and services (Araujo 2007) and, therefore, tend to make assumptions about the dominant logic of calculation and singularization characteristic of the conventional financial markets, homogenize this logic across different markets, and take its enactment (i.e., its performativity) for granted (Callon and Muniesa 2005; Muniesa and Callon 2008). In other words, this growing interest in the link between CSR and financial performance, which is now more like a futile exercise of chasing one's shadow, fails to ask the question: to what extent does the appropriation of the CSR paradigm into the financial market space fit the dominant market logic of calculation and singularization, and how could this appropriation of CSR be enabled and performed to fit the dominant financial market logic? Nowhere is this more evident than in the markets for responsible investments—for example, the inclusion of environmental, social, and governance (ESG) issues in investment decisions.

The market for responsible investment is one of the variants of the broader CSR and corporate social performance (CSP) agenda. It made its mark through the social responsible investment (SRI) practice, which has for a long time remained a niche market for investors interested in environmental, social, and governance issues. Although not often explicitly expressed, SRI—as part and parcel of the broader CSR agenda—is underscored by the quest to minimize negative and maximize positive corporate externalities. Throughout its history, the SRI practice has been trailed with a lot of interesting studies to ascertain how well such investments perform in relation to other forms of *mainstream* investments (cf. Orlitzky, Schmidt, and Rynes 2003), which may not necessarily share the same philosophy of internalizing corporate negative externalities. Although the academic literature on the link between corporate social performance and corporate financial performance is riddled with mixed findings, the case for mainstreaming SRI is on the rise. According to the Eurosif SRI Study (2005), "the global SRI market can be estimated to reach approximately €5 trillion" (58). Despite the interests behind the responsible investment movement and the bold forecast that it will "become mainstream within asset management by 2015, reaching between 15%–20% of total global Assets Under Management ($26.5 trillion) and a total revenue of approximately $53 billion" (Robeco Investment Management and Booz & Company 2007: 3), it is still at the fringes of the global financial market—a market estimated to be up to $140 trillion (more than three times the global GDP) at the end of 2005 (McKinsey Global Institute 2007).

We conjecture that one of the main reasons why the responsible investment market is struggling to become mainstreamed is the incompatibility of its underpinning philosophy (i.e., governance of externalities) with that of *mainstream* financial markets. However, this position is highly contestable and calls for some empirical inquiry. To understand this puzzle, therefore, this chapter draws insights from the extant literature on the sociology of financial markets—especially from the performativist perspectives of markets (MacKenzie and Millo 2003; Beunza and Stark 2003, 2004; Fligstein and Dauter 2007; Callon and Muniesa 2005; Muniesa and Callon 2008)—and seeks to unpack the barriers that may stand in the way of mainstreaming responsible investments. It pays specific attention to the question: to what extent does the foundational philosophy of the responsible investment practice, as part of the broader CSR culture, fit into the dominant financial market logic of calculation and singularization?

The sociotechnical perspective has been used extensively to study the emergence of different markets—for example, the wind power market (Karnoe 2004), the financial derivatives market (MacKenzie and Millo 2003), financial arbitrage (Beunza and Stark 2003, 2004), the mobile market (Simakova and Neyland 2008), and the carbon market (Callon 2009; Lohmann 2005)—but rarely has been applied to the study of markets for CSR.[1] Nonetheless, CSR still remains one of the undertheorized aspects of management studies. The novelty of this chapter, therefore, lies mainly in bringing together these disparate sets of literature to understand the dynamics of the responsible investment market, which could equally provide some useful insights into unlocking the inconclusive and often mixed results of studies on the relationship between corporate social performance and corporate financial performance in the literature. In so doing, it directly contributes to the urgent call to restore "to markets the political dimension that belongs to them and constitutes their organization as an object of debate and questioning" (Callon and Muniesa 2005: 1245).

The study is also empirically novel. Unlike most academic studies that are based on the meta-analysis of the academic literature, this study is primarily based on materials/documents, as well as focus group discussions, produced by the practitioners themselves. These practitioner groups include: fund managers associations, thank tanks, multinational institutions, accounting firms, consultancies, and so on. This is particularly interesting since the practice of CSR is well ahead of its theorization. It is anticipated that the findings presented in this text will be relevant to practitioners in the field of responsible investment and will offer some insights on the future direction of research in this area.

The chapter starts with a discussion on markets as diverse institutions with nonhomogenous logics and focuses specifically on the dominant logic of the conventional financial markets. It then systematically explores the research data to ascertain the overlap, or otherwise, between the governance logic of CSR and the dominant logic of the financial markets, and then it discusses the research evidence.

WHAT MARKET? INSTITUTIONS, LOGICS, AND PERFORMATIVITY

Markets are exchange institutions, which are prevalent in, and central to the functioning of, the contemporary economic world order. They are the *spaces* for the exchange of goods and services with their unique sets of logic, devices, networks, and artifacts. Although markets have been theorized as socially embedded, and therefore either constrained or enabled by social norms and institutions (Granovetter 1985), there is a tendency in the scholarship to confuse this understanding of markets, as series of social exchanges governed by social norms and institutions, with the idea of markets as institutions in themselves—with their specified "rules of the game" (North 1990). According to Loasby (1999: 107), "to confuse markets with exchange is a category mistake; it is a confusion of institutions and activities." Loasby argues that "an exchange is an event . . . ; it is something that happens. A market is a setting within which exchange may take place—a setting which refers to 'a group or groups of people, some of whom desire to obtain certain things and some of whom are in a position to supply what the others want' (Marshall 1919: 182)." This distinction between markets as institutions and markets as series of exchanges is very useful in accounting for the creation, sustenance, emergence, and performativity of markets (e.g., Holm 1995; Simakova and Neyland 2008) in both the institutionalist and social technical perspectives of markets.

Markets as institutions are, however, diverse (Kjellberg and Helgesson 2006). In other words, the market for commodities is different from the *money* markets as well as the *carbon* markets; at least, each of these markets is an arena for different market activities and exchanges. They are different calculative spaces with different forms of calculation (Callon and Muniesa 2005: 1231). As such, different markets are made up of different defining institutional logics—in other words, organizing principles that are sometimes in competition with each other. For instance, the market for corporate financial performance does not often factor in a firm's full social costs[2] in the calculation of its profit (Vogel 2005), while the market for responsible investment aims to completely do the opposite (i.e., internalize a firm's full social costs into its profit equation). This coexistence of diverse institutional logics is often referred to as institutional pluralism. Another good example of institutional pluralism is the case of a utility company, which through privatization inherits both the market logic of profit maximization and the regulatory (*governance*) logic of ensuring a competitive market in order to maximize social welfare (Jarzabzowski, Matthiesen, and Van de Ven 2009). In a similar trend, Reay and Hinings (2009) present the case of the health care system in Alberta, Canada, which had to cope with the uncomfortable coexistence of the competing logics of *business-like* logic and *medical professionalism* logic. Although institutional pluralism has been black boxed in accounts of institutional inertia and dynamics, some studies have begun to examine it in much detail and explore the strategies employed by entities trapped in such circumstance to cope with the complexities of institutional pluralism (e.g., Jarzabzowski, Matthiesen, and Van de Ven 2009; Reay and Hinings 2009). Accordingly, Lounsbury (2008) argues: "By focusing on how fields are comprised of multiple logics, and thus, multiple forms of institutionally-based rationality, institutional analysts can provide new insight into practice variation and the dynamics of practice." This also applies to the understanding of markets as dynamic institutions and diverse calculative spaces, which could be particularly interesting if applied to enhancing our knowledge of the coexistence of markets for CSR and the financial markets despite their seeming different underpinning logics.

From a performativity perspective, Callon and Muniesa (2005: 1245) define a market—in the neoclassical sense, which is a dominant framing of markets—as "a collective device for the evaluation of goods . . . [which] . . . is possible only if goods can be calculated by calculative agencies whose encounters are organized and stabilized to a greater or lesser degree." In its performativity, therefore, the market, as a collective device for the evaluation of goods, needs to socioconstructively objectify the good and singularize the outcomes of that objectification. Objectification, in the sense used by Callon and Muniesa (2005), implies some sort of tangibility and manipulability—that is, the good evaluated has to be "a thing" (Callon and Muniesa 2005). Both tangibility and manipulability allow the market system to compare and contrast. The comparability of data adds to the data quality. And one way to objectify the good evaluated is through quantification, which is central to neoclassical market logic. Through *singularization,* the objectified is brought together in a singular system—for example, the price mechanism—for it to leave the world of supply (i.e., the seller) and slot into the world of the buyer. It is thus "able to leave the calculative space and circulate elsewhere in an acceptable way (without taking with it the whole calculative apparatus)" (Callon and Muniesa 2005: 1231).

The performativity of the neoclassical market also requires agents and exchanges to be enacted. In this instance, both objectification and singularization are enacted by agents through (specialized) exchange media and platforms—for example, computer screens and networks, stock exchange floors, trading rooms and technologies, and so forth. Accordingly, "the co-production of singular and objectified properties requires the involvement of a large number of 'market professionals' (marketers, packagers, advertisers, designers, merchandisers, sellers, etc.)" (Callon and Muniesa 2005: 1234) because "the construction of markets is an accomplishment that depends on the mobilisation of different bodies of expertise" (Araujo 2007: 211). In sum, the singularization and the objectification attributes reinforce each other and strengthen the needs of the market upon which tangibility and comparability are built by agents and through exchanges. This association also supports the efficient market hypothesis, which assumes that the market internalizes information (i.e., quality data) in a way that supports both tangibility and comparability. In this regard, the effectiveness of markets, therefore, "stems from the fact that they make complicated calculations possible, and that these produce practical solutions to problems that could not otherwise be solved by purely theoretical reflection . . . [and] . . . to be calculated, economic goods have to be calculable" (Callon and Muniesa 2005: 1229, 1230). It is against this dominant logic of neoclassical performativity of markets that the responsible investment practice is often measured or anticipated to be calculated. But the question still remains: to what extent is the governance logic of the broad CSR agenda translatable into the objectification and singularization logic of the financial markets? Are CSR properties quantifiable and calculable?

EXPLORING THE MARKET FOR RESPONSIBLE
INVESTMENTS: PROSPECTS AND CHALLENGES

To understand the nature of the market for CSR and the challenges involved in mainstreaming the market for responsible investments, the data for this study were drawn from multiple practitioner sources—in other words, practitioners' reports, focus group discussions, and a Delphi panel session. The study searched for practitioners' reports in this field since 2000—given that much of the momentum in this field has been, mainly, since the turn of the 21st century—and identified 82 reports from accounting firms, investor associations, business coalitions, investment banks, multinational institutions, consultancies and think tanks, governments, and multistakeholder forums.

The choice of these practitioners' reports as data sources is not arbitrary. In addition to the fact that CSR practice is well ahead of the academic literature, the role of texts in the institutionalization of practices is very much acknowledged in the extant literature (Taylor et al. 1996). Phillips, Lawrence, and Hardy (2004), for instance, present one of the major step changes in management literature linking discourses directly to institutions. Social reality, it is argued, is constitutive of discourses. Without discourse, there is no social reality, and without understanding discourse, we cannot understand our reality, our experiences, or ourselves (Phillips and Hardy 2002). Drawing from Parker (1992), Phillips and Hardy (2002: 3) define discourse "as an interrelated set of texts, and the practices of their production, dissemination, and reception, that brings an object into being." In other words, the goal of discourse analysis is to ascertain the constructive effects of discourse through the structured and systematic study of texts (Hardy 2001; Phillips and Hardy 2002). In this regard, language becomes fundamental to institutionalization, and institutionalization occurs as actors interact and come to accept shared definitions of reality (Phillips, Lawrence, and Hardy 2004). Hence, it is through linguistic processes that definitions of reality are constituted (Berger and Luckmann 1966). Furthermore, Phillips and colleagues state that "institutions, therefore, can be understood as products of the discursive activity that influences actions" (2004: 635).

According to Phillips and colleagues, actions inform the formative processes of institutionalization and resultant institutions in turn inform, enable, and constrain actions. This interactive process is mediated by texts and discourses. Actions generate corresponding texts, but not every action is capable of generating texts that are widely disseminated and consumed. Phillips, Lawrence, and Hardy (2004: 642) theorize that only those actions that require organizational sense-making and that affect perceptions of an organization's legitimacy are more likely to result in the production of texts that are widely disseminated and consumed than actions that do not. The texts in turn inform discourses, which in turn inform institutions. However, not every text is capable of becoming embedded in discourses, except those "that are produced by actors who are understood to have a legitimate right to speak, who have resource power or formal authority, or who are centrally located in a field" (Phillips, Lawrence, and Hardy 2004: 644). In addition, "texts that take the form of genres, which are recognizable, interpretable, and usable in other organizations and texts that draw on other texts within the discourse and on other well-established discourses are more likely to become embedded in discourse than texts that do not" (2004: 644). In the same vein, they argue that not every discourse gives rise to institutions. Discourses that give rise to institutions are "coherent, structured and . . . supported by broader discourses and are not highly contested by competing discourses" (2004: 645).

Influenced by Phillips and colleagues (2004) and related literature, the criteria for selecting the texts used in this study are as presented here.

Criteria for Selecting the Report Documents

- Documents focused on the broad areas of ESG issues in investment decisions, project finance, and/or financial markets—including the following:
  - Sustainable finance
  - Responsible investments
  - CSR and corporate performance
  - CSR and investor behavior
  - Nonfinancial and/or extrafinancial performance
  - Sustainability and financial markets
- Documents produced mainly by practitioners—for example, consultancies, think tanks, industry associations, accounting firms, regulators, multinational institutions, multistakeholder groups, and so on; where published by academic institutions or by academics, the document should be understood as being addressed to practitioners and not meant for the academic audience
- Documents not published in academic journals
- Documents that were impactful—impact factor to be determined by practitioners' awareness of the document—for example, through citations or word-of-mouth reference
- Documents published from 2000 to date of study

A list of the 82 reports was sent to 36 experts in the field to advise on the relevance and impacts of these reports. The experts were also asked to identify other reports the study might have missed in the process. The intention here was to meta-analyze these reports with the aim of identifying the major issues involved in the integration of ESG risks in investment decisions. Out of the targeted 36 practitioner respondents, 18 responses were received. A good number of the reports presented to them were considered relevant and impactful; 13 extra reports were suggested through

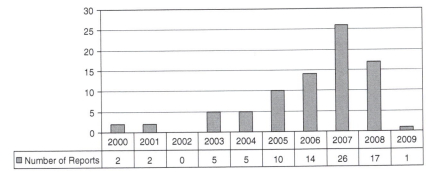

	2000	2001	2002	2003	2004	2005	2006	2007	2008	2009
▣ Number of Reports	2	2	0	5	5	10	14	26	17	1

Figure 5.1 Number of reports and annual trends.

this process, which were added to the mix. In total, the reports constituted well over four thousand pages; however, a sample of these (22)—those most mentioned by the respondents—were analyzed. A breakdown of the sources of the reports and the annual trend of the reports identified are presented in Figure 5.1.

In addition to the practitioners' reports, five focus group sessions were conducted in parallel in some financial cities of Europe (Frankfurt, Milan, Paris, Rome, and Stockholm). Each of the focus group sessions had an average of 15 discussants drawn from the different interest groups of fund managers, accounting firms, consultancies, CSR specialists, and so forth. The focus group discussions were facilitated by a group of experts drawn from academia and industry. Given the sensitivity around ESG issues—especially with regards to competitive, regulatory, and civil society pressures—these discussions were conducted in a safe environment to encourage honest conversations (i.e. openness and sharing of information). The focus group discussion sessions were governed by the Chatham House rule[3] and, as such, were not recorded—but notes were taken by the experts from academia and industry who observed the different sessions (see Figure 5.2).

DATA ANALYSIS

The notes generated from the focus group sessions and the practitioners' reports were then qualitatively analyses by Nvivo following a rigorous coding scheme developed by the researchers. The first set of findings yielded a number of themes ranging from the education and mind-set of the financial analysts involved in the making of markets to the market artifacts and technologies that shape the financial markets. Given the interest in understanding the underlying logics of the conventional financial markets and how they relate to the market for CSR, the researchers

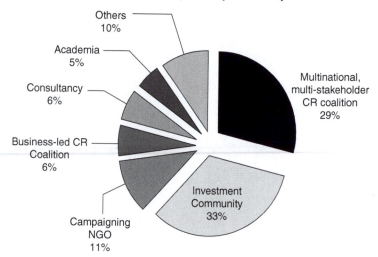

Figure 5.2 Percentage representation of reports by groups.

further narrowed down to those findings focusing mainly on the calculative attributes of the conventional financial markets and their implications
for the mainstreaming of the responsible investment practice. At the end
of this phase of the analysis, a Delphi[4] panel session was run to share the
findings of the study with experts in the field and also to get their feedback
on how to improve on the research. The Delphi panel session drew about
30 participants from the mainstream investment community, boutique
SRI community, academia, professional bodies, and the CR/sustainability
community. The researchers were all involved in the Delphi panel sessions,
and the suggestions/feedback from the sessions were further discussed and
reflected upon by the researchers immediately after the sessions, the next
day, while the feedback was still fresh. A sample of the issues identified
through the data analysis as some of the main areas where the market for
responsible investments is still struggling to align itself with the dominant
logic of the neoclassical financial markets are discussed in the following
sections.

EMPIRICAL FINDINGS

In this section we map the themes that emerged from the data analysis onto
the dominant logics of the financial markets (i.e., objectification, singularization, and transferability) highlighted earlier in the study in order to appreciate the seeming misalignment between the fundamental logics of the
two markets—markets for responsible investments and the *mainstream* financial markets.

Financial Market Logic 1: Objectification

One of the key features of the objectification logic is that market goods should be rendered quantifiable and calculable, which is often socially constructed in order to achieve some level of simplicity and comparability. The data show that the ESG issues present a very high degree of complexity, which makes them very difficult to articulate, assess, and integrate into investment decisions. This complexity is tied to the challenge involved in socially constructing the boundaries of ESG issues—in other words, what is in and what is out. Obviously, this is associated with the historical baggage ESG issues tend to inherit from the SRI trend. The SRI market has all sorts of issues embedded in it, including value-based funds (ethical funds) as well as positively and negatively screened funds. One could argue that it is difficult to point to an absolute morality (or ethics), which makes the entire drive toward ethical investment easily susceptible to relativist arguments and therefore subjective and not easily amenable to a market characterized by the quest for a socially constructed objectivity, comparability, and generalizability (Callon and Muniesa 2005). Reflecting on this confusion and complex identity, some fund managers noted:

> Part of our challenge as a movement is that we have a confusing persona in the marketplace. One minute we are talking about values and clients' ability to define ethical issues, another minute we are talking about ESG integration that could help in a risk-adjusted way. We merge all those together. Not surprisingly, clients, customers, consultants and everyone else, including ourselves, get confused. (Responsible Investor, "Responsible Investment Landscape 2008 Asset Owners": 6)

> Having found 16 different phrases to describe the kind of sustainability data that managers say they are now integrating into their mainstream analysis, it's hardly surprising people are confused and that integration is not moving as quickly as it could! If we want mainstreaming to accelerate going forwards, finding one or two consensus terms that embody what integration is about would be a very good move. (AXA, "Investment Managers Survey Report," 2008)

Given that the CSR logic is to regulate externalities and mitigate market failures, this complexity and uncertainty is further orchestrated by the fact that the CSR agenda upon which the ESG issues are founded is always expanding and adjusting to the demands of the time. The issues are constantly evolving and as such are difficult to pin down. For example, the issue of obesity and healthy eating has entered the CSR agenda, where it was not in the last decade or so, especially in the developed economies. The same can be said of other issues like climate change, water scarcity, and even immunization (e.g., PharmaFutures). This fluidity, while necessary in identifying and internalizing externalities arising from corporate actions and inactions, carries with it a significant amount of complexity and uncertainty, as expressed in the following comments:

> At the same time, the CR agenda continues to expand, with new theories about what is "responsible" business practice. What was once a simple set of ethical principles now embraces such issues as: resource use; greenhouse gas emissions; genetic modification; product pricing in developing countries; animal testing; ethical trading; and so on. In order to satisfy investor demands for information on such a diverse range of topics, SRI researchers demand an increasing quantity of information from companies on their policies and practices in all of these areas. . . . The widening scope of SRI analysis is obscuring efforts to focus down on the material issues. (Arthur D. Little, *Speaking the Same Language*, 2003: 6)

> The quest to unpack and address these complexities often leads to information overload, because. . . . Investors have limited time and resources to analyze corporate data . . . especially if that information has no clear link to investment decision-making . . . for it to effectively support an efficient market. (Boston College, "White Paper: Report on Project Findings Corporate Reporting of Social, Environmental, and Governance Information: What Investors Want," 2008: 4)

Financial Market Logic 2: Singularization and Financialization

Singularization logic aims to bring the goods rendered calculable and quantifiable into a singular system (e.g., a price mechanism), which is essential for the function of the conventional financial markets. The research data show that the issues around the singularization and financialization logic of the financial markets were expressed in three key ways: the (a) quality of data, (b) the materiality of data, and (c) the time horizon of data.

Quality of Data

As expressed in the following comments, the quality of CSR data required for responsible investment decisions and market quantification was often raised as one of the main obstacles constraining the mainstreaming of ESG issues.

> It was a common perception that most of the corporate material was of limited use for investment professionals, as it was (and still is today) typically communicated in prose style. Moreover, ESG data are often delivered to stakeholders as a separate paper report. . . . ESG information should be consistent and transparent. The information should be quantified and adequately explained. Comparisons with other organizations

should also be possible. For this reason, all material changes in the boundaries and scope of reporting, or the reporting periods, should be indicated and explained. The reported ESG-KPIs must be accurate (i.e. free from significant errors), plausible, and definitive, and not in contradiction with current measures. (European Federation of Financial Analysts Societies [EFFAS], "KPIs Reports," 2008)

The . . . reason for the scepticism of mainstream analysts is the lack of measures with which to compare CR performance between companies. Analysts are accustomed to using ratios and models to compare companies on a roughly equal basis, which helps to make portfolio decisions easier. (Arthur D. Little, *Speaking the Same Language*, 2003)

The argument, therefore, is that for ESG issues to be mainstreamed, they have to be amenable to these market demands of objectification and singularization (Callon and Muniesa 2005), as graphically explained here by an Investors Association body:

Integration of ESG is often viewed under a theoretical framework that, although currently under some scrutiny from the academic world, has been well-established through practical experience: namely that of "efficient markets." In short, this theory states that prices already reflect all known information relating to a share, and that the markets are in a state of equilibrium. All new information—and ESG represents an immense reservoir of additional information for financial analysts and investors . . . —has the potential to impact the fundamental assessment of an equity. This presupposes, of course—and this is where the work of DVFA [Society of Investment Professionals in Germany] is focused— that the data is quantified, comparable, and benchmarkable! This is what makes the data usable for every investment professional. (EFFAS, "KPIs Reports," 2008)

Notwithstanding, the need to meet the objectification and singularization demands of the market appears to be undermined by data inconsistencies and insufficiencies arising mainly from the differences of ESG data in terms of actors, industries, regions, and countries, as succinctly noted by the recent Goldman Sachs report and in one of the focus group sessions.

We are challenged by data inconsistencies, regional differences in policy focus, degrees of integration across the value chain, and diverse product portfolios across the companies in our ESG universe. We do not believe that sufficient quantifiable and comparable data exists to objectively measure several issues such as human rights, recruitment, training, local waste and water management and biodiversity. (Goldman Sachs Sustain, 2008)

It has often been highlighted that, depending upon the sector, the maturity of the company, its size, and its context (locality, events, regulation, environment) the stakes linked to ESG dimensions can be very different. For example, environmental considerations would be very secondary for banks but of high importance for manufacturing industry. However, not all manufacturing industries are exposed to the same environmental problems and responsibility in this field can present themselves in differing ways with different types of technology and levels of investment. The same for those who have to formulate CR policy—they vary according to the company, its sector, time, etc. (focus group, 2009)

Tied to this concern of data inconsistencies is the concern over the predictive reliability of data on ESG issues:

If a company is rated very highly based on its ESG criteria and its share price has gone up, you can't be sure the company's share price went up because of the ESG criteria or some other reason. Perhaps by observing the company and similar investments for an extended period of time the relationship may become more obvious; but presently, it isn't possible to do. (Phone interview with Alka Banerjee of Standard and Poor's, April 10, 2008; quote from Business Social Responsibility [BSR] report, "Environmental, Social and Governance: Moving to Mainstream Investing?" 2008: 9)

Materiality of Data

One of the vexing problems that has continued to haunt ESG matters is how to ascertain the issues that are material and those that are not. The materiality of these issues is at the center of the debate on the connection between corporate social performance (broadly defined as ESG issues) and corporate financial performance. For instance, WestLB (2007: 1) argued: "The link (of ESG information) to other financial variables (share price performance, valuation, profitability, growth) is much less pronounced, and only in a few cases do we have reason to believe that it goes beyond mere statistical coincidence."

It is worthwhile to point out that the materiality construct is not entirely an independent one. Materiality is rather perceived to be dependent on the other issues—such as quality of data, management processes, the methodologies and approaches employed, and even on the presence of a price system:

To traditional financial analysts, ESG factors are often material only when they carry a "price tag," a phenomenon that has been observable since the introduction of the European emissions trading system. (WestLB 2007: 11)

It was also emphasized that the materiality of "extrafinancial" factors does not necessarily support short-term performances (i.e., they are usually long-term focused), which are easier to calculate and singularize than long-term performances.

> The concept of extra-financial materiality aims not to identify the factors that have an impact of +/–5% on the results of the coming fiscal year, but rather to record those factors that can have an impact of, for example, 10%, 20% or 50% over the next five, 10 or 20 years, or that can even be decisive to the company's survival. (WestLB 2007: 7)

In support of this, BSR (2008: 3) commented: "Although many mainstream financial institutions, such as ABN AMRO and Goldman Sachs, have begun considering the effects of including ESG criteria as part of their fundamental financial analysis, investors are waiting for vetted proof of long-term materiality before fully incorporating the criteria." The ability to figure out the materiality of ESG issues, according to Arthur D. Little, is also dependent on the competence of the analysts: "Material CR issues are those that really affect value. Some SRI analysts have a poor understanding of the materiality of CR issues to shareholders' interests" (Arthur D. Little Consulting 2003: 4). All these are further compounded by the fact that in the "current definitions of trustee fiduciary duty, financial materiality and corporate disclosure requirements do not incorporate or ensure the integration of environmental, social and corporate governance issues into fundamental company analysis" (United Nations Environment Programme Finance Initiative [UNEPFI] 2004: 5).

Time Horizon of Data

Price is one of the essential elements of the neoclassical financial market and is a function of time. Therefore, time is an essential element in the investment decision equation. And this comes up often as one of the challenges in the way of mainstreaming ESG issues, especially as the financial markets are in the main skewed toward short-termism and ESG issues are often long-term oriented. There is a kind of default mode of thinking that expects attention to ESG issues in investment decisions to conform to short-term demands. In a survey conducted by EIRIS, it was found that:

> In the "top 10" sectors over 90% of investors surveyed believed that ESG issues would have some impact on the companies' value over the short to medium term (3–5 years); over a third considered the financial impact to affect over 10% of the value of companies; and around 10% considered over 25% of value to be at risk. (EIRIS 2006)

This creates a competitive tension and often a disparity between short-term and long-term investment time horizons, on one hand, and short-term and long-term investment interests. But most of the time, the short-term pressures tend to win against long-term interests and time horizons. However, the Chartered Financial Analyst (CFA) warned that:

> An excessive short-term focus combined with insufficient regard for long-term strategy can tip the balance in value-destructive ways for market participants, undermine the market's credibility, and discourage long-term value creation and investment. Such short-term strategies are often based on accounting-driven metrics that are not fully reflective of the complexities of corporate management and investment. (CFA 2006)

Financial Market Logic 3: Transferability (i.e., Agents, Artifacts, and Exchanges)

The transferability logic implies that markets require agents, artifacts, and exchanges to operate, and these could be politically motivated. The findings in this logic mainly fall under the following two categories: (a) power relations and (b) trust and accountability, which are essential for the functioning of financial markets.

Power Relations

In addition to the complexities engendered by the ESG issues, they also constitute an arena for contestations and power relations. These contestations and power relations in turn express themselves through different interests and interest groups. Unsurprisingly, in the literature and sometimes in everyday professional conversations on ESG issues, the investor community is often considered and treated as a homogenous group. This understanding in itself tends to occlude the differences in both interests and power relations that could exist amongst investors. A participant in one of the focus groups drew attention to the fact: "We should be careful here to recognize that investors are not an [*sic*] homogenous group. They are different and have different needs and therefore require different approaches."

Investors could also be differentiated in terms of their analytical inclinations—for example, either quantitative or qualitative oriented—as well as their professional identities. These analytical inclinations and differences in professional identities are themselves enough sources of contestation because "a quantitative investor/analyst would say that he can't use [a company's] data because they could not compare cross-sector—whereas a qualitative-based one would treat [the same data] as interesting insight into quality of management" (focus group discussant). There is also a tussle between the investment community and other professional groups. For instance, one of the participants in a focus group noted the following:

> People in a company have different views about their own CSR performance. For us SRI analysts help us to legitimize our own activity inside

the company. CSR manager and SRI analysts kind of team up against the rest of the managers.

It is also recognized that the three legs of ESG are not treated equally. In most cases, the G issues are prioritized over E and S issues, as confirmed the research findings of a think tank:

> Our findings suggest that asset managers' focus on ESG more often than not is limited to governance issues such as board structure and remuneration. Of the 22 asset managers that disclosed a policy on ESG issues 19 covered only corporate governance issues, while only F&C, Insight and Standard Life could explain their policy on environmental and social factors in any detail. Similarly, on corporate engagement, although the overall score for the 30 asset managers on ESG engagement was 53%, this fell to a mere 25% when environmental and social issues were considered separately from governance. It appears as though investment analysis of environmental and social risks/opportunities is confined to a small niche in the industry. This is a significant cause for concern as the risks associated with environmental and social mismanagement by companies can be as damaging to value as governance issues both in the short and the long run. . . . Although two thirds of the asset managers surveyed could demonstrate evidence of over 50 requests for change in company behaviour in relation to ESG issues; only one sixth (F&C, Insight, Aviva Investors, Schroders and Standard Life) could do the same once governance issues were removed. Evidence of success in securing change is also weaker in E&S than in ESG as a whole. (Fair Pensions, "Investor Responsibility," 2008)

Power relations and contestations may sometimes also take a transnational and political nature.

One reason why analysts, traders, and portfolio managers reject extrafinancial information is that it "has been defined exogenously. It is the result of a multi-stakeholder dialogue that is now being imposed on the closed 'capital market' system. Ultimately, incumbents fear that the objective of ESG is to change this system, and so their opposition should come as no surprise. It must, therefore, be made clear in each case what objectives are being pursued and what the underlying motives are" (WestLB 2007: 5).

The view that ESG issues are politically charged, as in the aforementioned quote, is further corroborated by this quote from an Investors Association body:

> There is a considerable conceptual and communicative gap between the more politically and human rights–motivated UN campaign, "Principles for Responsible Investments," and the day-to-day experience of sustainability in many companies. This disconnect cannot be remedied

by any legislative means, and no attempt should be made by legislatures to do so. The issue at hand is a translation of features and properties, which at first glance are difficult to grasp and too complex to quantify into indicators that the capital markets can understand, use for calculations, and relate to monetary figures. This type of modelling relies on the financial-analytical mindset of investment professionals. These are the people who will develop such models, and ultimately, the only ones who will recognize their usefulness. (EFFAS, "KPIs for ESG," 2008)

Trust and Accountability

All these challenges confronting the mainstreaming of ESG issues finally boil down to issues of trust and accountability—for example, amongst the different actors, firms, and even at the system level.

On the firm level, there is a seeming distrust of the credibility of management to represent ESG issues in decision making in ways that do not harm investors' interests. In this regard, most investors would expect that:

> The information, data, processes, and assigned competencies required for the preparation of ESG reports should be recorded, analyzed, documented, and disclosed in such a way that they would stand up to an internal and external audit or review. An independent audit by well-qualified third parties is a particularly good way to increase the assurance capability (i.e. perceived reliability) of the reported ESG-KPIs. This also serves to ensure the credibility and acceptance of ESG communication among the target groups. As a rule, external auditing carries the additional advantage that ESG reporting and ESG management can be improved based on the best practices referred to by the auditor. (EFFAS, "KPIs for ESG," 2008)

Ernst and Young (2007: 4) also noted: "Financial reputation is essentially about trust. The underlying question which needs to be clearly answered in the mind of the investor is whether they believe in management, their strategy and their ability to deliver." In other words, "the credibility of management, how they communicate and the quality of financial reporting are all paramount . . . [since] . . . financial reputation is primarily about building trust with, and demonstrating competence to investors" (Ernst and Young 2007: 3, 4).

Despite the fact that financial reputation is built on trust and accountability, "most fund managers scored very low on transparency, with only a few honourable exceptions" (Fair Pensions, "Investor Responsibility," 2008). This paradox of low transparency even when high transparency is needed to enhance financial reputation is not unrelated to the dilemma (i.e., the unintended burden of trust) that confronts managers, and which is aptly described by the following extracts:

As can be seen, companies appear to be reluctant to put hard numbers upon these issues or set themselves targets that can then be held against them in the future—not just in the environmental or social fields. Ironically, when taken to extremes, such fears of bad publicity can also make them appear closed or having something to hide in the eyes of journalists and other audiences. The lack of disclosure can itself lead to bad publicity as they gain a reputation for failing to reveal information. (Business in the Environment, "Investing in the Future," 2003)

There is no financial penalty for survey participation, the benefit is questionable and so it is often difficult to make the business case to disclose corporate information (Research Network for Business Sustainability 2008: 16)

This air of distrust extends to other actors and artifacts such as in Table 5.1.

In summary, therefore, these findings suggest that the foundational logics of responsible investments and the mainstream financial markets are fundamentally different, especially as the former is driven by the question to control corporate externalities and the latter is prone to failure due to its inability to internalize corporate externalities. Surprisingly, the extant literature on the relationship between corporate social performance and corporate financial performance appears to take the difference in the underpinning logics of the two spheres for granted. This invariably calls for a reexamination of the link between the broader CSR agenda, the functioning of markets, and the governance of corporate externalities.

Table 5.1 Distrust amongst various financial communities

Distrust for the	
SRI community	"The SRI community needs to become more credible to mainstream investors, and to justify its conviction that it can help investors to assess shareholder value more thoroughly." (Arthur D. Little Consulting 2003: 4)
Measurement metrics	"None of [the existing] frameworks have been observed long enough to conclusively show that they yield long-term outperformance." (BSR 2008: 8)
Rating agencies	"Organisations that conduct questionnaire surveys are not clear enough about whose interests they serve, or what they will do with the information they receive. Their analysis is often seen by companies as naive." (Arthur D. Little Consulting 2003: 4)

RETHINKING THE LINK BETWEEN CSR, MARKETS, AND CORPORATE EXTERNALITIES

Studies on the connection between corporate social responsibility and financial market outcomes have continued to generate mixed and inconclusive results. A significant proportion of the findings of these studies appear to assume that corporate social and financial performance share the same market logic and common exchange "currencies." We have reexamined this taken-for-granted assumption in the extant literature. Based on data drawn from the challenges of mainstreaming the market for responsible investments, we argue the case that corporate responsibility is a unique economic paradigm that will either need to develop its own market in order to be viable or will be easily susceptible to the dominant logic of calculation and singularization characteristic of the conventional financial markets. In other words, not everything about corporate responsibility is as measurable as the financial markets would ask for. Comparing what is rendered measurable, on one hand, and what is yet to lend itself to measurability, on the other hand, is a fundamental flaw in this literature. As such, corporate responsibility and financial performance will continue to run on competing logics until their different markets are distinctively articulated and/or aligned.

The extant literature on the link between corporate social performance and corporate financial performance has continued to be surprised by mixed and, at best, inconclusive results. Leveraging recent theoretical and empirical developments in social studies of finance (SSF), we have explored the assumption often made in the literature with regards to the link between corporate social and financial performances, which tends to apply a homogenized market logic and common exchange "currencies" to understanding corporate social actions, on one hand, and corporate financial performance, on the other. Institutional logics of legitimacy and calculativity are entangled in both domains at different intensities and combinations. In line with SSF theorizations, the text argues that the market for corporate financial performance is mainly driven and sustained by the logic of calculativity and singularization; while the market for corporate social actions thrives predominantly on the logic of legitimacy and the complexities of governing corporate externalities, it has yet to lend itself effectively to calculative practices and machines (artifacts) required by calculative agents to orchestrate its performativity. As such, some of the challenges highlighted by the financial market actors, in this regard, include lack of reliable and appropriate metrics/tools to measure ESG factors adequately, which makes comparability of firms along these lines difficult.

For there to be advances in the search for a credible link between corporate social performance and corporate financial performance, the performativity of the two needs to be harmonized through objectification, singularization, and appropriate agents and exchange mechanisms (Callon and Muniesa 2005). Thus, conflating the two logics and their performativity would be akin to the proverbial storing of new wine in an old wine skin and or the mistake of comparing apples to oranges. It is suggested that this distinction is necessary to resolve the inconclusive and mixed results generated so far and to advance research in this area of study. Otherwise, for there to be meaningful progress in the corporate social and financial performance debate, corporate responsibility as an economic paradigm needs to either develop its own market or allow itself to be fitted into the dominant logic of calculation and singularization characteristic of the corporate financial performance project. If not, corporate responsibility and the financial markets will continue to be strange bedfellows leading to very mixed and inconclusive results on the link between corporate social and finance performance.

6 Corporate Social Responsibility as a Private Governance Mechanism

Implications for CSR in Different Institutional Contexts

The meaning and practice of corporate social responsibility across cultures and national boundaries are central to the success of CSR in the context of globalization. In the recent past, some business scholars began to explore the contextual frameworks of CSR in different institutions and cultures.[1] For instance, the *Journal of Corporate Citizenship* ran special issues focusing on corporate social responsibility in Asia (2004), Africa (2005), and Latin America (2006). These studies challenge the underlying presumptuousness in the conceptualization of CSR principles in the West as universally applicable guidelines for business theory and practice. A recurring theme among the various studies is the claim that the understanding and practice of corporate social responsibility are to a reasonable degree predicated on sociocultural factors.

Matten and Moon (2008), for example, use the "explicit" and "implicit" models to explain the differences between Continental European and North American versions of corporate social responsibility practices. They suggest that within the explicit model of CSR, North American firms are vociferous about their contributions to society in the form of health care provision, education, employee welfare, and other social amenities. Contrarily, in the implicit model of CSR characteristic of Continental Europe, firms find it less attractive to report such provisions as contributions to the society, since such services and amenities are already taken care of by the national institutions of the countries in which they operate. The UK government's national health care service (the NHS) has been providing free health care service to its citizenry since the 1940s, and the German system has ensured that employees' welfare gets top priority in organizations through its codetermination approach to corporate governance.

In line with the socioeconomic differences inherent in the neoliberal capitalist systems, Maignan (2001) conducted a survey comparing French, German, and North American consumers' evaluations of the economic, legal, ethical, and philanthropic responsibilities of firms. The study finds that while US consumers highly value corporate economic responsibilities, French and German consumers are most concerned about businesses conforming to legal and ethical standards. Thus, Maignan suggests that these findings provide useful guidance for the efficient management of corporate social responsibility initiatives across borders and for further academic inquiries. In a similar study, Langlois and Schlegelmilch (1990) analyzed the usage and contents of corporate codes of ethics. Comparison of a sample of 600 large European companies contrasted with findings reported for similar US firms reveals that significantly fewer European than US firms adopted codes of ethics. In addition, the study shows striking differences in content between US and European codes of ethics, pointing to the existence of a distinctly European approach to codifying ethics.

There are also recorded differences between US and Asian understandings of corporate social responsibility. Burton, Farh, and Hegarty (2000) examined the orientation toward corporate social responsibility among 165 US and 157 Hong Kong business students. Although respondents from both countries exhibited little or no theoretical differences, there were nonetheless significant disparities in the types of responsibilities considered most important. Unlike their US counterparts, Hong Kong students accorded priority to economic responsibilities over noneconomic responsibilities. Orpen (1987) found similar differences between US and South African managers. He assessed the attitudes of 164 United States and 151 South African managers toward CSR. The US managers held significantly more favorable attitudes toward CSR. In addition, they agreed with more pro-responsibility arguments, whereas the South African managers agreed with more anti-responsibility arguments. The US managers felt that their society expected more corporate involvement in social responsibility activities than the South African managers. The results elucidate, in terms of the susceptibility of corporate social responsibility, differences in attitudes to cultural norms and values in the United States and South Africa.

In the four special issues of the *Journal of Corporate Citizenship* focusing on CSR in Asia (2004), Africa (2005), Latin America (2006), and developing economies (2006), scholars studied variations in CSR among various countries. Hamann and colleagues (2005) and Fig (2005) examined corporate social responsibility in South Africa and questioned the drift toward universalizing CSR. Kusku and Zarkada-Fraser (2004) compared CSR practices in Australia and Turkey and identified some key differences. Chapple and Moon (2005) reviewed CSR reporting in seven Asian countries. They found some variations in CSR practice across the Asian countries studied, which in their opinion were not reflective of the level of development of each of those countries, but rather the result of their different national business systems. This finding is counterintuitive to conventional wisdom as one would ordinarily expect the level of development of a country to correlate with its CSR practice (Jones 1999), since the prevalence of CSR theory and practice in the Western world is often attributed to economic prosperity. Even in the West, Worthington, Ram, and Jones (2006) found a different attitude to CSR among South Asian small enterprises in the United Kingdom. In sum, these studies suggest that the meaning and practice of corporate social responsibility is socioculturally embedded (Bennett 1998) and question the current trend toward the globalization of CSR practices through multinational corporations and multinational institutions.[2]

But are CSR practices suitable and relevant in all institutional contexts? To what extent and under what conditions are CSR practices complementary or noncomplementary governance mechanisms in weak institutional contexts? Articulating CSR as a market governance mechanism will have implications for both theory building and practice. First, it is no gainsaying that the capitalist political economy has taken advantage of globalization to become the dominant, as well as the idealized, global mode of economic coordination, especially following the decline of the competing socialist political economy model since the late 1980s (Kang 2006). Hence, the capitalist political economy has, to a large extent, become the global yardstick for assessing responsible and irresponsible business behaviors in the management literature, despite the differences in national socioeconomic cultures and institutions.

We argue that economic governance institutions will in most cases be configured to the tastes and preferences of a particular society. Consequently, economic systems can be classified as either weak or strong (Aguilera and Jackson 2003), a success or a failure (Wood and Frynas 2006), depending on how much they reflect the essential characteristics of the advanced capitalist political economies—in other words, in terms of functioning, independent, and free markets; governments; civil societies; and legislative institutions. It is therefore surprising that most major CSR theoretical frameworks and discourses in the management scholarship often assume strong institutional contexts in their accounts.

Aguilera and Jackson (2003: 247), for instance, developed "a theoretical model to identify and explain the diversity of corporate governance across advanced capitalist economies," while Matten and Moon (2008: 406) in their theorization of the explicit and implicit model of CSR assumed "some basic institutional prerequisites for CSR" founded on the essential characteristics of the advanced capitalist economies:

> First, we assume a functioning market in which corporations have discretion over their responses to market, social, or political drivers. Second, we assume functioning governmental and legal institutions that guarantee, define, and administer the market and act on behalf of society to address instances of market failure. Third, we assume that these institutions neither capture nor are captured by market actors. And fourth, we assume a civil society that institutionalizes and articulates social values and preferences, to which government and market actors respond. (Matten and Moon 2008: 406)

Even if one accepts the view that "CSR is located in wider responsibility systems in which business, governmental, legal, and social actors operate according to some measure of mutual responsiveness, interdependency, choice, and capacity" (Matten and Moon 2008: 407), it invariably leads to some uneasiness with regards to the role of so-called CSR practices in institutional contexts marred by inefficient markets, poor governance, and weak civil societies. The claim that CSR can be enacted where there are no "markets and business autonomy, as demonstrated by myriad cases of individual, family, tribal, religious, charitable, and feudal responsibility" (Matten and Moon 2008: 407), does not render irrelevant questions about the meaning and usefulness of CSR practices in different institutional contexts and cultures. Thus, the idea of developing CSR principles from within the theoretical framework of strong institutions (especially those of the West), with the intent to apply those principles in weak and fragile institutions, is problematic. In a weak institutional context, the government is weak, the market is inefficient, and firms that operate in such an environment tend to generate more negative externalities than otherwise.

Where attempts are made to articulate CSR as a market governance and public policy mechanism in the management literature, they have often assumed a global playing ground in the form of global public policy networks (e.g., Detomasi 2006). This view appears to place significant emphasis on globalization and its consequent global governance void (Scherer and Palazzo 2011) to the detriment of national governance spaces and political economies. Despite the intellectual attractiveness of this perspective, available evidence suggests that CSR practices can only "work, for *some* people, in *some* places, on *some* issues, *some* of the time" (Newell 2005: 556), and the effectiveness of current practices of corporate self-regulation in transnational social spaces (Morgan 2006) with little or no equivalent transnational governance mechanisms (Djelic and Quack 2008) is questionable (Graham and Woods 2006: 868). Moreover, acknowledging the homogenizing effects of globalization does not necessarily spell the end of nation states and the peculiarities of their economic governance institutional configurations. National business systems do not disappear, but rather find new and innovative ways of internalizing the influences of globalization while retaining their distinctiveness (Whitley 1999, 1998). National business systems, therefore, offer a very fertile ground for conceptualizing CSR as a public policy instrument.

The complex issues associated with globalization, coupled with growing concerns about poverty, corruption, inequalities, and sustainable development in most developing economies, challenge the role and purpose of multinational enterprises (MNEs) in the global world order. The globalization process and its consequent discontents tend to unsettle most familiar socioeconomic institutional arrangements, blurring the neat divide between the responsibilities of firms, markets, and nation states in both politics and economics (Stiglitz 2002). As a result, global firms appear to be directly or indirectly compelled by some external actors (e.g., NGOs, international organizations, and pressure groups) to fill in the transnational governance gap for nation states, especially in developing economies with weak and fragile institutions that are incapable of governing the activities of MNEs. MNEs are, therefore, encouraged to be more socially responsible and transparent in their practices. This subtle compulsion often reveals itself in the growing trend of CSR as self-regulation (Graham and Woods 2006; Brown and Woods 2007; Vogel 2008; Mattli and Woods 2009) and the private governance of corporate externalities (Crouch 2006).

Articulating CSR as a complementary governance mechanism suggests that it both shapes and is shaped by the other governance mechanisms within an institutional context. Although comparative CSR literature has in the main focused on how CSR practices are enabled and constrained by their institutional contexts (Matten and Moon 2008; Campbell 2007; Aguilera et al. 2007), it also sometimes positions firms and their CSR practices as passive recipients and responses, respectively, to the demands of their institutional contexts. While this might be true of CSR practices in most advanced capitalist economies with strong institutions[3] from which most of the CSR analytical frameworks have been framed, it is also recognized that firms are not just passive recipients of institutional norms and practices (DiMaggio and Powell 1983)—they are also institutional actors (Giddens 1984; Borsch 2004) and entrepreneurs (Lawrence and Suddaby 2007; Dahan, Doh, and Guay 2006; Crouch 2005) capable of setting a "hegemonic and pragmatic agenda" (Gray 2002).

A good example of this scenario would be the entrepreneurial influences of most MNEs on some organizational fields, especially in developing economies. The oil and gas sector in Nigeria, for instance, is heavily driven more by global rather than local practices (Ite 2004, 2005; Frynas, Mellahi, and Pigman 2006; Frynas 1999), since the major actors in the sector are MNEs who tend to retain their home country influences, albeit with slight modifications (Whitley 1999). In this regard, multinational actors could be conceived as institutional entrepreneurs "who skillfully use institutional logics to create or change institutions, in order to realize an interest that they value highly" (Leca and Naccache 2006: 634). And in such instances, "companies turn away from the national context and develop their own local governance structure. If the national institutional structure is seen as non-adequate or 'non-fitting' to deal with specific terms of competition, then the internal and external coordination of companies—in reaction to challenges posed by the market—is likely to deviate from the national structure" (Crouch, Schroder, and Voelzkow 2009).

An important sticking point in the international business literature at the moment is understanding to what extent MNEs retain their home country influences when they operate in developing economies characterized by fragmented (Whitley 1999) and segmented (Wood and Frynas 2006) national business systems. For instance, Amaeshi and Amao (2009) suggest that the behavior of MNEs in the Nigerian oil and gas sector is to a large extent influenced by their varieties of capitalism.

Amaeshi and Amao (2009) explore how the tradition and political culture of the home country of MNEs influence the CSR practices of these corporations when they operate outside their national or regional institutional contexts. The study focuses on a particular CSR practice (i.e., corporate expressions of code of conducts) of seven MNEs from three varieties of capitalism—coordinated (two), mixed (two), and liberal (three) market economies—operating in the oil and gas sector of the Nigerian economy. The study concludes that the corporate codes of conduct of these MNEs operating in Nigeria, to a large extent, reflect the characteristics of their home countries' model of capitalism, although with a certain degree of modifications. The home countries' model of capitalism is also found to have implications for the degree of adaptability of these MNEs' CSR practices to the Nigerian institutional context—with the mixed market economy model of capitalism adapting more flexibly than the liberal and coordinated market economies. Another study by Amao and Amaeshi (2008), citing the corporate governance scandal of Cadbury Plc Nigeria, suggest that MNEs are not always shielded from the dominant corrupt corporate practices of their host countries. Instead, they tend to reflect the dominant political culture of their host institutional contexts (Adegbite, Amaeshi, and Amao 2009).

While acknowledging the macroinstitutional influences, organizational behavior is also shaped from within and from below by the organizational culture, values, and leadership (Visser 2007; Hemmingway and Maclagan 2004). This is very central to the current CSR discourse. In this regard, CSR becomes a private governance mechanism for "maximizing the positive and minimizing the negative effects on social, environmental and economic issues and stakeholders."[4] Although it is not often mentioned in the management literature, the conventional business paradigm is subtly being challenged by the corporate responsibility and sustainability paradigm. The many discontents of globalization and particularly the current global crisis reinforce the view that something needs to change within the conventional business paradigm, and responsible business practices lie at the heart of this change. While this is possible, it raises moral questions as to whether firms strategically exploit lapses within their institutional contexts for their advantage or contribute to building and enhancing governance institutions for a more progressive society. Given this concern, we recognize the complementary function of CSR in capitalist economies and articulate CSR as any corporate practice that supports the institutional pillars of the capitalist political economy to create a "just and fair" society (Fligstein 1996), while a noncomplementary CSR is any corporate practice that undermines or crowds out the positive effects of any of these institutional pillars of the capitalist political economy (see Wiig and Kolstad's 2010 account of CSR in Angola, for example). Notwithstanding, these changes are more likely to be sticky rather than rapid or step changes given that large-scale and far-reaching changes would require "considerable institutional restructuring and realignment of major societal interests . . . [that] are unlikely to develop simply as a consequence of internationalization, or to occur within one or two decades" (Whitley 1999: 134). In relation to institutional changes relating to corporate governance structures, for instance, Vitols (2001: 339) argues that "these developments can be clearly characterized as incremental—rather than fundamental—changes in existing ownership, employee representation, and top management institutions."

Graham and Woods (2006: 868) argue that to make such voluntary governance mechanisms more effective, "government action—in the North and South—remains vital to effective regulation, by setting social goals and upholding the freedom of civil society actors to organize and mobilize. International organizations and legal instruments may be able to assist developing country governments in fulfilling these roles." Their suggestion fits in perfectly into what Midttun (2008) aptly describes as partnered governance. According to Midttun, most current global issues (e.g., climate change, human rights, and corruption) are no longer able to be governed by a single governance institution (e.g., markets, firms, and the state), especially as global economic entities continue to transverse territories with weak and fragile governance institutions. He therefore suggests a constructive, but complementary, mixture of public, market, voluntary, and civil regulatory mechanisms.

In that regard, CSR as a private governance of corporate externalities, therefore, serves as a complementary governance mechanism for the governance of global "wicked problems" (Churchman 1967) that neither markets, the civil society, nor the state, through hard regulation, could deal with in isolation. It is from this perspective that CSR needs to be appreciated as a practice with a distinct governance mechanism, which is not necessarily a profit-maximization mechanism, contrary to mainstream management thinking and expectations. In other words, despite the promises of CSR, it will be dangerous to rely on it in isolation from other complementary institutional configurations to drive institutional change and enable a progressive society in different institutional contexts.

Drawing from the challenges of accountability in global networks of production, we explore the limitations of CSR in the next chapter.

7 The Problem of Accountability in the Global Networks of Production

Corporate social responsibility is increasingly becoming a popular business concept in developed economies. As typical of other business concepts, it is on its way to globalization through practices and structures of the globalized capitalist world order, typified in multinational enterprises. However, CSR often sits uncomfortably in this capitalist world order as MNEs are often challenged by the global reach of their supply chains and the possible irresponsible practices inherent along these chains. The case of the BP oil spill of 2010 and the subsequent legal wrangles between BP, Halliburton, and Transocean exemplify the complexities surrounding the question of accountability in the global networks of production of MNEs.[1] The possibility of irresponsible practices along their supply chains and services puts global firms under pressure to protect their brands, even if it means assuming responsibilities for the practices of their suppliers.

Pressure groups understand this burden on firms and try to take advantage of the situation. This chapter seeks to challenge the often-taken-for-granted assumption that firms should be accountable for the practices of their suppliers by espousing the moral (and sometimes legal) underpinnings of the concept of responsibility. Except where corporate control and/or corporate grouping exist, it identifies the use of power as a critical factor to be considered in allocating responsibility in a firm–supplier relationship and suggests that the more powerful in this relationship has a responsibility to exert some moral influence on the weaker party. We highlight the use of codes of conduct, corporate culture, anti-pressure group campaigns, personnel training, and value reorientation as possible sources of wielding positive moral influence along supply chains.

The stakeholder theory of corporate social responsibility emphasizes a broad set of social responsibilities for business. Stakeholders, as used in this theory, refer to those individuals or groups who may affect or are affected by the organization (Freeman 1984, 1994; Clarkson 1995). They include a wide variety of interests and, as suggested by Mullins (2002), may be grouped under six main headings: employees, shareholders, consumers, government, community, and the environment, as well as groups such as suppliers, trade unions, business associates, and even competitors. In this regard, CSR can be broadly defined as an organization's commitment to operate in an economically and environmentally sustainable manner while recognizing the interests of its stakeholders.[2]

In line with this broader definition of CSR, global brands like Nike, GAP, Adidas, and McDonalds are often under intense pressure from groups working for responsible supply chain management. Much of this pressure is channeled through the supply chain, since the pressure groups sometimes find it difficult to reach the global brands directly. To this end, they rely on indirect tactics such as targeting the sourcing activities of these brands and their seeming exploitation of cheap labor conditions in developing countries. These attacks, which have been quite successful in recent times, hack on the reputation of these firms (e.g., Nike's case).[3] They engender negative public sentiments and invariably resentments toward the global brands following "irresponsible" behaviors along their supply chain. These negative perceptions of firms persist, irrespective of the locus of the "guilty" suppliers on the supply chain spectrum of the primary purchasing firm. This image tends to put firms under pressure to bear indefinite responsibilities for their wide and long supplier networks. Firms, therefore, do everything possible to protect their brands—including accounting for the seeming irresponsible behaviors of their suppliers, as shown in the current wave of social reports across industries.

There seems to be widespread agreement on some form of corporate responsibility for social issues. Nevertheless, the critical question is how to define or limit the scope of such responsibility within the context of the operations of MNEs. The enormity of corporate multinational power makes this an urgent and important task. The general conception of corporate social responsibility is extralegal (McWilliams and Siegel 2001). Apart from corporate social responsibility reports, firms including MNEs now appear to adhere to one code of conduct or another. These codes are usually voluntary initiatives by the firms, either alone or in association with other firms in the same or similar industry. Sometimes, other participants such as pressure groups and civil societies make input into the contents of such codes. However, most corporate codes of conduct have not properly addressed the issue of defining the limit of corporate responsibility for the activities of another corporation. For instance, the apparel industry code of conduct for US-based clothing and accessories corporations imposes a "duty" on such enterprises to ensure compliance with the code by their contractors, subcontractors, suppliers, and licensees.[4] This is clearly a nebulous obligation. Does this duty extend to all the levels and actors in the supply chain, irrespective of proximity or remoteness from the firm or MNE? Can the duty be applied to a situation where the MNE is not even in a position to control or influence a member of the supply chain? Is unlimited exposure to social responsibility a good idea for the business environment? How does social responsibility fit in with the concepts of corporate legal personality and independent existence of corporations? Is reconciliation possible?

One of the negative consequences of this pressure approach toward CSR adopted by pressure groups is the tendency to (inadvertently) promote the false notion that CSR practice is restricted only to large global firms and brands. Since most of the firms along the supply chains are likely to be small- and medium-scale enterprises (SMEs), this approach also exhibits the tendency of giving an inaccurate impression that SMEs are somehow shielded from engaging in CSR practices, which runs against the ethos of the CSR movement. On the contrary, there is a rising call for SMEs to participate in both CSR discourse and practice as well (Petts 1998; Spence 1999; Sarbutts 2003). This is where and why we think that arguing for and highlighting the limits of CSR practices along supply chains of global brands could be a way to curtail the excesses of pressure groups and their antics, as well as extend the reach of the call for SMEs to be equally socially responsible.

This chapter, therefore, examines whether firms should be responsible for the practices of their suppliers, the extent of this responsibility, and how they could effectively translate such responsibilities, if any, into practice. The chapter starts by situating firm–supplier relationships within the broader context of firm buying behavior and from that context evaluates the responsibilities of firms as customers to their suppliers—often times, the point that purchasing firms are customers is ignored in debates around responsible supply chain management. This does not focus on such ethical issues in purchasing as deception, bribery, price rigging, unsafe products, and public safety (Wood 1996: 185) since these are likely to arise from the internal environment of the purchasing firm and not necessarily from its relationship with its suppliers. In addition, it does not consider the intricacies of the economic dynamics characteristic of firm–supplier relationships. It focuses solely on espousing the moral (and sometimes legal) connotations of the concept of responsibility and what it means to be held responsible while relating these to firm–supplier relationships. In the main, the chapter attempts to set limits to responsibility in a supplier relationship by introducing the concepts of corporate control and corporate grouping as critical factors.

RESPONSIBILITY AS ACCOUNTABILITY: MEANING, CLARIFICATIONS, AND EXCEPTIONS

From ancient times, philosophers have struggled to unravel the wealth of meanings embedded in the term *responsibility* or the expression "to be held responsible." The term and the expression are both associated with the concept of morality. This is not surprising since the claim of morally responsible agents is one of the distinguishing characteristics of human rationality (Eshleman 2002). A comprehensive account of the philosophy of responsibility thus encapsulates nuances of moral responsibility, the status of a moral agent, and the conditions under which the actions of a moral agent may be considered responsible or irresponsible.

In the history of Western philosophy, substantive reflections on the notion of moral responsibility date back to the ancient Greek philosophers, especially Aristotle. In *Nichomachean Ethics* (BKIII), Aristotle assumes the criteria for moral agency to include the capacity for rational choice and deliberation. A responsible act is a voluntary act. Therefore, an agent is praiseworthy or blameworthy depending on his or her voluntary acts and disposition of character traits. For an act to qualify as a voluntary act, the agent must be both in full control of his or her action and must be rationally cognizant of the consequences of his or her action. Involuntary acts are thus those acts for which the agent should not be held responsible, either because they are executed out of ignorance, external coercion, or to avoid a greater evil (Cahn 2002). However, contemporary Western moral philosophy embodies varying and often conflicting notions of moral responsibility.

The Kantian idea of moral responsibility also stems from the conception of person as a moral agent. A moral agent or person is not only rational or capable of rational choice, but is one whose action is informed by a sense of duty. The sense of duty is codified in universal law principles, which Kant referred to as categorical imperatives. Therefore, a responsible or right action is not necessarily one that maximizes utility, but rather one that follows moral principles, which are capable of becoming universal moral laws (Cahn 2002: 752). Hence, for neo-Kantians and some other deontologists, a responsible or good moral agent ought to act in accordance with good moral principles irrespective of the consequences of such actions. The assumption here is that good moral principles lead to actions that invariably bring about good consequences. For consequentialists, however, a good or responsible action is one that brings about good consequences or maximizes utility (in the case of utilitarianism). Hence, the morality of an act is not dependent on moral principles prior to the action, but on the actual outcome of a particular act.[5]

In another sense, to be responsible may involve some sort of cause-and-effect relationship (e.g., gravity responsible for the fall of objects in space) or carry some sort of duties and or obligations that could be legal and moral (e.g., an *employed* schoolteacher's responsibility to teach). Since "to be morally [and legally] responsible for something, say an action, is to be worthy of a particular kind of reaction—praise, blame [punishment] or something akin to these—for having performed it" (Eshleman 2002: 1), the latter applies more to our arguments in this chapter than the former. Dwelling on the meaning of responsibility, the philosopher John Lucas (1993) wrote:

> Etymologically, to be responsible is to be answerable—it comes from the Latin *respondeo*, I answer, or the French *répondre*, as in RSVP. I can equally well say that I am answerable for an action or accountable for it. And if I am to answer, I must answer a question; the question is "Why did you do it?" and in answering that question, I give an account . . . of my action. So the central core of the concept of responsibility is that I

can be asked the question "Why did you do it?" and be obliged to give an answer.

In a similar effort, Craig (2000) defines *responsibility* as follows:

> To be responsible for something is to be answerable for it. We have prospective responsibilities, things it is up to us to attend to: these may attach to particular roles (the responsibilities of, for instance, parents or doctors), or the responsibilities we have as moral agents, or as human beings. We have retrospective responsibilities, for what we have done or failed to do, for the effects of our actions or omissions. Such responsibilities are often (but not always) moral or legal responsibilities.

However, can one be answerable for an action that lies beyond one's control? What if one's psychological and physical conditions do not permit one to give an account of one's actions, who should be accountable in this case? These questions raise the fundamental challenges of fatalism and determinism in relation to the concept of responsibility.

Responsibility in the sense used in this book is closely related to the concept of accountability. Drawing from the works of other academics (e.g., Gray, Owen, and Maunders 1987; Williams 1987; Roberts and Scapens 1985), Swift (2001: 17) characterizes accountability in both a broad and a narrow sense. Broadly speaking, he describes accountability as "the requirement or duty to provide an account or justification for one's actions to whomever one is answerable." In a narrow sense, Swift talks of accountability as "being pertinent to contractual arrangements only, . . . where accountability is not contractually bound there can be no act of accountability." Furthermore, borrowing from a later work of Gray and colleagues (1997), Swift notes that "essentially accountability is about the provision of information between two parties where the one is accountable, explains or justifies actions to the one to whom the account is owed." This form of accountability underlies the principal-agent relationship, which is central to the firm as an economic and legal entity. Despite the presence of semantic variations within the notion of accountability, the *duty to account* appears to convey a central meaning. The *duty to account* connotes the institution of rights and obligations and, as such, should be able to hurt if violated (Owen et al. 2000).

In the same line of thought, Gray, Owen, and Maunders (1988) explain that a firm's accountability to the wider society is inherent in a social contract between the society and the business group. The appropriation of the social contract theory here stems from the hypothesis that business derives its existence from the society. Although traditional social contract theories are hypothetical constructs, nevertheless, they are normative reference points in the justification of the legal use of coercive state or societal power on individual citizens and corporations. This idea of accountability inherent in the social contract is realized when market forces punish or reward corporate behavior (Swift 2001; Donaldson and Preston 1995). In this regard, Korten (2004) argues that the market by necessity needs information to be effective. Hence, corporations have the moral duty to produce necessary and complete information needed by the market to mete out punishment or dispense reward. This will constitute accountability to the market, which cannot be achieved through self-regulation.

The increasing demand for accountability from firms also extends to the activities within their supply chain (Mamic 2005). This extension of responsibility, in itself, is questionable: Is the supply chain of a firm *intrinsically* part of the firm? If it is, what becomes of the independence of the individual firms operating within a primary firm's supply chain? If it is not, is it appropriate to expect firms to account for actions outside their legal boundaries, thereby exposing them to unlimited responsibility for their supply chains? Why should one firm bear responsibilities for the practices of another firm? Are consumers responsible for the practices of the firms (e.g., supermarkets) they buy from? Are suppliers (in our case, supermarkets) not pressured to be responsible and ethical to the consumers at the micro level (individual buying behavior)? These questions assume more challenging postures, especially in cases where relationships between firms and suppliers are fundamentally economic and at arm's length (Sako 1992). As such, we see the apparent ascription of unlimited responsibility to account for suppliers' practices on the purchasing firms as inappropriate because it undermines corporate autonomy and independence.

In most legal systems, a corporation is recognized as a legal person. The principle of the independent legal existence of a corporation recognizes that a corporation is distinct from its members or shareholders. A corporation is regarded as neither an arm nor an extension of its members or shareholders. In *Dartmouth College v. Woodward* (1819), a corporation was described as "an artificial being, invisible, intangible, and existing only in contemplation of law." Corporate personality is now an established principle in most legal systems. Various decisions of the United States Supreme Court, for instance *Santa Clara County v. Southern P.R. Co* (1886) and *First National Bank v. Belotti* (1978), consistently confirmed the legal personality of corporations. Furthermore, the twin principles of corporate personality and separate legal existence of a corporation are the "cornerstone of English company law [and] a fundamental rule" (McGee, Williams, and Scanlan 2005: 99). An important component of these twin principles is the principle of limited liability under which the liability of the shareholders or members of a corporation is limited only to the value of their shareholding (*Salomon v. Salomon & Co.* 1897). In other words, it could be argued that the supply chain is not an extension of the firm and, as such, the purchasing firm should not bear any responsibilities for the practices of its suppliers. Suppliers, as firms, should bear responsibility for their actions. However, these are the general legal rules. In practice, there are exceptions to the general rules—for example, where there are some sorts of integrations (i.e., vertical or horizontal and even network) between the purchasing and supplying firms. To substantiate our argument for these exceptions, we draw insights from two related concepts in law—(a) control as limitation of corporate liability and (b) corporate group. These two concepts are, practically, exceptions to the twin principles of corporate legal personality and the separate existence of a corporation.

CONTROL

Relevant statutes usually contain their definitions of control (e.g., section 231 of the UK Employment Rights Act of 1996). Corporate control may exist in various forms. For example, where the management of one corporation can be appointed or removed by the management of another corporation, control appears to be in existence. In a situation where a corporation has no assets at all or has no assets within its area of operation and relies on the assets of the other corporation to do business, or where a corporation engaged in a risky venture sells its assets to a corporation in the same group (as happened in *Patrick Case*: Spender 2000: 38–43), corporate control may exist here too. The Australian *Patrick Case* illustrates this point. In that case, four members of a stevedoring group sold their business and other assets to another member of the group. The only asset left in each of the selling companies was a contract to supply labor to an upstream company in the same group. The upstream company later terminated this contract for supply of labor. The termination of that contract directly resulted in the insolvency of the four companies.

However, prior to the group restructuring, each member of the group employed its own workers and owned and operated its own stevedoring business. It was later pointed out that the main reason for the restructuring exercise was to "facilitate the termination of the employees' employment" (*Patrick Stevedores Operations No 2 Pty Ltd v. Maritime Union of Australia* 1998: 673; see Spender 2000:40). One other important result of the restructuring was that that same individual became the sole director of each of the four labor-supply companies. The applicable Australian corporation law, section 221, permitted sole directorship (Spender 2000: 40). The overall effect was that "although the legal entities who contracted with the employees did not change, the nature of the business and the viability of those companies had changed fundamentally" (Spender 2000: 41). The workers' union instituted an action against the corporate group (*Maritime Union of Australia v. Patrick Stevedores Operations No. 1 Pty Ltd* 1998; *Patrick Stevedores Operations No 2 Pty Ltd v. Maritime Union of Australia* 1998). An interlocutory injunction was granted against the members of the corporate group by both the court of first instance and the appellate court compelling the companies to treat the four labor-supply companies as their sole suppliers of labor. The companies were also required to treat the labor supply agreements as subsisting and valid (Spender 2000: 55). However, the litigation ended at the interlocutory stage when the parties reached settlement. The terms of settlement included the winding-up of the four labor-supply companies, the transfer of the workers' employment to the group holding company, and the termination of the labor supply contracts (Spender 2000: 55). In England today, it would not be possible for the kind of restructuring carried out by the Patrick group to dispense with the services of the employees of the four associated companies. The introduction of the concept of "associated employer" by section 231 of the Employment Rights Act 1996 prevents such actions (Milman 1999: 237). According to that statutory provision, two employers are associated if "one is a company of which the other (directly or indirectly) has control, or both are companies of which a third person (directly or indirectly) has control." This statutory provision is a clear case of disregard of the principle of independent existence of corporations.

Examples of such control may also exist where the businesses belong to the same corporate group or there is a parent-subsidiary relationship. In *Bowoto v. Chevron*, the claimants sued Chevron (now ChevronTexaco) for human rights abuses and for issuing false and misleading information on its practices in Nigeria under a military regime. In March 2004, the US (federal) District Court in San Francisco, California, rejected Chevron's arguments that (1) Nigeria is the proper forum for the trial of the case, (2) the alleged human rights abuses did not violate international law, and (3) Chevron could not be held responsible for the actions of its Nigerian subsidiary. In effect, in *Bowoto v. Chevron*, the court ruled that the separate personality of a subsidiary corporation does not constitute a bar to holding a corporation accountable for the actions of its overseas subsidiaries. The relevant control may also exist where, as in *Cape Industries v. Adams* (1990), the corporation knew of the risks but took steps to establish an asset-free undertaking for the risky business. In 1968, Cape Industries closed its main UK factory as a result of concerns for and the prevalence of asbestos-related disease, although its South African operations continued in such unsafe environment until 1979 (Meeran 2000: 263). The relevant South African and Namibian labor compensation laws provided only "a system of paltry compensation" and also precluded "claims against the employer" (Meeran 2000: 252).

Limitation of corporate liability is an issue of "compelling theoretical interest and practical importance" (Hohfeld 1909: 320). The exception to our general proposition of limiting responsibility to direct suppliers is where there is evidence of actual control by one corporation over another in the supply chain irrespective of their positions on the chain. Control may mean either "checking and supervising" or "determining-the-outcome" (Vagts 1980: 324). The first is control at the lower level while the second is a higher-level control. In this text, we adopt the higher level of control as the relevant factor. First, the level of "determining-the-outcome" requires less inquiry of details than "checking" or "supervising." Secondly, the usual relationship of firms is at that higher level, although it is possible for a firm to be involved in the details of the operations of another firm.

"Determining-the-outcome" is connected to the setting and monitoring of a general policy framework. Being in a position to set or monitor such policies is as good as actually setting or monitoring them. Where this control exists, the indication is that the relationship between the corporations is not a normal arms-length business relationship. Using control as the relevant factor for imposing responsibility has the distinct advantage of ensuring that a corporation does not avoid responsibility where such responsibility should be assumed. Otherwise, careful supply-chain organization may be capable of completely defeating the aims of CSR. Nothing prevents a corporation from establishing a supply-chain relationship, which ensures that the risky venture is carried out by an enterprise even lower than the direct supplier.

CORPORATE GROUPS

Corporations are generally permitted to own shares in other corporations. Corporate groups exist as a result of the ownership of shares by corporations in other corporations. The allocation of responsibility is one of the most controversial aspects of the law relating to corporate groups (Milman 1999: 224). There is a growing trend toward a departure from the strict application of the principles of corporate personality and separate corporate existence in the context of corporate groups. This approach appears to have influenced some English statutory provisions on corporate groups (*Littlewoods Mail Order Stores v. Inland Revenue Commissioners* 1969: 1241) such as consolidated accounts (Companies Act 1985, s.227), disclosure requirements (Companies Act 1985, ss.231, 232) and business report (Companies Act 1985, s.234, as amended by Part 1 of Company [Audit Investigations and Community Enterprise] Act 2004). Why should this legal approach not be extended to corporate social responsibility?

We advocate a single enterprise view of corporate groups. Single enterprise is an approach that treats the members of a corporate group as the same corporation. This approach reflects the actual and commercial reality of and in the operations of corporate groups. A suggestion has rightly been made for responsibility where "there is sufficient involvement in, control over and knowledge of the subsidiary operations" (Meeran 2000: 261). It appears that the trend is for corporations to be willing to argue in favor of separate companies as constituting a single economic unit whenever this may confer a perceived benefit, including right of action (an argument that was rejected by the court in *The Albazero* 1977), profit, or tax or other fiscal incentives (for instance, in *ICI v. Colmer* 1998 and *Bosal Holding BV* 2003). However, there appears to be a change in corporate attitude when social responsibility is in issue. For instance, in the *Bhopal* case (*Re Union*

Carbide Gas Plant Disaster at Bhopal India 1986, 1987), the defendant parent company disputed the argument of both the Indian government and the claimants that the parent was liable for the environmental disaster in issue regardless of the apparent legal separation between the parent and its Indian subsidiary.

It is important to recognize corporate groups as "a form of business organization *sui generis*" (Milman 1999: 219). One should not be oblivious of the fact that some corporations are "mere instrumentalities" (*Amoco Cadiz* 1984: 338) of other enterprises. There is no need to insist on the separate legal existence of the individual corporations in a corporate group. Such insistence on independent existence of the individual companies is certainly "not a true reflection of the economic reality [since] very often such groups are so intertwined with each other's affairs as to amount to little more than departments of one organization or entity" (McGee, Williams, and Scanlan 2005: 105). Artificialities are encouraged where the legal principle of separate existence is applied to corporate groups. For example, it is definitely not "the most honest way" of doing business where there is "the creation or purchase of a subsidiary with minimal liability which will operate with the parent's funds and on the parent's directions but not expose the parent to liability" (*Atlas Maritime Co. v. Avalon Maritime Ltd* (No 1) 1991: 779). In most cases of parent-subsidiary relationship, evidence shows that "subsidiaries are bound hand and foot to the parent company and must do just what the parent company says" (*DHN Food Distributors Ltd v. London Borough of Tower Hamlets* 1976: 860). The fact is that most historical accounts (for instance, Hovekamp 1991: 49–54) of the principle of separate existence of corporations strongly indicate that the principle was designed for the protection and encouragement of the individual shareholder, and not the corporate shareholder. In our view, therefore, firms in a dominant or controlling position in a corporate group should also be responsible for the activities of other firms in the group.

POWER AND INFLUENCE

A further probing into the different scenarios presented here resonates with what comes across as a common assumption that the more powerful in an economic relationship should bear the responsibilities of the weaker party (Reed 1999). On one hand, firms are readily perceived as more powerful than their suppliers and consequently are expected to assume responsibility for the practices of their suppliers. On the other hand, it is very plausible to conjecture that firms may also exert undue pressures on their suppliers, thereby forcing them to conform to their low cost targets at the expense of responsible business practices. As such, a firm's exercise of power over the supplier may have either a deontological or consequentialist outlook. Firms that enforce principles of responsible business practice from the standpoint of moral duty do so from a deontological perspective, while those that implement such principles in order to maximize profit do so from a consequentialist viewpoint. Using the example of the suppliers of UK clothing retailers, Jones and Pollitt (1998) show that an opportunistic abuse of power by retailers can lead to reductions in quality, lack of investment, lack of innovation, and even job losses and industry decline (Crane and Matten 2004).

Considering the enormity of corporate multinational power, encouraging responsible practices within their business networks would still count as a moral minimum. Since firms (especially multinational corporations) wield a lot of power—given the vast resources available at their disposal—it is morally justifiable and more sensible to expect them to use their power in a way that encourages suppliers to adhere to some reasonable standards of responsible practices. However, the *responsible use of power* applies to both the firm and the supplier given their relative power positions in the market (i.e., the powerful supplier—monopoly; and the powerful buyer—monopsony). But this influence, we suggest, should be limited to the interface between firms and their immediate suppliers. Our primary assumption here is that through ripple effects, the influence of the powerful firm will filter down the entire spectrum of the supply chain.

TRANSLATING RESPONSIBILITY IN SUPPLY CHAINS INTO PRACTICE: SOME MANAGERIAL SUGGESTIONS

The translation of responsibility in supply chains into practice will involve some sort of change management—as the status quo will be altered. Covey (1992), in his seminal book: *The Seven Habits of Highly Effective People*, suggests that it is essential to make the distinction between circle of control and circle of influence in any change management initiative. The circle of control relates to things we have complete control over, while the circle of influence relates to things we can seek to influence but do not have total control over. Following our position that purchasing firms should not bear responsibilities for the actions of suppliers and that firms in position of power should seek to positively influence the practices of their suppliers, it implies that firms can only act within their circle of influence while dealing with their suppliers. Some of the possible ways of exerting this influence may include, among others, corporate codes of conduct/standards, corporate culture, anti-pressure group campaigns,[6] and personnel development.

Codes of conduct/standards will state in clear terms the value orientation of the purchasing firm and its expectations from the suppliers. This can be mapped out in consultation with the direct suppliers or as an agreement between firms and new suppliers at the point of engagement. This form of consultation should be free from any form of stakeholder imperialism—a relationship whereby the stakeholders are only accorded instrumental values, solely for economic gains. Stakeholder imperialism does not give a voice to stakeholders and is characterized by unilateral communication (Crane and Livesey 2003) and unequal balance of power. It is not genuine; it is selfish, and firms engage in it because "it makes good business sense . . . [and] . . . helps companies to mitigate risk, protect corporate brand, and gain competitive advantage" (Deloitte Touche Tohmatsu 2002: 2 cited in Brown and Fraser 2004). Rather, the consultation should be characterized by *genuine intentions,* dialogue, engagement, trust, and fairness (Phillips 1997; Swift 2001). Firms engaging in this form of consultation understand that stakeholdership entails some form of intrinsic value. They enter into such a relationship for some ends that transcend the mere calculation and maximization of profits. It will then be the responsibilities of these immediate suppliers to pass on to their subsequent suppliers down the supply chain the culture of responsible business practice.

The principal purchasing firm also can institute a process that asks for periodic submission of ethical audit reports from suppliers as part of the engagement and ensure that any supplier found guilty by the auditors and/or the public would be named and shamed, which might even lead to the severance of relationship. In the same line of thought, purchasing firms can set up some sort of rewards for suppliers that continually meet the standards. Commenting on the relevance of the code of conduct in socially responsible supply chain management, Graafland (2002: 283) gives an account of how it is used in C&A:

> The code requires that suppliers respect the ethical standards of C&A in the context of their particular culture. Suppliers should have fair and honest dealings with all others with whom they do business, including employees, sub-contractors and other third parties. In addition to this general requirement, the code specifies detailed requirements related to employment conditions. For example, the use of child labor is absolutely unacceptable. Workers must not be younger than the legal minimum age and not less than 14 years. Wages must be comparable with local norms and comply with local laws. Furthermore, the code requires that suppliers make full disclosure to C&A of all facts concerning production and the use of sub-contractors. The suppliers are obliged to authorize [the auditors] to make un-announced inspections of the manufacturing facility.

According to Graafland, C&A (in the aforementioned example) severed relationships with suppliers that did not conform to the code.

Another possible way for a powerful firm to positively influence less powerful firms in its network is to serve as a role model to others through its ethical organizational culture. According to MacIntyre (1984), virtue is lived and not acted since one does not offer what one does not possess (*nemo dat quod non habet*). In this regard, Drumwright (1994) asserts that the success of socially responsible buying is to a large extent dependent on the organizational context within which the policies are made. In other words, to be able to influence suppliers effectively, the purchasing firm should exhibit a high level of ethical orientation that is permeated in its culture. Culture is to an organization what personality is to an individual. It is that distinctive formation of beliefs, values, work styles, and relationships (visible/invisible, said/unsaid) that distinguish one organization from another (Schein 1985: 9). But as there is abnormal personality, there is also the possibility of bad organizational culture. But what determines a good or bad culture? In our opinion, a good organizational culture is one that embodies these ethical dimensions of virtue, rights, justice, and utilitarianism. The presence or absence of these ethical dimensions determines the organization's ability to base its decisions, policies, systems, and processes on what is good and what is right (what ought to be) for its own sake (i.e., for the good of the society at large). This way, the purchasing firm will effectively serve as a role model to supplying firms for others to mimic. And theory confirms that firms have very high tendency to mimic other firms, especially successful ones (Powell and DiMaggio 1991).

A possible third option for a powerful firm to influence its supply chain is through personal training and value orientation. Crane and Matten (2004) distinguished two sets of ethical issues that arise in business-supplier relationship, viz. organizational level issues and individual level issues. At the organizational level are such issues as misuse of power, the question of loyalty, conflicts of interests, and preferential treatments. At the individual levels are such issues as bribery, unethical negotiation, and other personal factors. While some organizational issues can be addressed through the organizational culture, the individual-level issues can be influenced through personnel training in ethics and values. The purchasing firm can go a step further to extend this sort of training programs to the staff of their suppliers in order to minimize the rate of value frictions at the point of transaction. That way, both firm and suppliers will enjoy a more lasting relationship and earn a higher social capital base.

CONCLUSION

With the emergence of supranational economic ideologies in the West under the auspices of globalization, the dream of a deregulated global economic space is becoming a reality. Hence, MNEs rival existing nation states in the control of economic resources in the world. In this sense, MNEs are legitimate agents of justice and injustice and hence are liable to the same international principles governing economic and social corporations among states. However, multinational corporations often operate under intricate economic, social, and legal conditions within the territories of their subsidiary firms. Complex business laws and business structures differ from country to country, undermining the applicability of any emergent universal, moral-economic principles. These prevalent conditions, critics say, often allow multinationals the free moral space to maximize profits and trump existing ethical obligations.

We acknowledge that the aim of the chapter, as demonstrated, raises some moral issues. Some pertinent questions that keep resonating beyond our collective academic exercise are the following: Why limit the scope of responsibility of MNEs? Does limiting their scope of responsibility make CSR more effective along the supply chain or does it create a larger free moral space for MNEs to perpetrate irresponsible acts? While these questions are important, it is not surprising that global firms are currently under more pressure than ever to rescue their brands from possible charges of misconducts along their supply chain. The pressure groups understand this pressure and try to make the best use of it. It may not be surprising, also, to learn that sometimes the pressure groups use these opportunities to promote their agenda (e.g., the case of Shell and Greenpeace is well documented in the business ethics literature).[7]

Although Emmelhainz and Adams (1999) argue that the shift toward global supply and competition comes with an extended chain of responsibility on the part of individual firms, it would be theoretically inappropriate to hold any particular firm responsible for the practice of another firm unless it is established that the action of one firm *consequentially* leads to the action of another, particularly where the relationship is not at arm's length (e.g., through the concepts of control and corporate grouping as earlier discussed in the chapter). However, since firms are rational and free entities, this consequential link of actions and responsibilities would be more sensible where there is an obvious misuse of power on either of the parties involved. If not, it is our opinion that each firm should bear the responsibilities for its actions, albeit those firms in a position of power have the *deontological* duty to use power responsibly and the obligation to positively influence weaker parties possibly by setting standards, serving as role models, through anti-pressure group campaigns, and through personnel training and value orientation.

In the next chapter, we sum up the deontological duty of CSR as a business philosophy anchored on social justice (justice as fairness).

8 Corporate Social Responsibility as a Business Philosophy and an Expression of Social Justice
Justice as Fairness

THE IDEA OF SOCIAL JUSTICE IN POLITICAL PHILOSOPHY

Since our understanding of corporate social responsibility presupposes a conception of justice that does not view acts of corporate responsibility as simply charitable acts, but rather as legitimate expectations of citizens of the modern world, questions of justice homogonous to this approach border on how individuals in the modern state distribute the burdens and benefits of social and economic cooperation. Such questions would encompass what the law should permit or prohibit and how society as a whole should be regulated. In contemporary political philosophy, the works of the late American philosopher John Rawls take these questions of justice very seriously. Nevertheless, we are equally interested in the general exposition of the principles of utility (utilitarianism). This will help us understand some of the foundational, philosophical theories informing the corporate social responsibility debate. The goal of this chapter is to demonstrate that Rawls's contractarian notion of social justice (or justice as fairness) correlates with the ideals of CSR, while the dominant moral theory of the last century—namely, utilitarianism—may not. We proceed by tracing some theoretical and historical trajectories leading to the emergence of the social justice movement in the history of Western philosophy.

Philosophers have long sought generally acceptable and plausible answers to the question of justice or right, what the ancient Greek philosophers referred to as *dikaiosunē* ("doing right" or justice) or *dikaion* (right). Whether one is reading Plato's *Republic* (ca. 380 BC), Bentham's *Introduction to the Principles of Morals and Legislation* (1789), Rawls's *A Theory of Justice* (1971), Nozick's *Anarchy, State, and Utopia* (1974), or, more recently, Sandel's *Justice: What's The Right Thing to Do?* (2009), and so on, the theoretical and practical difficulty of dealing with the contents of justice remains the same, though the contexts may be different.

Though early Western philosophers dealt with questions of justice and right, "social justice," as we know it today, according to Jackson (2005) and Swift (2007), is a modern enterprise. Jackson writes that though social justice is an important ideal in contemporary political thought, it is nevertheless a newcomer to our political vocabulary. Furthermore, he explains that from a comparative standpoint, we know little about its "introduction into the political debate or its early theoretical trajectory" (Jackson 2005: 356). Similarly, Swift (2007) thinks that the idea of social justice is not only a recent development in Western philosophy, but also a controversial one:

> That idea [social justice] is relatively recent, creeping into use from about 1850 on, and not everybody likes it. It developed only as philosophers came to see society's key social and economic institutions, which crucially determine the distribution of benefit and burdens, as a proper object for moral and political investigation. Some philosophers aren't happy with it. People can act justly or unjustly, but what does it mean to say that society is just or unjust. Some politicians aren't crazy about it either. For them, those who talk about social justice tend to hold the mistaken belief that it is the state's job to bring about certain distributive outcomes, which means interfering with the individual freedom and the efficient working of a market economy. (Swift 2007: 9)

In addition, Jackson citing Miller's (1999) *Principles of Social Justice* claims that progressive, political philosophers or political economists, whose works reflected the growing public controversy about the role of the state in regulating economic and political institutions, seem to have introduced the term *social justice* into modern political discourse (Jackson 2005: 357).

Both Jackson (2005) and Swift (2007) see social justice as a movement whose goal is to empower the state to redistribute the benefits of social and economic cooperation to individuals disadvantaged by the unfair outcome of unregulated market forces or market distribution. For Jackson, the term *social justice* has a "substantive political content" because it calls on the state to alleviate poverty and reduce the economic and social inequalities existing among citizens (Jackson 2005: 360). Since the main thrust of the social justice debate is the distributive procedures of social and economic institutions, social injustice then arises from the failures of these institutions to attain an efficient and fair distribution of social and economic goods. As Simmons (2008: 69) notes, "social injustice will typically involve a defect in institutional rules that aims at or results in a morally improper distribution of basic social goods and burdens (hence the term distributive justice)."

No other book in contemporary political philosophy revitalized the debate about social justice more so than Rawls's *A Theory of Justice* (1971).[1] Even Robert Nozick, Rawls's colleague and ardent critic, writes in *Anarchy, State, and Utopia:* "A Theory of Justice is a . . . systematic work in political and moral philosophy which has not seen its like since the writings of John Stuart Mill, if then. . . . Political philosophers now must either work within Rawls' theory or explain why not" (Nozick 1974: 183). In *A Theory of Justice*, Rawls declares that "justice is the first virtue of social institutions, as truth is of systems of thought. A theory however elegant and economical must be rejected or revised if it is untrue; likewise laws and institutions no matter how efficient and well-arranged must be reformed or abolished if they are unjust" (Rawls 1971: 3). His aim, he says, is to develop a viable conception of social justice implicit in the social contract tradition, which, however, "generalizes and carries to a higher level of abstraction the familiar theory of the social contract as found, say, in Locke, Rousseau, and Kant" (Rawls 1971: 3).

Following the principle of liberal legitimacy, Rawls thinks that social, economic, or political cooperation must be predicated on the assumption that cooperating individuals consent to the terms of cooperation for their mutual benefit. Although he locates the ideals of justice in the classical tradition of virtue ethics, the principle of liberal legitimacy forms the moral basis for his contractarian approach—that is, "the liberal idea that the legitimacy of social rules and institutions depends on their being freely and publicly acceptable to all individuals bound by them" (Freeman 2007: 17). Prior to the publication of *A Theory of Justice,* most political philosophers considered the social contract theory obsolete since its method was widely dismissed by such powerful figures as David Hume and Jeremy Bentham (Freeman 2007: 8). By reviving the social contract tradition, Rawls is not interested in "whipping a dead horse," but rather hopes to develop a contract theory that is not only useful and relevant to contemporary political theory, but also "not subject to the objections often thought fatal to contract views and one that is superior to the long-dominant tradition of utilitarianism in moral and political philosophy" (Freeman 2007: 3–4).

RAWLS'S JUSTICE AS FAIRNESS

In *A Theory of Justice* (1971), Rawls presents democratic conceptions of person and society. Persons are free and equal citizens living in a society they see as a fair system of cooperation for their mutual benefit. In Rawls's human society, citizens practice "reciprocity of perspectives" by granting one another a fair share in the distribution of the benefits and burdens of socioeconomic cooperation. Given their nature as free and equal cooperating agents, citizens of Rawls's society must freely choose the principles of justice to regulate the basic structure (the social, economic, and political institutions of their society). An alien authority cannot impose the principles of justice on free citizens, nor should these principles derive from a higher, independent moral order. In the words of Freeman (2007: 30):

> Rawls's parties conceive of themselves as free, not in the sense that they may act on any desire they happen to have but in the sense that they are able to control, revise, and take responsibility for their final ends and desires by acting on and from reasonable and rational principles. Recognizing the deep-seated effects of basic social institutions on these

capacities and on their interests, they have a basic concern for how such institutions are designed. Not satisfied with the idea that these institutions answer to their desires for the accumulation of objects, Rawls's parties have a deeper interest in whether the institutions are structured so as to enable them to realize their reasoning capacities and whether the principles supporting these institutions can serve as a basis for the public justification among persons like themselves.

The aims of Rawls's contractarianism are not entirely new in political philosophy. In fact, much of his goals are rooted in Kantianism. For instance, in "The Contractual Basis for a Just Society," Kant writes that the lawful state must be grounded on three a priori principles: "1. The freedom of every member of society as a human being 2. the equality of each with all the others as a subject 3. the independence of each member of a commonwealth as a citizen" (Sterba 2003: 102).

Following Kant, Rawls, in *A Theory of Justice,* explores conditions under which free and rational individuals would agree to uphold cooperative institutions that are mutually advantageous to everyone (Freeman 2007: 9) and thus find a moral basis for the public justification of their political, social, and economic institutions. One way to articulate this arrangement is to design a hypothetical situation or thought experiment, which could then be applied to an actual society by using the method of a reflective equilibrium. Although Rawls's social contract doctrine does not presuppose the existence of an anthropological or historical condition, but rather a purely hypothetical one, it does call for some "bracketing" *epoché* or *Einklammerung* in a phenomenological sense.[2]

However, we do "devise basic institutions" (Freeman 2007: 42) in the real world. That is to say, "We cooperatively decide, through laws and willing acceptance of social and legal conventions, how the constitution, the economy, property, and so on are designed and fit together into one social scheme" (Freeman 2007: 42).

The relevance of Rawls's contractarian condition lies in its underlying phenomenological attitude, which enables citizens of a modern democratic society to express their autonomy as rational and reasonable persons working together to design a just society by being fair to everyone. Thus, Rawls hypothetical social contract theory, like Kantian contractarianism, has practical implications for the polity of modern democracies. Though Kant's original contract is merely an idea, it is nonetheless an idea with practical consequences. As Kant writes, "It can oblige every legislator to frame his laws in such a way that they could have been produced by the united will of a whole nation, and to regard each subject, insofar as he can claim citizenship, as if he had consented within the general will. This is the test of the rightfulness of every public law" (Sterba 2003: 105).

For Rawls, if we are to think about justice as fairness, we must first immerse ourselves (mentally) in a condition of strict equality. For example,

Rawls would want us to imagine a gathering of the representatives of opposing parties or groups in front of the United States Capitol. These may include the Republican, Democratic, and Independent parties, as well as free marketers, conservatives, social liberals, and representatives of corporations. The parties have come to choose principles that would govern the collective interest and well-being of the American people. Given their conflicting and competing political, economic, and religious ideologies, which principles would the party representatives choose?[3]

It would be a knotty task to get the members of Congress to reach a nonpartisan agreement on principles regulating the life of every United States citizen. Some members of Congress may favor one principle over another because of religion, gender, race, sexual orientation, or political ideology. For instance, some representatives (house members or senators) would oppose gay marriage because they represent conservative districts, while others may support increased social services for the poor because they represent constituencies with a high concentration of low-income people or the working class. Even libertarians and their conservative friends may part ways on culturally divisive issues such as right to life and abortion.

Furthermore, some representatives of big financial corporations on Wall Street, such as AIG, Bank of America, and oil giants BP, Chevron, Halliburton, and so on, may adhere to a certain right libertarianism, which promotes a laissez-faire market economy, while the social liberals representing Main Street would advocate for a government-regulated market economy. Social liberals may argue that although everyone recognizes that the free market is the most powerful, generative force of America's prosperity, it is, nevertheless, no free license to engage in reckless deregulatory practices. In the political arena, these representatives sometimes may reach consensus on less contentious issues, such as those that bear on national security or improving basic education for children.[4]

Now imagine that the members of Congress and other representatives of the various interest groups were to pass through a famous dark tunnel known as the "veil of ignorance" before entering the Capitol, one that inflicts a special form of temporary, dissociative amnesia on each party representative. Suddenly, they do not know any particular thing about themselves. They no longer know their political affiliations, economic interests, race, gender, sexual orientation, position in society, religion, talents, psychological dispositions, advantages or disadvantages, and so forth. All that the representatives now know is that they are members of Congress or representatives of interest groups choosing principles to govern a Western, democratic society. Rawls thinks that in this "original position" of equality, these representatives would only choose principles of justice that further their rational interest, since no one knows how he or she would fare in real life. The veil of ignorance and its bracketing effects ensure that the representatives adopt a conservative attitude toward risk and thus choose principles that allow the least undesirable conditions for the worst-off members of society. Rawls calls principles chosen in this hypothetically strict condition of equality, or original position, the "two principles of justice as fairness":

a. Each person has an equal claim to a fully adequate scheme of equal basic rights and liberties, which scheme is compatible with the same scheme for all; and in this scheme the equal political liberties, and only those liberties, are to be guaranteed their fair value.
b. Social and economic inequalities are to satisfy two conditions: first, they are to be attached to positions of offices open to all under conditions of fair equality of opportunity, and second, they are to be to the greatest benefits of the least advantaged members of society. (Rawls 1996: 5–6)

The two principles of justice have implications for both politicians and economists. The first principle of justice, which is known as the equal basic liberty principle, ensures that under reasonably favorable conditions—that is, in a functioning society with enough resources to permit the full exercise of these liberties (strong economies as opposed to weak ones)—citizens are guaranteed the same amount of basic liberties.

Rawls's basic liberties are, roughly speaking, political liberties—the right to vote and to be voted for, freedom of speech and assembly, liberty of conscience, freedom of person and the right to hold property, as well as freedom from arbitrary arrest (Rawls 1971: 61). The first principle of justice has lexical priority over the second principle. This means that in a society governed by justice as fairness, none of these basic principles can be traded off for other valued ends. As Sunstein (1997: 96) says:

> We might treat equal liberty as a reflection of the foundational commitment to equal dignity and respect and believe that we do violence to the way we value that commitment if we allow it to be compromised for the sake of greater social and economic advantages. On this view, the lexical priority of equal liberty is structurally akin to the refusal to allow a child to be traded for cash.

The basic liberties, for example, cannot be taken away from a given social group, even if doing so promotes economic efficiency. The priority of the basic liberties, however, does not imply that these liberties cannot be limited in any form. Rawls says that the basic liberties can be restricted among themselves in order to achieve a coherent scheme of liberties for all citizens. In other words, should the basic liberties come into conflict with one another, the institutional rules that define them must be adjusted to enable these liberties to fit into a coherent scheme (Rawls 1996: 295). Therefore, one can be denied a basic liberty in society for the sake of one or more basic liberties.

Nevertheless, a basic liberty cannot be denied to anyone for the sake of other public goods or valued ends, other than liberty itself. The first principle of justice also grants priority to rights of individuals over the demands of the political majority. As Rawls puts it: "The priority of the basic liberties implies that they cannot be justly denied to anyone, or to any group of persons, or even to all citizens generally, on grounds that such is the desire, or overwhelming preference, of an effective political majority, however strong and enduring" (Rawls 1996: 365).

The second principle of justice has two sections. The first section is generally referred to as the "fair equality of opportunity" principle, while the second section is known as the "difference principle." Again, among the second principles of justice, "fair equality of opportunity" has priority over the "difference principle." The fair equality of opportunity principle regulates, for instance, political offices, advertisements of jobs, and products for sale in society. It ensures that all positions are accessible to all citizens. Furthermore, it authorizes the government to ensure that employers meet requirements of fairness and equality when advertising job openings. For example, advertized positions should not contain racist, sexist statements, words or phrases that undermine fairness. With regard to firms' advertisement of products, sales, and services, the second principle of justice as fairness also mandates the government to regulate firms by demanding that they engage in full disclosure of information of the products and services being advertised. For the market to be efficient and competitive, it is essential that consumers be well informed about the products and services offered by firms. This would prevent, for instance, predatory lending or the covert marketing of potentially hazardous products to end users (Rawls 1996: 364–65).

Some economists and philosophers consider the last section of the second principle of justice controversial because, in their view, it calls for the toleration of some social and economic inequalities if doing so improves the situation of the worst off in society. Nonetheless, the difference principle does not call for inequalities as such, but rather recognizes the human condition in which through sheer brute luck and natural contingencies, social and economic inequalities exist among citizens in modern societies. It looks for ways to remedy some of the effects of these inequalities. The underlying idea is that Rawls sees society as a system of cooperation, where citizens reciprocally share the burdens and benefits that result from this cooperation. Rawls contends that citizens' chances in life neither must be absolutely determined by the social position in which they are born nor must a person's natural talents or lack of such absolutely determine his or her prospects in life. Rather, society should see one's place of birth and the distribution of natural talents as a matter of arbitrary contingency and, as such, mitigate the negative effects they may have on citizens' life prospects (Rawls 1971).

The unequal distribution of natural dispositions, which results in unequal distribution of wealth and positions in society, while not being erased entirely, may be allowed under the condition that it benefits the least advantaged members of society. Thus, Rawls regards the distribution of natural talents as a common societal asset because it is by nature arbitrary. We do not deserve our place in the distribution of native endowments. "Who would deny it?" Rawls asks. "Do people really think that they (morally) deserved to be born more gifted than others? Do they think that they (morally) deserved to be born a man rather than a woman, or vice versa? Do they think that they really deserved to be born into a wealthier rather than into a poorer family? No." (Rawls 2001: 74–75).

But to see the distribution of natural talents as a common asset does not mean that gifted people are not entitled to the benefits that their talents secure. Instead, the difference principle, as a principle of reciprocity, seeks ways to diminish the effects of this arbitrary distribution by reordering the basic structure of society. As a result, those who have much talent and those who have less complement each other in ways that benefit the entire society:

> Note that what is regarded as a common asset is the distribution of native endowments and not native endowments per se. It is not as if society owned individuals' endowments taken separately, looking at individuals one by one. To the contrary, the question of the ownership of our endowments does not arise; and should it arise, it is persons themselves who own their endowments: the psychological and physical integrity of persons is already guaranteed by the basic rights and liberties that fall under the first principle of justice. (Rawls 2001: 75)

In practical terms, what "common asset" represents are the different talents and dispositions that cooperating individuals have. Irrespective of whether these differences are variations in talents of the same kind or not, they serve a balancing function in society reminiscent of the "principle of comparative advantage" (Rawls 2001: 76). Consequently, justice as fairness as an egalitarian principle of justice could allow the government to tax very rich individuals in order to alleviate the situation of the worst off if they are active and contributing members of society.

On one hand, Rawls may have proposed an efficient redistributive theory of economic justice, given that economic inequality among United States citizens is greater than in most Western countries: "1 percent of Americans posses over a third of the country's wealth, more than the combined wealth of the bottom 90 percent of American families" and the "top 10 percent of American households take in 42 percent of all income and hold 71 percent of all wealth" (Sandel 2009: 58). On the other hand, Rawls's position is not welcome by libertarian groups in America. Unlike Rawls, whose theory of justice seeks to diminish the inequality arising from nature, libertarians argue that the fact of life is simple: life is naturally unfair, and any attempt to remedy this natural unfairness leads to infringements on the rights and liberties of individuals. In fact, according to Sandel (2009), Milton and Rose Friedman think that this fact of life is in itself actually a good thing:

Life is not fair. It is tempting to believe that government can rectify what nature has spawned. But it is also important to recognize how much we benefit from the very unfairness we deplore. . . . It is certainly not fair that Muhammad Ali should be able to earn millions of dollars in one night. But wouldn't it have been even more unfair to the people who enjoyed watching him if, in the pursuit of some abstract ideal of equality, Muhammad Ali had not been permitted to earn more for one night's fight . . . than the lowest man on the totem pole could get for a day's unskilled work on the docks. (Sandel 2009: 165)

Rawls's theory rejects the idea that it is wrong for the government to intervene in society by ordering the basic structure of society so as to mitigate the negative effects of the unequal distribution of natural talents and other fortuities of social life. Society does not have to be complacent about natural inequalities in order to be fair. The libertarian economist Milton Friedman favors deregulation of markets and loose governance mechanisms for markets (unfettered markets) as an expression of the fundamental rights of people to exercise total control over their property, as long as they respect the rights (including contractual rights and obligations) and the property of others. Most libertarians advocate for a minimal state (Sandel 2009: 60).

Robert Nozick, for example, thinks that Rawls's difference principle will stifle competition in a free market economy and usher in a welfare state with a large proportion of "lazy folks" or the less endowed (the least disadvantaged). In *Anarchy, State, and Utopia* (1974), Nozick worries that Rawls's difference principle favors the less endowed over the well endowed. He doubts that the rich and the endowed would have a strong incentive under a Rawlsian model to join in the cooperative scheme: "No doubt, the difference principle presents terms on the basis of which those less well endowed would be willing to cooperate. (What better terms could they propose for themselves?) But is this a fair agreement on the basis of which those worse endowed could expect the willing cooperation of others?" (Nozick 1974: 192).

Under his "entitlement theory of justice," Nozick views "justice as fairness" as defective because it begins by looking at the outcomes or patterns of distribution of social and economic goods, or the patterns of this distribution over time, rather than considering whether the dealings that brought about those outcomes were just. For Nozick, any distribution of economic or social goods is just if everyone partaking in such distribution is entitled to or merits their share (Blowfield and Murray 2008: 64). An adequate scheme of distributive justice must meet two requirements, namely, the justice of initial holdings and the justice of transfer:

The first asks if the resources you used to make your money were legitimately yours in the first place. (If you made a fortune selling stolen goods, you would not be entitled to the proceeds). . . . The second asks

if you made your money either through free exchanges in the marketplace or from gifts voluntarily bestowed upon you by others. If they answer to both questions is yes, you're entitled to what you have, and the
state may not take it without your consent. Provided no one starts out
with ill-gotten gains, any distribution that results from a free market
is just, however equal or unequal it turns out to be. (Sandel 2009: 63)

Nozick's entitlement theory, however, does not reject the idea of a rectifi-
catory justice in regard to remedying, let's say, past injustices brought about
by colonialism or slavery. In such instances, the government may use taxation or other available methods to bring about justice (Sandel 2009: 63).
Responding to Nozick and other critics, Rawls denies that justice as fairness
will lead to the kind of socialist, welfare state they envision, since the "least
advantaged" under the difference principle are not defined as the handi-
capped or the most depressed, but rather the least skilled workers in the
lowest income class (Rawls 2001: 59–65; Freeman 2007: 104–5). Furthermore, Rawls says that the least disadvantaged should not be seen, if all goes
well, as "the unfortunate and unlucky—objects of our charity and compas-
sion, much less pity—but those to whom reciprocity is owed as a matter
of political justice among those who are free and equal citizens along with
everyone else" (Rawls 2001: 139). The least advantaged are able-bodied
men and women who are contributing actively to society in ways that are
mutually advantageous and consistent with everyone's self-respect.

The idea of "reciprocity of perspectives," which the difference principle
embodies, is itself grounded on the notion that social cooperation is always
a productive activity. Thus, if there is no cooperation, then nothing will
be produced, and, consequently, there will be no benefits or burdens to be
shared (Rawls 2001). Contrary to the presumptions of his critics, Rawls
thinks that the kind of society resulting from justice as fairness would be
a private propertied, market economy or "property owing democracy"
that is a midway between laissez-faire capitalism and welfare socialism.
He rejects laissez-faire capitalism because it secures only formal equality
for citizens while rejecting fair value of the equal political liberties and fair
equality of opportunity. The goals of laissez-faire capitalism "are economic
efficiency and growth constrained only by a rather social minimum" (Rawls
2001: 137).

Rawls also rejects welfare-state capitalism because it too does not guarantee the fair value of political liberties to citizens. As the name may suggest,
welfare-state capitalism, according to Rawls, may provide some equality of
opportunity, as well as satisfy a decent social minimum in welfare services,
but still allows substantial inequalities to occur in the area of the ownership
of property, concentrating wealth, the control of the economy, and the government in the hands of a few (Rawls 2001: 137–38).

Contrarily, the basic structure of a property-owning democracy spreads
the wealth around and in so doing hinders a small segment of society from

controlling the government and the economy. Rawls's new paradigmatic, political society—property-owning democracy—achieves this sustained sharing of capital and larger participation of the citizenry in directing the political life of the state not by redistributing income at the end of each year (through the award of stimulus checks, for example), "but rather by ensuring the widespread ownership of productive assets and human capital (that is, education and trained skills) at the beginning of each period, all this against a background of fair equality of opportunity" (Rawls 2001: 139).

A society that practices justice as fairness, Rawls believes, will benefit both the rich and the poor. The rich will benefit by living in a less antagonistic society, while the poor will benefit by having decent life prospects and by being in a better position than they would have been under an alternative arrangement. Therein lies the incentive for cooperation.

JUSTICE AS FAIRNESS AND UTILITARIANISM

Rawls considers utilitarianism the dominant moral theory in the 20th century. However, viewed as a form of justice, he insists that utilitarianism not only fails to address the pertinent issues of justice in the modern world, but also serves as the foundational principle for proponents of "turbo-capitalism" to vindicate and disastrously accelerate the social, economic, and institutional inequalities found in modern democracies. For Rawls, the principles of utility are irreconcilable with the ideals of a well-ordered democratic society governed by the principles of justice as fairness. As a normative doctrine, Rawls sees classical utilitarianism as a form of universalistic hedonism or eudemonistic, consequentialist theory since it teaches that the end of human conduct is happiness and the discriminating norms for distinguishing a right conduct from a wrong one are pleasure and pain (Rawls 1971). Jeremy Bentham (1748–1832), perhaps the earliest scholar to articulate the principles of the doctrine in a more systematic and coherent form, presents the tenets in *The Introduction to the Principles of Morals and Legislation*:

> Nature has placed mankind under the governance of two sovereign masters, pain and pleasure. It is them alone to point out what we ought to do, as well as determine what we shall do. On the one hand the standard of right and wrong, on the other the chain of causes and effects, are fastened to their throne. They govern us in all we do, in all we say, in all we think: every effort we can make to throw off our subjection, will serve but to demonstrate and confirm it. In words a man may pretend to abjure their empire: but in reality he will remain subject to it all the while. (Bentham 1970: 11)

Classical utilitarianism in its early development was based on simple rules, a collection of empirical data obtained through inquiry into human nature and the motivation of human behavior. It was a systematic approach in the observation and explication of human conduct by means of simple scientific and rational analysis (Smart and Williams 1973: 149). This simple methodology points to utilitarianism as a form of ethics that captures the imagination of rational individuals. It simply says we all ought to be happy by seeking and maximizing the pleasurable while minimizing the unpleasurable or the painful. As Rawls writes in *A Theory of Justice:* "It is natural to think that rationality is maximizing something and in morals it must be the good. Indeed, it is tempting to suppose that it is self-evident that things should be arranged so as to lead to the most good" (Rawls 1971: 24–25).

From the simple fact that everyone desires pleasure and happiness, and abhors pain and unhappiness, classical utilitarianism draws this conclusion: the moral issue of goodness can ultimately be understood in terms of the principle of the greatest happiness or good for the greatest number. The good is hence attained in a society or achieved when the aggregate of pleasure outnumbers the aggregate of pain. Therefore, in order to arrive at the right action in a society, the interests of different individuals have to be added together with the view of producing the greatest amount of happiness overall.

The contrast between the Rawls theory of social justice and classical utilitarianism is in essence a contrast between a teleological theory and a deontological one. For teleological theories, "the good is defined independently from the right, and then the right is defined as that which maximizes the good" (Rawls 1971: 24).

Teleological doctrines therefore are consequentialist in nature. Classical utilitarianism is a consequentialist moral theory according to which the only value is the happiness of sentient beings, especially humans. Consequentialism as a form of ethics states that the moral value of any action lies in its consequences. It is with reference to their consequences that actions, and indeed social institutions, law, and practices, are to be justified (Smart and Williams 1973). Thus, actions that produce desirable consequences are deemed good, even if the relationship between a moral agent and the value of his/her action is merely instrumental. Rawls sees classical utilitarianism mostly in its contemporary form, as represented by Henry Sigwick's *The Methods of Ethics* (1907). A fair interpretation of this contemporary form of classical utilitarianism defines the good as the satisfaction of rational desires. A society is rightly ordered, and therefore just, when its major institutions are arranged so as to achieve the greatest net balance of satisfaction summed over all the individuals belonging to it (Rawls 1971: 22). For Rawls, utilitarianism as an aggregate-maximizing, economic principle sacrifices equality and social justice since it does not matter to utilitarians how "the sum of satisfactions is distributed among individuals. The correct distribution is whatever yields the maximum fulfillment" (Rawls 1971: 26).

In addition, utilitarians appeal to impartiality in order to extend a method of individual practical rationality to society as a whole (Rawls

1971: 26–27). Impartiality combined with sympathetic identification allows a hypothetical observer to experience the desires of others as if they were his own and to compare alternative courses of action according to their conduciveness to a single maximand made possible by equal consideration and sympathy.

The significant fact is that in this procedure, appeals to equal consideration have nothing to do with impartiality between persons. What are really being given equal consideration are the desires or experiences of separate persons (Rawls 1971: 61).

Rawls develops his theory of social justice—justice as fairness—consciously in opposition to utilitarianism. Most of Rawls's criticisms of utilitarianism in *A Theory of Justice* are chiefly against classical utilitarianism. Much of the acclaimed dominance of utilitarianism in moral philosophy, according to Rawls, rests on the inability of previous theories of justice to stand up to the utilitarian challenge. Such theories owe their failure to the fact that they dwelt much on pointing out the obscurities and apparent incongruities amidst utilitarian principles, rather than on constructing alternative, workable, and systematic moral conceptions capable of posing a powerful challenge to utilitarianism. The result of the failure of these moral theories in combating squarely the influence of utilitarianism, Rawls claims, leaves one with the choice of two extremes in moral theory: utilitarianism and an "incoherent jumble of ideas and principles" known as intuitionism (Kymlicka 1990: 50): "The doctrine that there is an irreducible family of first principles, which have to be weighed against one another by asking ourselves which balance, in our considered judgment, is most just" (Rawls 1971: 34).

In justice as fairness, which Rawls sees as a superior alternative to utilitarianism, the role of intuitionism is limited by the contractarian choice situation (Grcic 1980: 15). To demonstrate the failure of utilitarianism, he compares it directly to justice as fairness on four major points.

THE CHOICE SITUATION

Rawls takes us back to the hypothetical original position, where he places the principles of utility side by side with the two principles of justice as fairness. Here he takes utilitarianism to task for failing to pass the fairness test of his thought experiment. He believes that the representatives in the original position, acting under the influence of the veil of ignorance, would rank the alternative principles available for choice by their worst possible outcomes. Therefore, the representatives would eschew principles of justice that simply maximize aggregate utility or welfare (utilitarianism) in favor of those that guarantee basic liberties. The representatives would rather follow what Rawls calls the "maximin rule" and choose principles that come with minimal risks: principles that guarantee everyone a decent life prospect, irrespective of the contingencies of birth or socioeconomic status. They would consider the principles of utility too precarious an option, since no one in the original position would willingly risk sacrificing his or her basic liberties and equal share of primary social goods for the possible maximization of the greater utility of others:

> In this respect the two principles of justice have a definite advantage [over utilitarianism]. Not only do the parties protect their basic rights but they insure themselves against the worst eventualities. They run no chance of having to acquiesce in a loss of freedom over the course of their life for the sake of a greater good enjoyed by others, an undertaking that in actual circumstances they might not be able to keep. (Rawls 1971: 176)

THE CONCEPTION OF JUSTICE AS IMPARTIALITY

For Rawls, violation of basic liberties cannot be justified on the grounds that such an action promotes the general welfare of society. He claims that utilitarianism by contrast does not conceive of justice as independent of utility. Rather, as a teleological doctrine, utilitarianism defines the good (or utility) independently from the right, whereby it sees the good as the satisfaction of rational desire. Utilitarianism then identifies the right as whatever maximizes utility. Consequently, it considers rules, individual acts, or institutional undertakings as right if they produce the most good or maximize utility.

Rawls's arguments against utilitarianism and its definition of utility as the satisfaction of rational desire stem from the question of distributive justice. Accordingly, a utilitarian society is just when it achieves the greatest aggregate of "satisfactions" or utility for most citizens, regardless of how these satisfactions are distributed among persons in society. Rawls believes that utilitarianism condones the violation of the liberty of a few for the greater utility of the many. In contrast to utilitarianism, justice as fairness accords priority to liberty and rights over an increase in aggregate utility. In a society governed by justice as fairness, each member enjoys an inviolability of basic liberties and rights, which even the welfare of the majority cannot override (Rawls 1971: 28).

Furthermore, Rawls derides the utilitarian conception of justice as impartiality. By so doing, he adds Adam Smith and David Hume to the list of the early proponents of classical utilitarianism (Sen 2009: 137). Under the utilitarian view of justice as impartiality, a social system may be said to be right (or just) when an ideally impartial and sympathetic spectator approves it from a general point of view. This is someone who happens to be in possession of all the relevant knowledge of the circumstances and whose own interest is not at stake.

The ideal spectator responds to each citizen's desires and aspirations one by one, as if they were his or her own, and approves their individual desires sympathetically. The ideal spectator makes each citizen's desires and satisfactions, when summed together, represent the most appropriate aggregate of utility in society: an act that defines justice from the point of view of impartiality and benevolence (Rawls 1971: 186).

If a just society is one meeting the approval of such an ideal, fictitious observer or person, then in Rawls's view, utilitarianism clearly misconstrues impersonality as impartiality (Rawls 1971: 183–92). Therefore, the ideal impartial, sympathetic spectator construct for defining justice would be implausible, since such an ideal would only be realized in a society of perfect altruists. Rawls contends that his justice as fairness proves to be superior to utilitarianism in defining justice as impartiality because the original position guarantees impartiality. The persons or parties in the original position are to choose the principles of justice under the veil of ignorance, creating a situation of impartiality.

THE CONCEPTION OF SOCIETY AND INTEGRITY OF PERSONS

Perhaps Rawls's greatest criticism of utilitarianism lies in how utilitarians view persons and society. Rawls asserts that one major flaw of utilitarianism is that it does not take seriously the distinctions between persons as integral selves. Utilitarianism, he says, breaks down the distinctions between persons as citizens while aggregating human desires and interests into one large conglomerate (Rawls 1971: 27).

Thus, utilitarianism could permit gross inequalities if such acts produce the best consequences for the majority of people. Simmons (2008: 74–75) echoes Rawls's view:

> Utilitarians count happiness (and unhappiness) in their calculus regardless of the source of that happiness so in (say) determining the justice of slavery, the slaveholder's pleasure (including sadistic pleasures) would have to be weighed against the slaves' pains in the calculus. Even if utilitarian calculation reliably yielded the conclusion that slavery was unjust or wrong (since the slaves' pains always outweighed the slaveholder's pleasures), utilitarianism would have reached this conclusion for the wrong reasons, overlooking the facts that the slaves' lives and happiness are not simply counters to be tossed into and weighed against others in an impersonal calculus and that the pleasure the slaveholder takes in his slaves' suffering makes enslavement worse from the moral viewpoint, not better.

Utilitarians may counter with the claim that utilitarianism views individuals as moral equals; as Bentham and Mill said, "everybody to count for one, nobody for more than one" (Simmons 2008: 75) in the utilitarian calculus. However, this claim to formal equality still leaves room to bend everyone's happiness to the requirements of "social expediency" (Simmons 2008: 75). Justice as fairness advocates for not just equal distribution of social goods, but for the regulation of the basic structure of society in a way that favors the fair treatment of individuals (Simmons 2008: 75).

In the utilitarian society, the individual is subordinate to society. By contrast, justice as fairness regards citizens as distinctive persons, endowed with inviolable rights and basic liberties, which even the welfare of a majority cannot trump. In this sense, justice as fairness treats the individual in society as an end, rather than as a means to other people's ends. Besides, while utilitarianism views society as a fictitious body composed of individuals as its members, justice as fairness, Rawls maintains, sees society as a system of cooperation that offers reciprocity of advantages to its members, neglecting neither the less nor the more favored members.

THE SOCIAL BASIS OF SELF-RESPECT

Rawls thinks that people will find it difficult in a utilitarian society to become confident of their own worth, since they only have instrumental moral values. To regard persons as means to other persons' ends is to impose lower life prospects upon them. On the contrary, he claims, justice as fairness provides a social basis for self-respect. Persons in the original position express their respect for one another by choosing the two principles of justice. Moreover, when persons publicly affirm these principles in the real world, they express their desire to treat one another not as means, but as ends in themselves. For Rawls, self-respect is an important primary social good without which a person's sense of self as a citizen is lost; losing that, "nothing may seem worth doing. . . . All desire and activity becomes empty and vain, and we sink into apathy and cynicism" (Rawls 1971: 440).

In a utilitarian society, Rawls continues, people will experience loss of self-esteem, a weakening of their sense of motivation in pursuing their goals, since some must forgo their basic rights and liberties for the greater utility of others. As a result, a utilitarian society would not be stable for the right reasons because citizens, whose rights and liberties have been violated, would most likely develop a deep feeling of resentment, rather than a feeling of identification with the greater social good (Rawls 1971: 183–92).

JUSTICE AS FAIRNESS AND UTILITARIANISM: IMPLICATIONS FOR CORPORATE SOCIAL RESPONSIBILITY

What implications do justice as fairness and utilitarianism have for corporate social responsibility? Firms are constituent parts of the larger market and, as such, belong to what Rawls calls the basic structure of society—social, economic, and political institutions. The externalities that corporations produce, positive or negative, play a role in determining the life prospects of members of the society. It is hardly surprising that justice as fairness would take special interest in the regulation of corporations. Rawls justice as fairness can serve as a platform for citizens of the modern world to view CSR differently. From the lens of justice as fairness, CSR would become a means through which society could take advantage of the resources of firms to achieve social justice. This way, the bond between society and business would become stronger, enabling corporations to benefit from local patronage and support (Blowfield and Murray 2008: 64). Justice as fairness encourages corporations to engage in active citizenship, which redefines CSR as the legitimate expectations of citizens, rather than a philanthropic engagement of firms with the larger society.

Utilitarianism, on the other hand, as a form of consequentialist ethics, is one of the foundational principles of present-day capitalism. From a utilitarian standpoint, markets promote general welfare. A marketer's action is good if it promotes the utility of the many, bad if it brings about a reduction in utility. As Blowfield and Murray (2008: 62–63) point out: "In a utilitarian theory of justice, actions are neither good nor bad in themselves, but only in terms of what they bring about, captured in Bentham's (1789) view that 'good' acts are those that bring the greatest happiness to the largest number of people."

As we noted earlier, Rawls's strongest criticism of utilitarianism is that the theory is unable to recognize persons as distinct individuals and integral selves, rather than as means to the ends of others. Thus, utilitarians would allow firms to lay off workers with ease or pay workers only minimum wages if the economic efficiency such acts bring about promotes the welfare of the larger society or the majority of those affected by the activities of the firm (Blowfield and Murray 2008: 63). Since the interest of the individual is subordinate to the interest of the majority, the good of the majority can be used to justify serious harm to the few: "Thus, in the context of corporate responsibility, it is the aggregate benefit of a company's actions that matters, rather than any disbenefit to particular individuals or entities" (Blowfield and Murray 2008: 63).

In the cost-benefit analysis used often by governments or corporations, the utilitarian ideal of translating all moral goods into a single currency of value is also evident. Sandel (2009) uses the case of the tobacco company Philip Morris in the Czech Republic to illustrate this. In an attempt to dissuade the Czech government from hiking the tax on tobacco, Philip Morris commissioned a cost-benefit analysis of the effect of smoking for the Czech government. Taking cigarette tax and premature deaths associated with smoking together, Philip Morris demonstrated to the Czech government that it stood to gain rather than lose money from citizens smoking cigarettes: "Although smokers impose higher medical costs on the budget while they are alive, they die early, and so save the government considerable sums in health care, pensions, and housing for the elderly" (Sandel 2009: 42). According to Sandel, when the cost-benefit analysis became public, it turned into a PR disaster for Philip Morris: "Tobacco companies used to deny that cigarettes killed people. . . . Now they brag about it" (Sandel 2009: 42).[5] Utilitarian cost-benefit analyses that see the premature death of some citizens of the Czech Republic as steam for the economy do not capture the moral intuition of most reasonable people.

While utilitarianism, as an aggregate-maximizing principle of justice, would only support the self-regulation of corporations in the name of CSR if the consequences maximize aggregate utility, justice as fairness would ensure that firms are accountable to stakeholders. Since justice as fairness considers the market an integral part of the basic structure of society, we can argue that firms operating in the marketplace are thus accountable to society at large (society can be seen in some sense as the primary stakeholder of firms). This argument is all the more compelling because society bears the burden of negative externalities generated by corporations. Recently, this new way of viewing corporations has inspired grassroots social movements in the United States and other parts of the world. The Occupy Wall Street (OWS) movement, for example, recognizes the enormity of corporate power in influencing the political, economic, and social lives of citizens, as well as the responsibility corporations owe society. We believe that justice as fairness can serve as a foundational moral theory for the discourse on stakeholder justice and for the embedding of corporate social responsibility principles in business organizations, while utilitarianism may not. This understanding of CSR is reflected in Article 7 of the Global Manifesto, which implicitly acknowledges the role of corporate social responsibility in resolving national and global public choice problems as follows:

> Justice and the rule of law constitute reciprocal presuppositions. Responsibility, rectitude, transparency, and fairness are fundamental values of economic life, which must always be characterised by law-abiding integrity. All those engaged in economic activity are obliged to comply with the prevailing rules of national and international law. Where deficits exist in the quality or the enforcement of legal norms in a particular country, these should be over-ruled by self-commitment and self-control; under no circumstances may one take advantage of them for the sake of profit.

In that regard, CSR becomes a form of partnered governance (Midtunn 2008) that provides an effective and efficient mechanism for the governance of local and global "wicked problems" (Churchman 1967) that neither markets, the civil society, nor the state through hard regulation could deal with in isolation. However, this highly novel governance mechanism is yet to be extensively explored empirically. For example, it is yet not clear how collaborative or partnered governance mechanisms work in practice and how they contribute to strengthening the local governance of global economic institutions in developing economies. Neither is there a clear understanding of what institutional configurations are required for the effective and efficient functioning of such governance mechanisms in weak and fragile institutions and how partnered governance complements or contradicts other existing economic governance theories, especially in the context of the current global governance void. In addition, given the varied interest groups involved, partnered governance is likely not a smooth process and therefore could create a fertile ground for conflicts.

Notes

CHAPTER 1

1. In the course of writing this book, the European Commission revised the 2002 definition of CSR. It now defines CSR in simpler terms as "the responsibility of enterprises for their impacts on society" (European Commission 2011). This definition is closer to our description of CSR as a private governance of corporate externalities.
2. It's this cliché, in our view, that erroneously gave Adam Smith a near-mythical status among laissez faire economists as the father of deregulation.
3. A free rider is someone who consumes a public good or a resource without paying for it, or who pays a lot less than his or her fair share. A very simple example would be an individual who makes use of an available public transportation system but does not pay for the services provided by the system.
4. Herbert Simon, winner of a Nobel Prize in economics, also shares this view. See Donaldson 1982: 166–67.

CHAPTER 2

Part of this chapter is from K. Amaeshi, "Stakeholder Management: Theoretical Perspectives and Implications," in *Construction Stakeholder Management*, ed. E. Chinyio and P. Olomolaiye (Oxford: Wiley-Blackwell, 2010), pp. 13–40.

1. See the Canadian Business for Social Responsibility (CBSR) website at http://www.cbsr.bc.ca/what_is_csr/index.cfm (accessed April 8, 2003).

CHAPTER 3

1. United Nations General Assembly, "Declaration on the Right and Responsibility of Individuals, Groups and Organs of Society to Promote and Protect Universally Recognized Human Rights and Fundamental Freedoms," 1999, UN Doc.A/Res/53/144.
2. United Nations Sub-Commission on the Promotion and Protection of Human Rights, "Human Rights Principles and Responsibilities for Transnational Corporations and Other Business Enterprises," 2002, UN Doc.E/CN.4/Sub.2/2002/XX, E/CN.4/Sub.2/WG.2/WP.1.

3. *Doe v. Unocal Corp.*, 963 F. Supp. 880 (C.D. Cal. 1997).
4. *Wiwa v. Royal Dutch Petroleum Company and Shell Transport and Trading Company*, 226 F 3d 88 (2nd Cir. 2000); No. 96 Civ. 8386 (S.D.N.Y 1998).
5. *National Coalition Government of the Union of Burma v. Unocal, Inc.*, U.S. Dist. Lexis 2097 (1997), *Observer v. United Kingdom* (1992), 14 EHRR 153.
6. *The Presbyterian Church of Sudan v. Talisman Energy and the Republic of Sudan*, 374 F Supp. 2d 331 (2005).
7. *The Social and Economic Rights Action Centre for Economic and Social Rights v. Nigeria*, ACHPR, Comm. No. 155/96 (2001), paras. 60, 70.
8. European Parliament, "Resolution on EU Standards for European Enterprises Operating in Developing Countries: Towards a European Code of Conduct," 1999, European Parliament Resolution A4–0508/98, 1999 C 104/180.
9. Ibid.
10. United Nations, "Norms on the Responsibilities of Transnational Corporations and Other Business Enterprises with Regard to Human Rights," 2003, UN Doc. E/CN.4/Sub.2/2003/12/Rev.2 (2003).

CHAPTER 4

1. In the free and perfectly competitive market, the firm maximizes profit at a point where marginal revenue equals marginal cost and price (MR = MC = P).
2. Social costs = private costs (cost to the firm) + external costs (cost to the society not borne by the firm).
3. Ecosystem Valuation, "Glossary," http://www.ecosystemvaluation.org/glossary.htm.
4. Moreover, it is also acknowledged that the state does not enjoy a monopoly of wisdom and may sometimes get things wrong (including the First and Second World Wars) or be hijacked by some elite groups, as is evident in some developing democracies.

CHAPTER 5

1. Some notable exceptions here include Déjean, Gond, and Leca (2004) and Igalens and Gond (2005).
2. Social costs = private costs (cost to the firm) + external costs (cost to the society not borne by the firm).
3. The Chatham House Rule reads as follows: "When a meeting, or part thereof, is held under the Chatham House Rule, participants are free to use the information received, but neither the identity nor the affiliation of the speaker(s), nor that of any other participant, may be revealed." The world-famous Chatham House Rule may be invoked at meetings to encourage openness and the sharing of information. See Chatham House, "Chatham House Rule," http://www.chathamhouse.org.uk/about/chathamhouserule.
4. The objective of most Delphi applications is the reliable and creative exploration of ideas or the production of suitable information for decision making. The Delphi method is based on a structured process for collecting and distilling knowledge from a group of experts by means of a series of questionnaires

interspersed with controlled opinion feedback (Adler and Ziglio 1996). According to Helmer (1977), Delphi represents a useful communication device among a group of experts and thus facilitates the formation of a group judgment. Culled from: Illinois Institute of Technology, http://www.iit.edu/-it/delphi.html.

CHAPTER 6

1. See, for example, Orpen 1987; Langlois and Schlegelmilch 1990; Bennett 1998; Jones 1999; Quazi and O'Brien 2000; Maignan 2001; Kusku and Zarkada-Fraser 2004; Hamann et al. 2005; Fig 2005; Chapple and Moon 2005; Amaeshi et al. 2006.
2. These multinational bodies tend to work from the assumption that the global economic system is converging. While the global economic system convergence theory seems plausible, it has been confirmed that business practices are socially and contextually bound.
3. For instance, the governance of corporate negative externalities such as child labor, environmental pollution, employee welfare, consumer protection, and labor conditions are already hardwired in the institutional governance of most advanced capitalist economies, while these are still issues in most developing (or weak) capitalist economies. However, this allows firms in advanced capitalist economies to look for innovative and creative ways of coping with the tensed interactions amongst the different institutional governance mechanisms.
4. Accenture, "Sustainability," https://microsite.accenture.com/sustainability/Pages/default.aspx.

CHAPTER 7

1. See Introduction for more details.
2. http://www.cbsr.bc.ca/what_is_csr/index.cfm.
3. Nike and its subcontractors are often accused of inhumane labor and business practices in Asian factories where Nike products are made. See: *"Kasky v. Nike* and Its Implications for CSR," http://www.csrpolicies.org/CSRResources/CSRBriefs/csrbriefs_nike.html.
4. Clean Clothes Campaign, "Code of Labour Practices for the Apparel Industry Including Sportswear," http://www.cleanclothes.org/codes/ccccode.htm.
5. Deontology is an ethical theory that sees an action as right or wrong depending on whether such actions follow established moral principles or not. Consequentialism, on the contrary, is an ethical theory that considers the moral value of an action from the standpoint of its consequences. Thus, a good action is one that brings about good consequences, while a bad action is one that results in bad consequences.
6. The anti-pressure group campaign option is basically geared toward the global firms reclaiming power from the pressure groups and shifting public attention to the responsibilities of firms within their supply chains and the need for them to be held accountable for their practices as independent firms with legal and moral rights/duties.
7. For example see Bowie and Dunfee (2002) and Zyglidopoulos (2002).

CHAPTER 8

1. Rawls, who was a professor of philosophy at Harvard University until his death in 2002, remains perhaps the most important American philosopher since John Dewey. His theory of justice continues to influence the discourse on political theory and practice in North American universities and elsewhere around the world.

2. Husserl's bracketing, or *Einklammerung* in German, is a phenomenological attitude that brackets most presuppositions of ordinary life in order to arrive at pure consciousness. This method is similar to Rawls's original position.

3. See also Sandel 2009: 140–42.

4. See also Sandel 2009.

5. Some utilitarians may dispute the way Sandel presented this analysis as a misappropriation of utilitarian principles. The psychological cost of death to the community, which seems to have been relegated to the background in this analysis, would have featured prominently for the utilitarian aggregating pain and pleasure in the cost-benefit analysis (see Sandel 2009: 43).

Bibliography

Ackerman, B. A., and A. Alstott. *The Stakeholder Society*, New Haven, CT: Yale University Press, 1999.

Adegbite, Emmanuel., Kenneth Amaeshi, and Olufemi Amao. "Mafia Politics and Shareholder Activism in Nigeria." European Group for Organization Studies Conference, ESADE, Barcelona, 2009.

Adler, M., and E. Ziglio. *Gazing into the Oracle: The Delphi Method and Its Implications for Social Policy and Public Health*. London: Jessica Kingsley Publishers, 1996.

Agle, B. R., R. K. Mitchell, and J. A. Sonnenfeld. "Who Matters to CEOs? An Investigation of Stakeholder Attributes and Salience, Corporate Performance, and CEO Values." *The Academy of Management Journal* 42, no. 5 (1999): 507–25.

Aguilera, R. "Corporate Governance and Director Accountability: An Institutional Comparative Perspective." *British Journal of Management* 16, no. 1 (2005): 39–53.

Aguilera, Ruth, and G. Jackson. "The Cross-National Diversity of Corporate Governance: Dimensions and Determinants." *Academy of Management Review* 28, no. 3 (2003): 447–65.

Aguilera, Ruth V., Deborah E. Rupp, Cynthia A. Williams, and Jyoti Ganapathi. "Putting the S Back In Corporate Social Responsibility: A Multilevel Theory of Social Change in Organizations." *Academy of Management Review* 32, no. 3 (2007): 836–63.

Allinson, Robert. E. "Ethical Values as Part of the Definition of Business Enterprise and Part of the Integral Structure of the Business Organization." *Journal of Business Ethics* 17 (1998).

Alpay, Guven, Muzaffer Bodur, Hakan Ener, and Cem Talug. "Comparing Board-Level Governance at MNEs and Local Firms: Lessons from Turkey." *Journal of International Management* 11, no. 1 (2005): 67–86.

Amable, Bruno. *The Diversity of Modern Capitalism*. Oxford: Oxford University Press, 2003.

Amaeshi, K. M. "Mind Your Business: Should Companies Be Responsible for the Practices of Their Suppliers?" In *Proceedings of the ERP Environment Business Strategy and the Environment Conference*, September 2004, Devonshire Hall, University of Leeds, UK.

Amaeshi, Kenneth. "International Financial Institutions and Discursive Institutional Change: Implications for Corporate Social Responsibility in Developing Economies." *Journal of Change Management* 11, no. 1 (2011): 111–28.

Amaeshi, Kenneth. "Exploring the Institutional Embeddedness of Corporate Stakeholding and Social Responsibility: A Comparative Political Economy Perspective." Unpublished PhD thesis, Warwick Business School, University of Warwick, 2007.

Amaeshi, Kenneth, and Bongo C. Adi. "Reconstructing the Corporate Social Responsibility Construct in Utlish." *Business Ethics: A European Review* 16, no. 1 (2007): 3–18.

Amaeshi, Kenneth., Bongo C. Adi, Chris Ogbechie, and Olufemi Amao. "Corporate Social Responsibility in Nigeria: Western Mimicry or Indigenous Influences?" *Journal of Corporate Citizenship* 24 (Winter 2006): 83–99.

Amaeshi, Kenneth, and Olufemi Amao. "Corporate Social Responsibility in Transnational Spaces: Exploring the Influences of Varieties of Capitalism on Expressions of Corporate Codes of Conduct in Nigeria." *Journal of Business Ethics* 86, no. 2 (2009): 225–39.

Amaeshi, Kenneth, and A. Crane. "Stakeholder Engagement: A Mechanism for Sustainable Aviation." *Corporate Social Responsibility and Environmental Management* 13, no. 5 (2006): 245–60.

Amao, Olufemi. "Corporate Social Responsibility, Multinational Corporations and the Law in Nigeria: Controlling Multinationals in Host States." *Journal of African Law* 52 (2008a): 89–113.

Amao, Olufemi. "The African Regional Human Rights System and Multinational Corporations: Strengthening Host State Responsibility for the Control of Multinational Corporations." *International Journal of Human Rights* 12, no. 5 (2008b):761–88.

Amao, Olufemi, and Kenneth Amaeshi. "Galvanising Shareholder Activism: A Prerequisite for Effective Corporate Governance and Accountability in Nigeria." *Journal of Business Ethics* 82, no. 1 (2008):119–30.

Anderson, Gavin W. *Constitutional Rights After Globalization*. Oxford and Portland, Oregon: Hart Publishing, 2005.

Anderson, Gavin W. "Corporate Governance And Constitutional Law: A Legal Pluralist Perspective." In *Global Governance And The Quest For Justice. Volume II: Corporate Governance*, edited by S. MacLeod, 27–47. Oxford: Hart, 2006.

Andriof, J., B. Husted, S. Waddock, and S. S. Rahman. "Introduction." In *Unfolding Stakeholder Thinking: Theory, Responsibility and Engagement*, edited by J. Andriof, S. Waddock, B. Husted, and S. S. Rahman, 9–16. Sheffield: Greenleaf, 2002.

Andriof, J., and S. Waddock. "Unfolding Stakeholder Engagement." In *Unfolding Stakeholder Thinking: Theory, Responsibility and Engagement*, edited by J. Andriof, S. Waddock, B. Husted, and S. S. Rahman, 19–42. Sheffield: Greenleaf, 2002.

Appadurai, A. "Globalization and the Research Imagination." *International Social Science Journal* 51, no. 160 (1999): 229–38.

Araujo, L. "Markets, Market-making and Marketing." *Marketing Theory* 7, no. 3 (2007): 211–26.

Arthur D. Little Consulting. "Speaking the Same Language: Improving Communications between Companies and Investors on Corporate Responsibility." Report, 2003.

Aupperle, Kenneth. E. "An Empirical Measure of Corporate Social Orientation." *Research in Corporate Social Performance and Policy* 6 (1984): 27–54.

Bainbridge, Stephen M. *The New Corporate Governance in Theory and Practice*. New York: Oxford University Press, 2008.

Baines, Tim. "Integration of Corporate Social Responsibility through International Voluntary Initiatives." *Indiana Journal of Global Legal Studies* 16, no. 1 (2009): 223–48.

Baldwin, Robert. "Is Better Regulation Smarter Regulation?" *Public Law* 485 (2005): 485–511.

Baldwin, Robert, Colin Scott, and Christopher Hood. "Introduction." In *A Reader on Regulation*, by Robert Baldwin, Colin Scott, and Christopher Hood. Oxford: Oxford University Press, 1998.

Bansal, P. "Evolving Sustainably: A Longitudinal Study of Corporate Sustainable Development." *Strategic Management Journal* 26 (2005): 197–218.

Barnard, Catherine, Simon Deakin., and Richard Hobbs. *Reflexive Law, Corporate Social Responsibility and the Evolution of Labour Standards: The Case of Working Time.* Cambridge: ESRC Centre for Business Research, University of Cambridge, 2004.

Baron, David P. "A Positive Theory of Moral Management, Social Pressure, and Corporate Social Performance." *Journal of Economics and Management Strategy* 18, no.1 (2009):7–43.

Barrett, Richard. *Liberating the Corporate Soul: Building a Visionary Organization.* Boston: Butterworth-Heinemann, 1998.

Baucus, M., and J. Near. "Can Illegal Corporate Behaviour Be Predicted?" *Academy of Management Journal* 34 (1991): 9–36.

Baumol, William J. *Business Behavior, Value and Growth.* New York: Macmillan, 1967.

Beckert, Jens. "The Social Order of Markets." *Theory and Society* 38, no. 3 (2009): 245–69.

Beer, Chris. *To What Extent Do Stakeholders Have Intrinsic Moral Rights in Relation to the Management of the Corporation?* European Business Ethics Network, UK chapter (EBEN-UK) 2003 Essay Competition 1st Position Award-Winning Paper.

Beliveau, B., M. Cottrill, and H. O'Neill. "Predicting Corporate Social Responsiveness." *Journal of Business Ethics* 13, no. 9 (1994): 731–38.

Bennett, R. "Corporate Philanthropy in France, Germany and the UK: International Comparisons of Commercial Orientation towards Company Giving in European Nations." *International Marketing Review* 15, no. 6 (1998): 458–75.

Bentham, Jeremy. *An Introduction to the Principles of Morals and Legislation.* London: Anthlone Press, 1970.

Berger, P., and T. Luckmann. *The Social Construction of Reality: A Treatise in the Sociology of Knowledge.* London: Penguin Books, 1966.

Bergin, Tom, and Greg Roumeliotis. "BP Challenges Halliburton Court Request on Spill." *Reuters*, January 3, 2012. http://www.reuters.com/article/2012/01/03/us-bp-halliburton-idUSTRE80200S20120103.

Berle, Adolf A. "The Impact of the Corporation on Classical Economic Theory." *Quarterly Journal of Economics* 79 (1965): 25–40.

Berman, Shawn, Andrew C. Wicks, Suresh Kotha, and Thomas M. Jones. "Does Stakeholder Orientation Matter? The Relationship between Stakeholder Management Models and Firm Financial Performance. *Academy of Management Journal* 42, no. 5 (1999).

Beunza, D. "Tools of the Trade: The Socio-Technology of Arbitrage in a Wall Street Trading Room." *Industrial and Corporate Change* 13, no. 2 (2004): 369–401.

Bird, Frederick B., and James A. Waters. "The Moral Muteness of Managers." *California Management Review* (Fall 1989): 73–88.

Birkinshaw, Julian, Gary Hamel, and Michael J. Mol. "Management Innovation." *Academy of Management Review* 33, no. 4 (2008): 825–45.

Blowfield, Mick. "Ethical Sourcing: A Contribution to Sustainability or a Diversion?" *Sustainable Development* 8, no. 4 (2000): 191–200.

Blowfield, Michael, and Jedrzej George Frynas. "Editorial Setting New Agendas: Critical Perspectives on Corporate Social Responsibility in the Developing World." *International Affairs* 81, no. 3 (2005): 499–513.

Blowfield, Michael, and Alan Murray. *Corporate Responsibility: A Critical Introduction.* Oxford: Oxford University Press, 2008.

Boiral, O. "The Certification of Corporate Conduct: Issues and Prospects." *International Labour Review* 142, no. 3 (2003): 317–340.

Borsch, A. "Globalisation, Shareholder Value, Restructuring: The (Non)-transformation of Siemens." *New Political Economy* 9, no. 3 (2004): 365–87.

Bowie, Ngman. "A Kantian Theory of Capitalism." *Business Ethics Quarterly* 1, no. 1 (1998): 37–60.

Bowie, Ngman E., and Thomas Dunfee. "Confronting Morality in Markets."*Journal of Business Ethics* 38, no. 4 (2002): 281–93.

Bowman, S. R. The Modern Corporation And American Political Thought. Law, Power, And Ideology. University Park, PA: The Pennsylvania State University Press, 1996.

Braithwaite, John, and Peter Drahos. *Global Business Regulation*. Cambridge: Cambridge University Press, 2000.

Branson, Douglas M. "Corporate Governance 'Reform' and the New Corporate Social Responsibility." *University of Pittsburgh Law Review* 62, no. 4 (2001): 605–48.

Broder, John M. "U.S. Acts to Fine BP and Top Contractors for Gulf Oil Spill."*New York Times,* October 13, 2011, A18.

Brown, Dana L., and Ngaire Woods. *Making Global Self-Regulation Effective in Developing Countries.* Oxford: Oxford University Press, 2007.

Brown, Judy, and Michael Fraser. "Competing Discourses in Social and Environmental Accounting: An Overview of the Conceptual Landscape." Victoria University of Wellington Working Paper Series, 2004.

Brown, Judy, and Michael Fraser. "Approaches and Perspectives in Social and Environmental Accounting: An Overview of the Conceptual Landscape." *Business Strategy and the Environment* 15 (2006): 103–17.

Brühl, T. and V. Rittberger. "From International To Global Governance: Actors, Collective Decision-Making, And The United Nations In The World Of The Twenty-First Century." In *Global Governance and the United Nations System,* edited by V. Rittberger, 1–47). Tokyo: United Nations University Press, 2004.

BSR: 2008, Environmental, Social and Governance: Moving to Mainstream Investing.

Buenza, Daniel, and David Stark. "The Organization of Responsiveness: Innovation and Recovery in the Trading Rooms of Lower Manhattan." *Socio-Economic Review* 1, no. 2 (2003): 135–64.

Buenza, Daniel, and David Stark. "Tools of the Trade: The Socio-Technology of Arbitrage in a Wall Street Trading Room." *Industrial and Corporate Change* 13, no. 1 (2004): 369–401.

Buhmann, Karin. "Integrating Human Rights in Emerging Regulation of Corporate Social Responsibility: The EU Case." *International Journal of Law in Context* 7, no. 2 (2011): 139–79.

Burdeau, Cain. "BP Accuses Halliburton over Gulf Spill." *Independent,* December 7, 2011. http://www.independent.co.uk/news/world/americas/bp-accuses-halliburton-over-gulf-spill-6273185.html.

Burton, B. K., J-L. Farh, and W. H. Hegarty. "A Cross -cultural Comparison of Corporate Social Responsibility Orientation: Hong Kong vs. United States Students." *Teaching Business Ethics* 4 (2000): 151–67.

Cahn, Steven M. *Classics of Political and Moral Philosophy.* New York: Oxford University Press, 2002.

Callon, Michel. "Civilizing Markets: Carbon Trading between in Vitro and in Vivo Experiments." *Accounting, Organizations and Society* 34, no. 3–4 (2009): 535–48.

Callon, Michel, and Fabian Muniesa. "Peripheral Vision: Economic Markets as Calculative Collective Devices." *Organization Studies* 26, no. 8 (2005): 1229–50.

Campbell, John L. "Why Would Corporations Behave in Socially Responsible Way? An Institutional Theory of Corporate Social Responsibility." *Academy of Management Review* 32, no. 3 (2007): 946–67.

Campbell, Tom. "The Normative Grounding of Corporate Social Responsibility: A Human Rights Approach." In *The New Corporate Accountability: Corporate Social Responsibility and the Law,* by Doreen J. McBarnet, Aurora Voiculescu, and Tom Campbell, 529–64. Cambridge: Cambridge University Press, 2007.

Carroll, Archie B. "A Three Dimensional Conceptual Model of Corporate Social Performance." *Academy of Management Review* 4 (1979): 497–505.

Carroll, Archie B. "The Pyramid of Corporate Social Responsibility: Toward the Moral Management of Organizational Stakeholders." *Business Horizons* 34, no. 4 (1991): 39–48.

Carroll, Archie B. *Business and Society: Ethics and Stakeholder Management.* Cincinnati, OH: South-Western, 1993.

Carroll, Archie B. "Managing Ethically with Global Stakeholders: A Present and Future Challenge." *Academy of Management Executive* 18, no. 2 (2004): 114–19.

Carroll, Archie B., and Ann Buchholtz. *Business and Society: Ethics and Stakeholder Management.* Cincinnati, OH: South-Western, 1999.

Cassel, D. "Human Rights Business Responsibilities in the Global Marketplace." *Business Ethics Quarterly* 11, no. 2 (2001): 261–74.

Cerne, A. "Like A Bridge Over Troubled Water: Discourses Integrating Corporate Social Responsibility And Growth In International Business." *Journal of Interdisciplinary Economics* 23, no. 2 (2011): 177–200.

Chang, Ha-Joon. *Globalisation, Economic Development and the Role of the State.* Penang: Third World Network, 2003.

Chapple, W., and J. Moon. "Corporate Social Responsibility (CSR) in Asia: A Seven-Country Study of CSR Web Site Reporting." *Business and Society* 44, no. 4 (2005): 415–39.

Chartered Financial Analyst (CFA). "Breaking the Short-term Cycle: Discussion and Recommendations on How Corporate Leaders, Asset Managers, Investors, and Analysts Can Refocus on Long-term Value." CFA Institute Report, 2006.

Chiu, Iris H.Y. "Standardization in Corporate Social Responsibility Reporting and a Universalist Concept of CSR?—A Path Paved with Good Intentions." *Florida Journal of International Law* 22, no. 3 (2010): 61–400.

Churchman, C.W. "Wicked Problems." *Management Science* 4, no. 14 (1967): B141–42.

Clapham, Andrew. "The Question of Jurisdiction under International Criminal Law over Legal Persons: Lessons from the Rome Conference on an International Criminal Court." In *Liability of Multinational Corporations under International Law,* by Menno T. Kamminga and Saman Zia-Zarifi, 139–95. The Hague: Kluwer Law International, 2000.

Clapham, Andrew. *Human Rights Obligations of Non-State Actors.* Oxford: Oxford University Press, 2006.

Clapham, Andrew, and Scott Jerbi. "Categories of Corporate Complicity in Human Rights Abuses." *Hastings Int and Comp. L.R.* 24 (2001): 339–49.

Clark, Gordon L., and Dariusz Wójcik. *The Geography of Finance: Corporate Governance in the Global Marketplace.* Oxford: Oxford University Press, 2007.

Clark, T., and L.L. Knowles. "Globalization and the Role of the Global Corporation." *Journal of International Management* 9, no. 4 (2003): 361–72.

Clarke, Thomas. "Introduction: Theories of Governance—Reconceptualizing Corporate Governance Theory after the Enron Experience." In *Theories of Corporate Governance: The Philosophical Foundations of Corporate Governance,* by Thomas Clarke, 1–30. London: Routledge, 2004.

Clarkson, Max. B. "A Stakeholder Framework for Analyzing and Evaluating Corporate Social Performance." *Academy of Management Review* 20 (1995): 92–117.

Clinard, Marshall B. *Corporate Corruption. The Abuse of Power.* New York: Praeger, 1990.

Cohen, A. "Bureaucratic Internalization: Domestic Governmental Agencies and the Legitimization of International Law." *Georgetown Journal of International Law* 36, no. 4 (2005): 1079–1144.

Collier, Jane. "Theorising the Ethical Organization." *Business Ethics Quarterly* 8, no. 4 (1998): 621–54.

Collins, Hugh. "Ascription of Legal Responsibility to Groups in Complex Patterns of Economic Integration." *Modern Law Review* 53 (1990): 731.

Covey, Stephen R. *The Seven Habits of Highly Effective People: Restoring the Character Ethic.* New York: Simon & Schuster, 1992.

Craig, Edward. *Prospective and Retrospective Responsibility. The Concise Routledge Encyclopedia of Philosophy.* London: Routledge, 2000.

Craig, R., and J. Amernic. "Enron Discourse: The Rhetoric of a Resilient Capitalism." *Critical Perspectives on Accounting* 15, no. 6–7 (2004): 813–52.

Crane, Andrew. "Facing the Backlash: Green Marketing and Strategic Reorientation in the 1990s." *Journal of Strategic Marketing* 8, no. 3 (2000): 277–96.

Crane, Andrew, and Sharon Livesey. "Are You Talking to Me? Stakeholder Communication and the Risks and Rewards of Dialogue." In *Unfolding Stakeholder Thinking,* edited by Jorg Andriof, 39–52. Sheffield, UK: Greenleaf Publishing, 2003.

Crane, Andrew, and Dirk Matten. *Business Ethics: A European Perspective; Managing Corporate Citizenship and Sustainability in the Age of Globalization.* Oxford: Oxford University Press, 2004.

Crane, Andrew, Dirk Matten, and Jeremy Moon. *Corporations and Citizenship.* Cambridge: Cambridge University Press, 2008.

Crouch, Colin. *Capitalist Diversity and Change: Recombinant Governance and Institutional Entrepreneurs.* Oxford: Oxford University Press, 2005.

Crouch, Colin. "Modelling the Firm in Its Market and Organizational Environment: Methodologies for Studying Corporate Social Responsibility." *Organization Studies* 27, no. 10 (2006): 1533–51.

Crouch, Colin, Martin Schroder, and Helmut Voelzkow. "Regional and Sectoral Varieties of Capitalism." *Economy and Society* 38, no. 4 (2009): 654–78.

Cumming, J. F. "Engaging Stakeholders in Corporate Accountability Programmes: A Cross Sectoral Analysis of UK and Transnational Experience." *Business Ethics: A European Review* 10, no. 1 (2001): 45–52.

Cutler, A. Claire. "Private International Regimes and Interfirm Cooperation." In *The Emergence of Private Authority in Global Governance,* edited by Rodney Bruce Hall and Thomas Biersteker, 3–28. Cambridge: Cambridge University Press, 2002.

Cutler, A. Claire, Virginia Haufler, and Tony Porter. "Private Authority in International Affairs." In *Private Authority and International Affairs.* Albany: State University of New York Press, 1999a.

Cutler, A. Claire, Virginia Haufler, and Tony Porter, eds. *Private Authority and International Affairs.* Albany: State University of New York Press, 1999b.

Dahan, N., J. Doh, and T. Guay. "The Role of Multinational Corporations in Transnational Institution Building: A Policy Network Perspective." *Human Relations* 59, no. 11 (2006): 1571–1600.

Dal Bó, Ernesto. "Regulatory Capture: A Review." *Oxford Review of Economic Policy* 22, no. 2 (2006): 203–24.

Darke, P., G. Shanks, and M. Broadbent. "Successfully Completing Case Study Research: Combining Rigour, Relevance and Pragmatism." *Information Systems Journal* 8, no. 4 (1998): 273–89.

De Backer, Koen, and Leo Sleuwagen. "Does Foreign Direct Investment Crowd Out Domestic Entrepreneurship? *Review of Industrial Organization* 2, no. 1 (2003): 67–102.

Deeg, Richard, and Gregory Jackson. "The State of the Art: Toward a More Dynamic Theory of Capitalist Variety." *Socio-Economic Review* 5 (2007): 149–79.

Déjean, Frédérique, Jean-Pascal Gond, and Bernard Leca. "Measuring the Unmeasured: An Institutional Entrepreneur Strategy in an Emerging Industry."*Human Relations* 57, no. 6 (2004): 741–64.

Deloitte Touche Tohmatsu (now Deloitte). *Sustainability Reporting and Assurance—Trends, Challenges and Perspectives*. Denmark: Deloitte & Touche, 2002.

DesJardins, J. "Corporate Environmental Responsibility." *Journal of Business Ethics* 17, no. 8 (1998): 825–38.

Detomasi, David A. "The Multinational Corporation and Global Governance: Modelling Global Public Policy Networks." *Journal of Business Ethics* 71, no. 3 (2006): 321–34.

Deva, S. "Human Rights Violations By Multinational Corporations And International Law: Where From Here?" *Connecticut Journal of International Law* 19 (2003): 1–57.

Devinney, Timothy M. "Is the Socially Responsible Corporation a Myth? The Good, the Bad, and the Ugly of Corporate Social Responsibility." *Academy of Management Perspectives* 23, no. 2 (2009): 44–56.

DiMaggio, Paul. J., and Walter W. Powell. "The Iron Cage Revisited: Institutional Isomorphism and Collective Rationality in Organizational Fields." *American Sociological Review* 48, no. 2 (1983): 147–60.

Dine, Janet, and Kristine Shields. "Corporate Social Responsibility: Do Corporations Have a Responsibility to Trade Fairly?" In *Perspectives on Corporate Social Responsibility*, edited by Nina Boeger, Rachel Murray, and Charlotte Villiers, 144. Cheltenham, Glos, UK: Edward Elgar, 2008.

Djelic, Marie-Laure, and Sigrid Quack. "Institutions and Transnationalization." In *The SAGE Handbook of Organizational Institutionalism*, edited by Royston Greenwood, Christine Oliver, Roy Suddaby, and Kerstine S. Andersson. Los Angeles: SAGE, 2008.

Djelic, Marie-Laure, and Kerstin Sahlin-Andersson. "Dynamics of Soft Regulations." In *Transnational Governance: Institutional Dynamics of Regulation*, by Marie-Laure Djelic and Kerstin Sahlin-Andersson. Cambridge: Cambridge University Press, 2006.

Donaldson, Thomas. *Corporations and Morality*. Englewood Cliffs, NJ: Prentice Hall, 1982.

Donaldson, Thomas, and Lee E. Preston. "The Stakeholder Theory of the Corporation: Concepts, Evidence and Implications." *Academy of Management Review* 20 (1995): 65–91.

Dore, R. *Stock Market Capitalism: Welfare Capitalism, Japan and Germany versus the Anglo-Saxons*. Oxford: Oxford University Press, 2000.

Drumwright, Minette. "Socially Responsible Organizational Buying." *Journal of Marketing* 58, (1994): 1–19.

Dunning, John H. *Global Capitalism at Bay*. London: Routledge, 2001.

EIRIS. "Valuing ESG Issues: A Survey of Investors." Report, 2006.

Emmelhainz, Margaret A., and Ronald J. Adams. "The Apparel Industry Response to 'Sweatshop' Concerns: A Review and Analysis of Codes of Conduct." *Journal of Supply Chain Management* (Summer 1999): 51–57.

Engwall, Lars. "Enterprises in Field of Governance." In *Transnational Governance: Institutional Dynamics of Regulation*, edited by Marie-Laure Djelic and Kerstin Sahlin-Andersson,161–65. Cambridge: Cambridge University Press, 2006.

Ernst and Young. "Financial Reporting: KPMG's Survey of Leading Investors." Report, 2007.

Eshleman, Andrew. "Moral Responsibility." In *The Stanford Encyclopedia of Philosophy* (summer edition), edited by Edward N. Zalta, 2002. http://plato.stand ford.edu/archives/sum2002/entries/moral-responsibility.

European Commission. "Green Paper: Promoting a European Framework for Corporate Social Responsibility (COM 2001, 366)." 2002. http://eur-lex.europa.eu/LexUriServ/site/en/com/2001/com2001_0366en01.pdf.

European Commission. "Corporate Social Responsibility: A New Definition, a New Agenda for Action." 2011. http://europa.eu/rapid/pressReleasesAction.do?reference=MEMO/11/730.

Eurosif: 2005, Eurosif SRI Study.

Evan, William, and R. E. Freeman. "A Stakeholder Theory for the Modern Corporation: Kantian Capitalism." In *Ethical Theory and Business,* edited by Tom Beauchamp and Norman Bowie. Englewood Cliffs, NJ: Prentice Hall, 1988.

Farnell, Derrick. "Without Answerability: Disentangling the Two Forms of Moral Responsibility." DerrickFarnell.com. http://www.derrickfarnell.org/articles/Responsibility_without_Answerability.htm.

Ferran, Ellis. "Corporate Law, Codes and Social Norms—Finding the Right Regulatory Combination and Institutional Structure." *Journal of Corporate Law Studies,* no. 2 (2001).

Fig, D. "Manufacturing Amnesia: Corporate Social Responsibility in South Africa." *International Affairs* 81, no. 3 (2005): 599–617.

Fishbein, Martin, and I. Ajzen. *Belief, Attitude, Intentions and Behavior: An Introduction to Theory and Research.* Boston: Addison-Wesley, 1975.

Fisher, Josie. "Social Responsibility and Ethics: Clarifying the Concepts." *Journal of Business Ethics* 52, no. 4 (2004): 391–400.

Fiske, S. T., and S. E. Taylor. *Social Cognition.* Reading, MA: Addison-Wesley, 1984.

Fiss, Peer C., and Edward J. Zajac. "The Diffusion of Ideas over Contested Terrain: The (Non)adoption of a Shareholder Value Orientation among German Firms." *Administrative Science Quarterly* 49 (2004): 501–34.

Flagstein, Neil, and Luke Dauter. "The Sociology of Markets." *Annual Review of Sociology* 33, no. 1 (2007): 105–28.

Flanagan, William, and Gail Whiteman. "AIDS Is Not a Business: A Study in Global Corporate Responsibility—Securing Access to Low-Cost HIV Medications." *Journal of Business Ethics* 73 (2007): 65–75.

Fligstein, Neil. "Markets as Politics: A Political-Cultural Approach to Market Institutions." *American Sociological Review* 61, no. 4 (1996): 656–73.

Fligstein, Neil. *The Architecture of Markets: An Economic Sociology of Twenty-First-Century Capitalist Societies.* Princeton: Princeton University Press, 2002.

Fligstein, Neil, and L. Dauter. "The Sociology of Markets." *Annual Review of Sociology* 33, no. 1 (2007): 105–28.

Francioni, F. "Exporting Environmental Hazard through Multinational Enterprises: Can the State of Origin Be Held Responsible?" In *International Responsibility for Environmental Harm,* edited by F. Francioni and T. Scovazzi, 275–98. London: Graham & Trotman, 1991.

Frank, N. Crimes Against Health And Safety. New York: Harrow & Heston, 1985.

Freedman, Judith. "The Tax Avoidance Culture: Who Is Responsible? Governmental Influences and Corporate Social Responsibility." *Current Legal Problems* 59, no. 1 (2006): 359–390.

Freeman, R. Edward. *Strategic Management: A Stakeholder Approach.* Boston: Pitman, 1984.

Freeman, R. Edward. "The Politics of Stakeholder Theory: Some Future Directions." *Business Ethics Quarterly* 4, no. 4 (1994): 409–21.

Freeman, R. Edward, and W. M. Evan. "Corporate Governance: A Stakeholder Interpretation." *The Journal of Behavioral Economics* 19, no. 4 (1990): 337–59.

Freeman, R. Edward, and J. McVea. "A Stakeholder Approach to Strategic Management." In *The Blackwell Handbook of Strategic Management,* edited by M. Hitt, E. Freeman, and J. Harrison, 189–207. Oxford: Oxford University Press, 2001.

Freeman, Samuel Richard. *Justice and the Social Contract: Essays on Rawlsian Political Philosophy.* Oxford: Oxford University Press, 2007.

Friedman, A. L., and S. Miles. *Stakeholders: Theory and Practice.* Oxford: Oxford University Press, 2006.

Friedman, Milton. *Capitalism and Freedom.* Chicago: University of Chicago Press, 1962.

Friedman, Milton, and Rose D. Friedman. *Free to Choose: A Personal Statement.* New York: Harcourt Brace Jovanovich, 1980.

Friedman, Richard B. "On the Concept of Authority in Political Philosophy." In *Authority,* edited by Joseph Raz. New York: New York University Press, 1990.

Frynas, Jedrzej George. *Oil in Nigeria: Conflict and Litigation between Oil Companies and Village Communities.* Munster: Lit Verlag, 1999.

Frynas, Jedrzej George, Kamel Mellahi, and Geoffrey Allen Pigman. "First Mover Advantages in International Business and Firm-Specific Political Resources." *Strategic Management Journal* 27, no. 4 (2006): 321–45.

Fulop, G., R. D. Hisrich, and K. Szegedi. "Business Ethics and Social Responsibility in Transition Economies." *Journal of Management Development* 19, no. 4 (2000): 5–31.

Gago, R. F., and M. N. Antolin. "Stakeholder Salience in Corporate Environmental Strategy." *Corporate Governance* 4, no. 3 (2004): 65–76.

Gainet, C. 2011. "Exploring The Impact Of Legal Systems And Financial Structure On Corporate Responsibility." *Journal of Business Ethics* 95 (2011): 195–222.

Gatewood, E., and A. B. Carroll. "The Anatomy of Corporate Social Response." *Business Horizons* 24, no. 1 (1981): 9–16.

Ghoshal, S. "Bad Management Theories Are Destroying Good Management Practices." *IEEE Engineering Management Review* 33, no. 3 (2005): 79–91.

Giddens, A. *The Constitution of Society: Outline of the Theory of Structuration.* Cambridge: Polity Press, 1984.

Goodpaster, Kenneth E. "The Concept of Corporate Responsibility." *Journal of Business Ethics* 2, no. 1 (1983): 1–22.

Graafland, Johan J. "Sourcing Ethics in the Textile Sector: The Case of C&A." *Business Ethics: A European Review* 11, no. 3 (2002): 282–94.

Graham, David, and Ngaire Woods. "Making Corporate Self-Regulation Effective in Developing Countries." *World Development* 34, no. 5 (2006): 868–83.

Granovetter, M. "Economic Action and Social Structure: A Theory of Embeddedness." *American Journal of Sociology* 91, no. 3 (1985): 481–510.

Grant, W. Business And Politics In Britain, Revised Edition. Basingstoke: Macmillan, 1993.

Gray, Robert. "The Social Accounting Project and Accounting Organizations and Society Privileging Engagement, Imaginings, New Accountings and Pragmatism over Critique?" *Accounting, Organizations and Society* 27, no. 7 (2002): 687–708.

Gray, Rob, Colin Dey, Dave Owen, Richard Evans, and Simon Zadek. "Struggling with the Praxis of Social Accounting: Stakeholders, Accountability, Audits and Procedures." *Accounting, Auditing & Accountability Journal* 10, no. 3 (1997): 325–64.

Gray, Rob, Dave Owen, and Carol Adams. *Accountability: Changes and Challenges in Corporate Social and Environmental Reporting.* Hemel Hempstead, England: Prentice Hall, 1996.

Gray, Rob, Dave Owen, and K. T. Maunders. *Corporate Social Reporting: Accounting and Accountability.* Englewood Cliffs, NJ: Prentice Hall, 1987.

Gray, Rob, Dave Owen, and Keith Maunders. "Corporate Social Reporting: Emerging Trends in Accountability and the Social Contract." *Accounting, Auditing & Accountability Journal* 1, no. 1 (1988): 6–20.

Grcic, Joseph Matthew. *John Rawls and the Social Contract Tradition.* South Bend, IN: University of Notre Dame, 1980.

Greening, D. W., and B. Gray. "Testing a Model of Organizational Response to Social and Political Issues." *Academy of Management Journal* 37, no. 3 (1994): 467–98.

Günther, Jutta. "FDI as a Multiplier of Modern Technology in Hungarian Industry." *Intereconomics* 37, no. 5 (2002): 263–69.

Hall, Peter A. "The Evolution of Varieties of Capitalism in Europe." In *Beyond Varieties of Capitalism: Conflict, Contradictions, and Complementarities in the European Economy,* edited by Bob Hancké, Rhodes Martin, and Mark Thatcher. Oxford: Oxford University Press, 2008.

Hall, Peter A., and Daniel W. Gingerich. *Varieties of Capitalism and Institutional Complementarities in the Macroeconomy: An Empirical Analysis.* Max Planck Institute for the Study of Societies Cologne, MPIfG Discussion Paper 04/5, September 2004.

Hall, Peter A., and David W. Soskice, eds. *Varieties of Capitalism: The Institutional Foundations of Comparative Advantage.* Oxford: Oxford University Press, 2001.

Hall, Rodney B., and Thomas J. Biersteker. "The Emergence of Private Authority in the International System." In *The Emergence of Private Authority in Global Governance,* edited by Rodney B. Hall and Thomas J. Biersteker. Cambridge: Cambridge University Press, 2002.

Hamann, R., T. Agbazue, P. Kapelus, and A. Hein. "Universalizing Corporate Social Responsibility? South African Challenges to the International Organization for Standardization's New Social Responsibility Standard." *Business and Society Review* 110, no. 1 (2005): 1–19.

Hancké, Bob, Martin Rhodes, and Mark Thatcher. "Introduction: Beyond Varieties of Capitalism." In *Beyond Varieties of Capitalism: Conflict, Contradictions, and Complementarities in the European Economy,* edited by Bob Hancké, Martin Rhodes, and Mark Thatcher. Oxford: Oxford University Press, 2007.

Handley, K., T. Clark, R. Fincham, and A. Sturdy. "Researching Situated Learning: Participation, Identity and Practices in Client–Consultant Relationships." *Management Learning* 38, no. 2 (2007): 173–91.

Hardy, C. "Researching Organizational Discourse." *International Studies of Management and Organization* 31, no. 3 (2001): 25–47.

Hardy, C., N. Phillips, and S. R. Clegg. "Reflexivity in Organization and Management Theory: A Study of the Production of the Research 'Subject.'" *Human Relations* 54, no. 5 (2001): 531–60.

Harris, Richard, Qian Cher Li, and Mary Trainor. "Is a Higher Rate of R&D Tax Credit a Panacea for Low Levels of R&D in Disadvantaged Regions?" *Research Policy* 38, no. 1 (2009): 192–205.

Harrison, Jeffery G., and R. E. Freeman. "Stakeholders, Social Responsibility, and Performance: Empirical Evidence and Theoretical Perspectives." *Academy of Management Journal* 42, no. 5 (1999): 479–85.

Hart, Stuart L., and Clayton M. Christensen. "The Great Leap: Driving Innovation from the Base of the Pyramid" *Sloan Management Review* 44, no. 1 (2002): 51–56.

Haufler, Virgina. *A Public Role for the Private Sector. Industry Self-Regulation in a Global Economy.* Washington, DC: Carnegie Endowment for International Peace, 2001.

Heal, Geoffrey. "Corporate Social Responsibility: An Economic and Financial Framework." *The Geneva Papers on Risk and Insurance Issues and Practice* 30, no. 3 (2005): 387–409.

Heidegger, Martin. *What Is Called Thinking?* New York: Harper & Row, 1968.

Held, David, Anthony McGrew, David Goldblatt, and Jonathan Perraton. *Global Transformations: Politics, Economic, and Culture.* Cambridge, UK: Polity Press, 1999.

Hemingway, Christine A. "Personal Values as a Catalyst for Corporate Social Entrepreneurship." *Journal of Business Ethics* 60, no. 3 (2005): 233–49.

Hemingway, Christine A., and P. W. Maclagan. "Managers' Personal Values as Drivers of Corporate Social Responsibility." *Journal of Business Ethics* 50, no. 1 (2004): 33–44.

Hemphill, T.A. and W. Lillevik, W. "The Global Economic Ethic Manifesto: Implementing A Moral Values Foundation In The Multinational Enterprise." *Journal of Business Ethics* 101 (2011): 213–230.

Hepple, B. "A Race to the Top? International Investment Guidelines and Corporate Codes of Conduct." *Comparative Labour Law and Policy Journal* 20 (1999): 347–363.

Henderson, David. *Misguided Virtue: False Notions of Corporate Social Responsibility.* London: Institute of Economic Affairs, 2001.

Hess, David. "Social Reporting: A Reflexive Law Approach to Corporate Social Responsiveness." *Journal of Corporation Law* 25, no. 1 (1999): 41–84.

Heugens, P. P.M.A.R., F. A. J. Van Den Bosch, and C. B. M. Van Riel. "Stakeholder Integration: Building Mutually Enforcing Relationships." *Business & Society* 41, no. 1 (2002): 36–60.

Hill, C.W.L., and T. M. Jones. "Stakeholder-agency Theory." *Journal of Management Studies* 29 (1992): 131–54.

Hirst, Paul, and Grahame Thompson. *Globalization in Question: The International Economy and the Possibilities of Governance.* Cambridge, UK: Polity Press, 1996.

Hohfeld, Wesley. N. "Nature of Stockholders' Individual Liability for Corporate Debts." *Colum. L. Rev.* 9 (1909): 285.

Holm, Petter. "The Dynamics of Institutionalization: Transformation Processes in Norwegian Fisheries." *Administrative Science Quarterly* 40, no. 3 (1995): 398–422.

Hovekamp, Herbert. *Enterprise and American Law, 1836–1937.* Cambridge, MA: Harvard University Press, 1991.

Hull, Clyde Eiríkur, and Sandra Rothenberg. "Firm Performance: The Interactions of Corporate Social Performance with Innovation and Industry Differentiation." *Strategic Management Journal* 29, no. 7 (2008): 781–89.

Human Rights Watch. The Price Of Oil, Corporate Responsibility And Human Rights Violations In Nigeria's Oil Producing Communities. New York: Human Rights Watch, 1999.

Hussain, S. "The Ethics of 'Going Green': The Corporate Social Responsibility Debate." *Business Strategy and the Environment* 8, no. 4 (1999): 203–10.

Idemudia, Uwafiokun. *Corporate Partnerships and Community Development in the Nigerian Oil Industry: Strengths and Limitations.* Markets, Business and Regulation Programme Paper No. 2. Geneva: United Nations Research Institute for Social Development, 2007.

Idemudia, Uwafiokun. "Oil Companies and Sustainable Community Development in the Niger Delta, Nigeria: The Issue of Reciprocal Responsibility and Its Implications for Corporate Citizenship Theory and Practice." *Sustainable Development* (2011).

Igalens, Jacques, and Jean-Pascal Gond. "Measuring Corporate Social Performance in France: A Critical and Empirical Analysis of ARESE Data." *Journal of Business Ethics* 56, no. 2 (2005): 131–48.

Ite, Uwem E. "Multinationals and Corporate Social Responsibility in Developing Countries: A Case Study of Nigeria." *Corporate Social Responsibility and Environmental Management* 11, no. 1 (2004): 1–11.

Ite, Uwem E. "Poverty Reduction in Resource-rich Developing Countries: What Have Multinational Corporations Got to Do with It?" *Journal of International Development* 17, no. 7 (2005): 913–29.

Jackson, Ben. "The Conceptual History of Social Justice." *Political Studies Review* 3, no. 3 (2005): 356–73.

Jackson, Gregory. "Stakeholders under Pressure: Corporate Governance and Labour Management in Germany and Japan." *Corporate Governance: An International Review* 13, no. 3 (2005): 419–28.

Jägers, Nicola M.C.P. *Corporate Human Rights Obligations: In Search of Accountability.* Anterwerpen, Oxford and New York: Intersentia, 2002.

Jamali, Dima. "The Case for Strategic Corporate Social Responsibility in Developing Countries." *Business and Society Review* 112, no. 1 (2007): 1–27.

Jarzabkowski, P., J. Matthiesen, and A. Van de Ven. "Doing Which Work? A Practice Approach to Institutional Pluralism." In *Institutional Work: Actors and Agency in Institutional Studies of Organization*, edited by T. Lawrence, R. Suddaby, and B. Leca, 284–316. Cambridge: Cambridge University Press, 2009.

Jawahar, I. M, and G. L. McLaughlin. "Toward a Descriptive Stakeholder Theory: An Organizational Life Cycle Approach." *Academy of Management Review* 26, no. 3 (2001): 397–414.

Jayne, M. R., and G. Skerratt. "Socially Responsible Investment in the UK: Criteria That Are Used to Evaluate Suitability." *Corporate Social Responsibility and Environmental Management* 10, no. 1 (2003): 1–11.

Jensen, Michael C. "Value Maximization, Stakeholder Theory, and the Corporate Objective Function." *Business Ethics Quarterly* 12, no. 2 (2000): 235–56.

Jensen, Michael C. "Value Maximisation, Stakeholder Theory, and the Corporate Objective Function." *European Financial Management* 7 (2001): 297–317.

Jensen, Michael C. "Value Maximisation, Stakeholder Theory, and the Corporate Objective Function." *Journal of Applied Corporate Finance* 22, no. 1 (2010): 32–42.

Johnson, R. B., and A. J. Onwuegbuzie. "Mixed Methods Research: A Research Paradigm Whose Time Has Come." *Educational Researcher* 33, no. 7 (2004): 14–26.

Jones, I. W., and M. G. Pollitt. "Ethical and Unethical Competition: Establishing the Rules of Engagement." *Long Range Planning* 31, no. 5 (1998):703–10.

Jones, M. T. "The Institutional Determinants of Social Responsibility." *Journal of Business Ethics* 20 (1999): 163–79.

Jones, Marc T. and P. Fleming. "Unpacking Complexity Through Critical Stakeholder Analysis: The Case of Globalization." Business and Society 42 no. 4 (2003): 430–455.

Jones, Thomas M. "Instrumental Stakeholder Theory: A Synthesis of Ethics and Economics." *Academy of Management Review* 20 (1995): 404–37.

Jones, Thomas M., W. Felps, and G. A. Bigley. "Ethical Theory and Stakeholder-related Decisions: The Role of Stakeholder Culture." *Academy of Management Review* 32, no. 1 (2007): 137–55.

Jordana, Jacint, and David Levi-Faur. "The Politics of Regulation in the Age of Governance." In *The Politics of Regulation: Institutions and Regulatory Reforms for the Age of Governance*, by Jacint Jordana and David Levi-Faur, 1–28. Cheltenham, UK: E. Elgar, 2004.

Joseph, Sarah. "An Overview of the Human Rights Accountability of Multinational Enterprises." In *Liability of Multinational Corporations under International Law*, by Menno T. Kamminga and Saman Zia-Zarifi, 75–93. The Hague: Kluwer Law International, 2000.

Kaku, Ryuzaburo. "The Path of Kyosei." *Harvard Business Review*, (July–August 1997): 57–61.

Kaler, John. "Morality and Strategy in Stakeholder Identification." *Journal of Business Ethics* 39, (2002): 91–99.

Kaler, John. "Differentiating Stakeholder Theories." *Journal of Business Ethics* 46 (2003): 71–83.

Kamminga, Menno, and Saman Zia-Zarifi. "Introduction." In *Liability of Multinational Corporations under International Law*, edited by Menno T. Kamminga and Saman Zia-Zarifi, 1–13. The Hague: Kluwer Law International, 2000.

Kamp, A., and P. Hagedorn-Rasmussen. "Diversity Management in a Danish Context: Towards a Multicultural or Segregated Working Life." *Economic and Industrial Democracy* 25, no. 4 (2004): 525–54.

Kang, Nahee. "A Critique of the 'Varieties of Capitalism' Approach." Nottingham University Business School, 2006. http://www.nottingham.ac.uk/business/ICCSR/pdf/ResearchPdfs/45-2006.pdf.

Kang, Nahee, and Moon, Jeremy. "Conceptualising National Variations and Change in CSR: An Exploration of the State-Led Model." Paper presented at the Society for the Advancement of Socio-Economics (SASE) conference on "Capitalism in Crisis," Sciences Po, Paris, 2009.

Karnoe, Peter. "The Dynamics of Framing in Transactional Spaces: The Co-Creation of Worth, Calculative Devices and Calculative Agencies in the Danish Wind Power Market." Copenhagen Business School Working Paper 18, 2004.

Kassinis, George, and Nikos Vafeas. "Stakeholder Pressures and Environmental Performance." *Academy of Management Journal* 49, no. 1 (2006): 145–59.

Kaufman, Christine. *Globalisation and Labour Rights. The Conflict between Core Labour Rights and International Economic Law.* Oxford: Hart, 2007.

Kaufmann, Daniel, Art Kraay, and Massimo Mastruzzi. "Governance Matters V: Aggregate and Individual Governance Indicators for 1996–2005." Social Science Research Network, 2008. http://papers.ssrn.com/sol3/papers.cfm?abstract_id=930847.

Kaul, I.G., and M.A. Stern. *Global Public Goods: International Cooperation in The 21st Century.* New York: Oxford University Press, 1999.

Kay, J. "The Stakeholder Corporation." In *Stakeholder Capitalism*, edited by G. Kelly, D. Kelly and A. Gamble, 125–141. London: Macmillan, 1997.

Kelly, G., D. Kelly, and A. Gamble, eds. *Stakeholder Capitalism.* Houndmills, Basignstoke: Macmillan, 1997.

King, Andrew. "Cooperation between Corporations and Environmental Groups: A Transaction Cost Perspective." *Academy of Management Review* 32, no. 3 (2007): 889–900.

Kjellberg, H., and C. Helgesson. "Multiple Versions of Markets: Multiplicity and Performativity in Market Practice." *Industrial Marketing Management* 35, no. 7 (2006): 839–55.

Kline, John M. "International Regulation of Transnational Business, Providing the Missing Leg of Global Investment Standards." *Transnational Corporations* 2, no. 1 (1993):153–64.

Knill, Christoph, and Dirk Lehmkuhl. "Private Actors and the State: Internationalization and Changing Patterns of Governance." *Governance* 15, no. 1 (2002): 41–63.

Kobrin, Stephen J. "Private Political Authority and Public Responsibility: Transnational Firms and Human Rights." *Business Ethics Quarterly* 19, no. 3 (2009): 349–74.

Konz, Gregory N.P., and Francis X. Ryan. "Maintaining an Organizational Spirituality: No Easy Task." *Journal of Organizational Change Management* 12, no. 3 (1999): 200–10.

Korhonen, Jouni. "The Dominant Economics Paradigm and Corporate Social Responsibility." *Corporate Social Responsibility and Environmental Management* 9, no. 1 (2002): 67–80.

Korten, David C. "The Responsibility of Business to the Whole," 2004. http://www.islandnet.com/plethora/mai/responsibility.html.

Kramer, H. "The Philosophical Foundations of Management Rediscovered." *Management International Review* 15, nos. 2–3 (1975): 47–55.

Krugman, Paul. "On Economic Hooliganism." *New York Times*, May 15, 2011. http:/www.nytimes.com/2011/05/15/magazine/paul-krugman-how-the-financial-crisis-was-wasted.html?pagewanted=1&_r=1&sq=paul krugman on the financial crisis&st=cse&scp=2.

Küng, Hans. *The Economic Crisis Requires a Global Ethic: The Manifesto for a Global Economic Ethic.* New York: Global Ethic Symposium, 2009.

Kuschnik, Bernhard. "On the Difficulties of Legally Regulating Multinational Enterprises." *European Business Law Review* 19, no. 5 (2008): 895–908.

Kusku, F., and A. Zarkada-Fraser. "An Empirical Investigation of Corporate Citizenship in Australia and Turkey." *British Journal of Management* 15 (2004): 57–72.

Kymlicka, Will. *Contemporary Political Philosophy: An Introduction.* Oxford: Clarendon Press, 1990.

Kysar, Douglas A. "Preferences for Processes: The Process/Product Distinction and the Regulation of Consumer Choice." *Harvard Law Review* 118, no. 2 (2004): 525–642.

Langlois, C. C., and B. B. Schlegelmilch. "Do Corporate Codes of Ethics Reflect National Character? Evidence from Europe and the United States." *Journal of International Business Studies* 21, no. 4 (1990): 519–39.

Lantos, Geoffrey P. "The Boundaries of Strategic Corporate Social Responsibility." *Journal of Consumer Marketing* 18, no. 7 (2001): 595–632.

Lawrence, T. B., and R. Suddaby. "Institutions and Institutional Work." In *Handbook of Organization Studies*, 2nd ed., edited by S. R. Clegg, C. Hardy, W. R. Nord, and T. Lawrence, 215–54. London: Sage, 2007.

Leader, S. "Human Rights Risks And New Strategies For Global Investment." Journal of International Economic Law 9 (2006): 657–705.

Leca, B., and P. Naccache. "A Critical Realist Approach to Institutional Entrepreneurship." *Organization* 13, no. 5 (2006): 627–51.

Lee, Min-Dong Paul. "Configuration of External Influences: The Combined Effects of Institutions and Stakeholders on Corporate Social Responsibility Strategies." *Journal of Business Ethics* 102 (2011): 291–98.

Li, Shaomin, Mark Fetscherin, Ilon Alon, Christoph Latteman, and Kuang Yeh. "Corporate Social Responsibility in Emerging Markets." *Management International Review* 50, no. 5 (2010): 635–54.

Lipschutz, Ronnie D., and Cathleen Fogel. "Regulation for the Rest of Us?" Global Civil Society and the Privatization of Transnational Regulation." In *The Emergence of Private Authority in Global Governance*, edited by Rodney Bruce Hall and Thomas J. Biersteker. Cambridge: Cambridge University Press, 2002.

Liptak, Adam. "Justices, 5–4, Reject Corporate Spending Limit." *New York Times*, January 21, 2010.

Loasby, Brian J. *Knowledge, Institutions, and Evolution in Economics.* London: Routledge, 1999.

Lodge, Martin. "Accountability and Transparency in Regulation: Critiques, Doctrines and Instruments." In *The Politics of Regulation: Institutions and Regulatory Reforms for the Age of Governance*, edited by Jacint Jordana and David Levi-Faur. Cheltenham, UK: E. Elgar, 2004.

Lohmann, Larry. "Marketing and Making Carbon Dumps: Commodification, Calculation and Counterfactuals in Climate Change Mitigation." *Science as Culture* 14, no. 3 (2005): 203–35.

Lounsbury, M. "Institutional Rationality and Practice Variation: New Directions in the Institutional Analysis of Practice." *Accounting, Organizations and Society* 33, nos. 4–5 (2008): 349–61.

Lowi, Theodore J. "American Business, Public Policy, Case Studies and Political Theory." *World Politics* 16, no. 4 (1964): 677–715.

Lucas, J.R. *Responsibility.* Oxford: Oxford University Press, 1993.

Macey, J.R. "Public choice: The theory of the firm and the theory of market exchange." Cornell Law Review 74 (1988): 43–77.

MacIntyre, Alasdair. *After Virtue: A Study In Moral Theory,* 2nd ed. Notre Dame, Indiana: University of Notre Dame Press, 1984.

MacKenzie, Donald, and Yuval Millo. "Constructing a Market, Performing Theory: The Historical Sociology of a Financial Derivatives Exchange." *American Journal of Sociology* 109, no. 1 (2003): 107–45.

Mackey, Alison, Tyson B. Mackey, and Jay B. Barney. "Corporate Social Responsibility and Firm Performance: Investor Preferences and Corporate Strategies." *Academy of Management Review* 32, no. 3 (2007): 817–35.

MacLeod, Sorcha. "The United Nations, Human Rights and Transnational Corporations: Challenging the International Legal Order." In *Perspectives on Corporate Social Responsibility,* edited by Nina Boeger, Rachel Murray, and Charlotte Villiers, 65–84. Cheltenham, Glos, UK: Edward Elgar, 2008.

Maignan, Isabelle. "Consumers' Perceptions of Corporate Social Responsibilities: A Cross-cultural Comparison." *Journal of Business Ethics* 30 (2001): 57–72.

Maignan, Isabelle, O. C. Ferrell, and G.T.M. Hult. "Corporate Citizenship: Cultural Antecedents and Business Benefits." *Journal of the Academy of Marketing Science* 27, no. 4 (1999): 455–69.

Mamic, Ivanka. "Managing Global Supply Chain: The Sports Footwear, Apparel and Retail Sectors." *Journal of Business Ethics* 59, no. 1–2 (2005): 81–100.

Marcoux, A.M. "Balancing Act." In Contemporary Issues in Business Ethics, 4th ed., edited by J.R. DesJardins and J.J. McCall, 92–98. Belmont, California: Wadsworth, 2000.

Marques, Jose C., and Peter Utting. *Corporate Social Responsibility and Regulatory Governance: Toward Inclusive Development?* New York: Palgrave Macmillan, 2009.

Marquis, Christopher, Mary Ann Glynn, and Gerald F. Davis. "Community Isomorphism and Corporate Social Action." *Academy of Management Review* 32, no. 3 (2007): 925–45.

Martiny, D. "Traditional Private and Commercial Law Rules under the Pressure of Global Transactions: the Role of an International Order." In Rules and Networks: the Legal Culture of Global Business Transactions, edited by R. Applebaum, W.L.F. Felstiner, and V. Gessner, 123–155. Oxford: Hart Publishing, 2001.

Matten, Dirk, and A. Crane. "Corporate Citizenship: Towards an Extended Theoretical Conceptualization." *Academy of Management Review* 30, no. 1 (2005): 166–79.

Matten, Dirk, and Jeremy Moon. "Implicit and Explicit CSR: A Conceptual Framework for a Comparative Understanding of Corporate Social Responsibility." *Academy of Management Review* 33, no. 2 (2008): 404–24.

Mattli, Walter, and Ngaire Woods, eds. *The Politics of Global Regulation.* Princeton, NJ: Princeton University Press, 2009.

McBarnet, Doreen J. "After Enron, Corporate Governance, Creative Compliance and the Uses of Corporate Social Responsibility." In *Governing the Corporation,* edited by Justin O'Brien. Chichester, England: John Wiley & Sons, 2005.

McBarnet, Doreen J. "Corporate Social Responsibility: Beyond Law, through Law, for Law: The New Corporate Accountability." In *The New Corporate Accountability: Corporate Social Responsibility and the Law,* edited by Doreen J. McBarnet, Aurora Voiculescu, and Tom Campbell. Cambridge: Cambridge University Press, 2007.

McBarnet, Doreen, and Marina Kurkchiyan. "Corporate Social Responsibility through Contractual Control? Global Supply Chains and 'Other-Regulation.'" In *The New Corporate Accountability: Corporate Social Responsibility and the Law,* edited by Doreen J. McBarnet, Aurora Voiculescu, and Tom Campbell. Cambridge: Cambridge University Press, 2007.

McGee, Andrew. "The Regulation of Insurance." In *Regulating Enterprise: Law and Business Organizations in the UK,* edited by David Milman. Oxford, UK, and Porland, OR: Hart Publishing, 1999.

McGee, Andrew, Christina Williams, and Gary Scanlan. *The Law of Business Organizations.* Exeter: Law Matters, 2005.

McKinsey Global Institute. "Mapping the Global Capital Market Third Annual Report," 2007. http://jwc.shfc.edu.cn/jryj/Upfiles/2007122184824187.pdf.

McLaren, Duncan. "Global Stakeholders: Corporate Accountability and Investor Engagement." *Corporate Governance* 12, no. 2 (2004): 191–201.

McLeay, Fiona. "Corporate Codes of Conduct and the Human Rights Accountability of Transnational Corporations: A Small Piece of a Larger Puzzle." In *Transnational Corporations and Human Rights,* edited by Olivier De. Schutter, 219–40. Oxford: Hart Publishing, 2006.

McNichol, Jason. "Transnational NGO Certification Programs as New Regulatory Forms: Lessons from the Forestry Sector." In *Transnational Governance: Institutional Dynamics of Regulation,* edited by Marie-Laure Djelic and Kerstin Sahlin-Andersson. Cambridge: Cambridge University Press, 2006.

McWilliams, Abagail, and Donald Siegel. "Corporate Social Responsibility: A Theory of the Firm Perspective." *Academy of Management Review* 26, no. 1 (2001): 7–127.

Meeran, Richard. "Liability of Multinational Corporations: A Critical Stage in the UK." In *Liability of Multinational Corporations under International Law,* edited by Menno T. Kamminga and Saman Zia-Zarifi, 251. The Hague; London; Boston: Kluwer Law International, 2000.

Metcalf, Cherie. "Corporate Social Responsibility as Global Public Law: Third Party Rankings as Regulation by Information." *Pace Environmental Law Review* 28, no. 1 (2010): 145–99.

Meyer, Klaus E. "Perspectives on Multinational Enterprises in Emerging Economies." *Journal of International Business Studies* 35, no. 4 (2004): 259–76.

Michalet, Charles-Albert. "Transnational Corporations and the Changing International Economic System." *Transnational Corporations* 3, no. 1 (1994): 6–22.

Midttun, Atle. "Partnered Governance: Aligning Corporate Responsibility and Public Policy in the Global Economy." *Corporate Governance* 8, no. 4 (2008): 406–18.

Miller, D. *Principles of Social Justice.* Cambridge, MA: Harvard University Press, 1999.

Mills, Stuart L., ed. *Corporate Violence: Injury and Death for Profit.* Totowa, NJ: Rowman & Littlefield, 1987.

Milman, David. "Regulation of Business Organizations into the Millennium." In *Regulating Enterprise: Law and Business Organizations in the UK,* edited by David Milman, 1. Oxford, and Portland, OR: Hart Publishing, 1999.

Mitchell, R., B. Agle, and D. Wood. "Towards a Theory of Stakeholder Identification: Defining the Principle of Who and What Really Counts." *Academy of Management Review* 22, no. 4 (1997): 853–86.

Mokhiber, Russell. *Corporate Crime and Violence: Big Business Power and the Abuse of the Public Trust.* San Francisco: Sierra Club, 1988.

Möllering, Guido. *Trust: Reason, Routine, Reflexivity.* Amsterdam: Elsevier, 2006.

Moon, Jeremy. "New Governance in Australian Schools: A Place for Business Social Responsibility?" *Australian Journal of Public Administration* 55, no. 1 (1998): 55–67.

Moon, Jeremy. "The Social Responsibility of Business and New Governance." *Government and Opposition* 37, no. 3 (2002): 385–408.

Moon, Jeremy, Nahee Kang, and Jean-Pascal Gond. "Corporate Social Responsibility and Government." In *The Oxford Handbook of Business and Government,* edited by David Coen, Wyn Grant, and Graham K. Wilson. New York: Oxford University Press, 2010.

Moon, Jeremy, and David Vogel. "Corporate Social Responsibility, Government and Civil Society." In *The Oxford Handbook of Corporate Social Responsibility,* edited by Andrew Crane, Abagail Williams, Dirk Matten, Jeremy Moon, and Donald S. Siegel. Oxford: Oxford University Press, 2008.

Morgan, G. "Transnational Actors, Transnational Institutions, Transnational Spaces: The Role of Law Firms in the Internationalisation of Competition Regulation." In *Transnational Regulation in the Making,* edited by M-L. Djelic and K. Sahlin-Anderson, 139–160. Cambridge: Cambridge University Press, 2006.

Morss, Elliot. "The New Global Players: How They Compete and Collaborate." *World Development* 19, no. 1 (1991).

Morth, Urika. "Soft Regulation and Global Democracy." In *Transnational Governance: Institutional Dynamics of Regulation,* edited by Marie-Laure Djelic and Kerstin Sahlin-Andersson. Cambridge: Cambridge University Press, 2006.

Muchlinski, Peter T. "Human Rights and Multinationals—Is There a Problem?" *International Affairs* 77, no. 1 (2001): 31–48.

Muchlinski, Peter. *Multinational Enterprises and the Law,* 2nd ed. Oxford: Oxford University Press, 2007a.

Muchlinski, Peter. *The New Corporate Accountability: Corporate Social Responsibility and the Law.* By Doreen J. McBarnet, Aurora Voiculescu, and Tom Campbell, 431–58. Cambridge: Cambridge University Press, 2007b.

Mullins, Laurie J. *Management and Organizational Behavior.* London: Pitman, 1989.

Mullins, Laurie J. *Management and Organisational Behaviour,* 6th ed. London: Financial Times Prentice Hall, 2002.

Muniesa, Fabian, and Michel Callon. "Economic Experiments and the Construction of Markets." In *Do Economists Make Markets?: On the Performativity of Economics,* edited by Donald A. MacKenzie, Fabian Muniesa, and Lucia Siu. Princeton, NJ: Princeton University Press, 2008.

Munro, R. "Alignment and Identity Work: The Study of Accounts and Accountability." In *Accountability: Power, Ethos and the Technologies of Managing,* edited by Rolland Munro and Jan Mouritsen, 1–19. London: Thompson Business Press, 1996.

Murphy, Craig. *International Organization and Industrial Change: Global Governance since 1850.* New York: Oxford University Press, 1994.

Newell, Peter. "Managing Multinationals: The Governance of Investment for the Environment." *Journal of International Development* 13, no. 7 (2002): 907–19.

Newell, Peter. "Citizenship, Accountability and Community: The Limits of the CSR Agenda." *International Affairs* 81, no. 3 (2005): 541–57.

Nicholls, Alex, and Charlotte Opal. *Fair Trade: Market-Driven Ethical Consumption.* London: SAGE, 2005.

North, D. C. *Institutions, Institutional Change and Economic Performance.* Cambridge: Cambridge University Press, 1990.

Nussbaum, Alexander (Sascha) K. "Ethical Corporate Social Responsibility (CSR) and the Pharmaceutical Industry: A Happy Couple?" *Journal of Medical Marketing* 9, no. 1 (2009): 67–76.

O'Dwyer, B. "The Construction of a Social Account: A Case Study in an Overseas Aid Agency." *Accounting, Organizations and Society* 30, no. 3 (2005): 279–96.

Oetzel, Jennifer, and Jonathan P. Doh. "MNEs and Development: A Review and Reconceptualization." *Journal of World Business* 44, no. 2 (2009): 108–20.

Ogus, A. I. *Regulation: Legal Form and Economic Theory.* Oxford: Clarendon Press, 1994.

Okoye, Adaeze. "Theorising Corporate Social Responsibility as an Essentially Contested Concept: Is a Definition Necessary?" *Journal of Business Ethics* 89, no. 4 (2009): 613–27.

Oppenheim, Lassa F. *International law*. London: Longman, 1905.

Organization for Economic Cooperation and Development, *Overview of Selected Initiatives and Instruments Relevant to Corporate Social Responsibility*. Paris: Organization for Economic Cooperation and Development, 2008.

Orlitzky, M., F. L. Schmidt, and S. L. Rynes. "Corporate Social and Financial Performance: A Meta-Analysis." *Organization Studies* 24, no. 3 (2003): 403–41.

Orpen, C. "The Attitudes of United States and South African Managers to Corporate Social Responsibility." *Journal of Business Ethics* 6, no. 2 (1987): 89–96.

Ostry, Silvia. "The Domestic Domain: The New International Policy Arena." *Transnational Corporations* 1, no. 1 (1992): 7.

Osuji, Onyeka K. "Fluidity Of Regulation-CSR Nexus: The Multinational Corporate Corruption Example." *Journal of Business Ethics* 103 (2011): 31–57.

Owen, David L., Tracey A. Swift, Christopher Humphrey, and Mary Bowerman. "The New Social Audits: Accountability, Managerial Capture or the Agenda of Social Champions?" *European Accounting Review* 9, no. 1 (2000): 81–98.

Pallot, June. "The Legitimate Concern with Fairness: A Comment." *Accounting, Organizations and Society* 2, no. 16 (1991): 201–8.

Parker, I. *Discourse Dynamics: Critical Analysis for Social and Individual Psychology*. London: Routledge, 1992.

Parkinson, John. "Corporate Governance and the Regulation of Business Behaviour." In *Global Governance and the Quest for Justice*, by Sorcha MacLeod, 1–26. Oxford: Hart, 2006.

Passas, N. "Lawful but Awful: 'Legal Corporate Crimes.'" *Journal of Socio-Economics* 34, no. 6 (2005): 771–86.

Patriotta, G., and K. Starkey. "From Utilitarian Morality to Moral Imagination: Reimagining the Business School." *Journal of Management Inquiry* 17, no. 4 (2008): 319–27.

Peters, Guy B. "Shouldn't Row, Can't Steer: What's a Government to Do?" *Public Policy and Administration* 12, no. 2 (1997): 51–61.

Petts, Judith. "Environmental Responsiveness, Individuals and Organizational Learning: SME Experience." *Journal of Environmental Planning and Management* 41, no. 6 (1998): 711–30.

Pfeffer, J. *Power in Organizations*. Boston, MA: Pitman, 1981.

Phillips, Nelson, and C. Hardy. *Discourse Analysis: Investigating Processes of Social Construction*. Thousand Oaks, CA: Sage, 2002.

Phillips, Nelson, Thomas B. Lawrence, and Cynthia Hardy. "Discourse and Institutions." *Academy of Management Review* 29 (2004): 635–52.

Phillips, Robert A. "Stakeholder Theory and a Principle of Fairness." *Business Ethics Quarterly* 7, no. 1 (1997): 51–66.

Phillips, Robert. *Stakeholder Theory and Organizational Ethics*. San Francisco, CA: Berrett-Koehler, 2003.

Phillips, Robert A., and Joshua D. Margolis. "Toward an Ethics of Organizations." *Business Ethics Quarterly* 9, no. 4 (1999): 619–38.

Porter, Michael. "CSR—A Religion with too Many Priests? *European Business Forum* 15 (2003).

Porter, Michael E., and Mark R. Kramer. "The Competitive Advantage of Corporate Philanthropy." *Harvard Business Review* 80, no. 12 (2002): 56–68.

Portes, Alejandro, and William Haller. "The Informal Economy." In *The Handbook of Economic Sociology*, 2nd ed., by Neil J. Smelser and Richard Swedberg. Princeton, NJ: Princeton University Press, 2005.

Posner, Richard A. *A Failure of Capitalism: The Crisis of '08 and the Descent into Depression*. Cambridge, MA: Harvard University Press, 2009.

Powell, Walter W., and Paul DiMaggio. *The New Institutionalism in Organizational Analysis*. Chicago: University of Chicago Press, 1991.

Prahalad, C. K., and Allen Hammond. "Serving the World's Poor, Profitably." *Harvard Business Review* 80, no. 9 (2002): 48–57.

Quazi, A. M., and D. O'Brien. "An Empirical Test of a Cross-national Model of Corporate Social Responsibility." *Journal of Business Ethics* 25 (2000): 33–51.

Radaelli, Claudio M., and Fabrizio De Francesco. *Regulatory Quality in Europe: Concepts, Measures and Policy Processes*. Manchester, England: Manchester University Press, 2007.

Ramamurti, Ravi. "Developing Countries and MNEs: Extending and Enriching the Research Agenda." *Journal of International Business Studies* 35, no. 4 (2004): 277–83.

Ramasastry, Anita. "Corporate Complicity: From Nuremberg to Rangoon—An Examination of Forced Labor Cases and Their Impact on the Liability of Multinational Corporations." *Berkeley Journal of International Law* 20 (2002): 91–159.

Rapakko, Timo. *Unlimited Liability in Multinationals*. The Hague: Kluwer, 1997.

Ratner, Steven. "Corporations and Human Rights: A Theory of Legal Responsibility." *Yale Law Journal* 111, no. 3 (2001): 443.

Raustiala, Kal. "The Architecture of International Cooperation: Transgovernmental Networks and the Future of International Law." Virginia Journal of International Law 43, no. 1 (2002): 1.

Rawls, John. *A Theory of Justice*. Oxford: Oxford University Press, 1971.

Rawls, John. *Political Liberalism*. New York: Columbia University Press, 1996.

Rawls, John. *Justice as Fairness: A Restatement*. Edited by Erin Kelly. Cambridge, MA: Harvard University Press, 2001.

Reay, T., and C. R. Hinings. "Managing the Rivalry of Competing Institutional Logics." *Organization Studies* 30, no. 6 (2009): 629–52.

Redmond, Paul. "Transnational Enterprise and Human Rights: Options for Standard Setting and Compliance." *International Lawyer* 37, no. 1 (2003): 69–102.

Reed, Darryl. "Three Realms of Corporate Responsibility: Distinguishing Legitimacy, Morality and Ethics." *Journal of Business Ethics* 21, no. 1 (1999): 23–25.

Reed, Darryl. "Corporate Governance Reforms in Developing Countries." *Journal of Business Ethics* 37, no. 3 (2002): 223–47.

Reese, Jon. "Money | Mail Online." *Mail Online*, September 27, 2008. http://www.dailymail.co.uk/money/index.html.

Reichman, Jerome H., and Rochelle C. Dreyfuss. "Harmonization without Consensus: Critical Reflections on Drafting a Substantive Patent Law." *Duke Law Journal* 57 (2007): 85–103.

Research Network for Business Sustainability. "Knowledge Forum on Valuing Business Sustainability." Report, 2008.

Rest, James R. *Moral Development: Advances in Research and Theory*. New York: Praeger, 1986.

Reynolds, Scott J., Frank C. Shultz, and David Hekman. "Stakeholder Theory and Managerial Decision-Making Constraints and Implications of Balancing Stakeholder Interests." *Journal of Business Ethics* 64 (2006): 285–301.

Rhodes, R.A.W. "Understanding Governance: Ten Years On." *Organization Studies* 28, no. 8 (2007): 1243–64.

Richardson, Benjamin J. "Keeping Ethical Investment Ethical: Regulatory Issues for Investing for Sustainability." *Journal of Business Ethics* 87, no. 4 (2009): 555–72.

Richter, Ulf H. "Drivers of Change: A Multiple-Case Study on the Process of Institutionalization of Corporate Responsibility among Three Multinational Companies." *Journal of Business Ethics* 102 (2011): 261–79.

Rieth, L. "Corporate Social Responsibility In Global Economic Governance: A Comparison Of The OECD Guidelines And The UN Global Compact." In *New Rules For Global Markets – Public And Private Governance In The World Economy,* edited by S. A. Schirm, 177–192. Basingstoke, UK: Palgrave Macmillan, 2004.

Ritchie, J., and J. Lewis. *Qualitative Research Practice: A Guide for Social Science Students and Researchers.* London: Sage, 2003.

Rivoli, P. and S. Waddock. "First They Ignore You . . . : The Time-Context Dynamic And Corporate Responsibility." California Management Review 53, no. 2 (2011): 87–104.

Robeco Investment Management and Booz & Company. "Responsible Investing: A Paradigm Shift—from Niche to Mainstream," 2007. http://www.robeco.com/eng/images/Whitepaper_Booz&co%20SRI_final_tcm143–113658.pdf.

Roberts, John, and Robert Scapens. "Accounting Systems and Systems of Accountability: Understanding Accounting Practices in Their Organizational Contexts." *Accounting, Organizations and Society* 10, no. 4 (1985): 443–56.

Roberts, Sarah. "Supply Chain Specific? Understanding the Patchy Success of Ethical Sourcing Initiatives." *Journal of Business Ethics* 44, no. 2/3 (2003): 159–70.

Rodriguez, Peter, Donald S. Siegel, Amy Hillman, and Lorraine Eden. "Three Lenses on the Multinational Enterprise: Politics, Corruption, and Corporate Social Responsibility."*Journal of International Business Studies* 37, no. 6 (2006): 733–46.

Rogowski, Ralf, and Ton Wilthagen. *Reflexive Labour Law: Studies in Industrial Relations and Employment Regulation.* Deventer, Netherlands: Kluwer Law and Taxation Pub., 1994.

Rosenau, James N. "Governance, Order and Change in World Politics." In *Governance without Government: Order and Change in World Politics,* edited by James N. Rosenau and Ernst Otto Czempiel, 1–29. Cambridge: Cambridge University Press, 1992.

Rowley, T. J. "Moving beyond Dyadic Ties: A Network Theory of Stakeholder Influences." *The Academy of Management Review* 22, no. 4 (1997): 887–910.

Ruggie, John G. "Business and Human Rights: The Evolving International Agenda." *Journal of International Law* 101, no. 4 (2007): 819–40.

Rugman, A. M., and A. Verbeke. "Commentary on 'Corporate Strategies and Environmental Regulations: An Organizing Framework.'" *Strategic Management Journal* 19, no. 4 (1998): 377–87.

Saha, M., and G. Darnton. "Green Companies or Green Con-panies: Are Companies Really Green, or Are They Pretending to Be." *Business and Society Review* 110, no. 2 (2005): 117–58.

Sako, Mari. *Prices, Quality and Trust: How Japanese and British Companies Manage Buyer Supplier Relations.* Cambridge: Cambridge University Press, 1992.

Sandel, Michael J. *Justice: What's the Right Thing to Do?* New York: Farrar, Straus and Giroux, 2009.

Sarbutts, Nigel. "Can SMEs 'Do' CSR? A Practitioner's View of the Ways Small- and Medium-Sized Enterprises Are Able to Manage Reputation through Corporate Social Responsibility." *Journal of Communication Management* 7, no. 1 (2003): 340–47.

Sauvant, Karl P. and Victoria Aranda, "The International Legal Framework for Transnational Corporations." In *Transnational Corporations: The International Legal Framework,* edited by A.A. Fatouros, 83–115. London: Routledge, 1994.

Schein, Edward. *Organizational Culture and Leadership.* San Francisco: Jossey-Bass, 1985.

Scherer, Andreas G., and Guido Palazzo. "Toward a Political Conception of Corporate Responsibility—Business and Society Seen from a Habermasian Perspective." *Academy of Management Review* (2007): 1096–120.

Scherer, Andreas G., and Guido Palazzo. "The New Political Role of Business in a Globalized World: A Review of a New Perspective on CSR and its Implications for the Firm, Governance, and Democracy." *Journal of Management Studies* 48, no. 4 (2011): 899–931.

Scherer, Andreas G., Guido Palazzo, and Dorothee Baumann. "Global Rules and Private Actors: Toward a New Role of Transnational Corporation in Global Governance." *Business Ethics Quarterly* 16, no. 4 (2006): 505–32.

Schneider, B. R. "Hierarchical Market Economies and Varieties of Capitalism in Latin America." *Journal of Latin American Studies* 41 (2009): 553–75.

Schwartz, Mark S., and Archie Carroll. "Corporate Social Responsibility: A Three-Dimensional Domain Approach." *Business Ethics Quarterly* 13 (2003): 503–30.

Scott, W. R. "The Adolescence of Institutional Theory." *Administrative Science Quarterly* 32, no. 4 (1987): 493–511.

Scott, W. R. *Institutions and Organizations*. Thousand Oaks, CA: Sage, 1995.

Scott, W. R., and J. W. Meyer. "The Organization of Societal Sectors." In *Organizational Environments: Ritual and Rationality*, edited by J. W. Meyer and W. Richard Scott, 129–53. Beverly Hills, CA: Sage, 1983.

Selznick, Phillip. *Regulatory Policy and the Social Sciences*. Edited by Roger G. Noll. Berkeley: University of California Press, 1985.

Sen, Amartya. *The Idea of Justice*. Cambridge, MA: Belknap Press of Harvard University Press, 2009.

Servais, Jean-Michel. *International Labour Law*. The Hague: Kluwer Law International, 2005.

Shane, Scott, and Sankaran Venkataraman. "The Promise of Entrepreneurship as a Field of Research." *Academy of Management Review* 25, no. 1 (2000): 217–26.

Shelton, D. "Environmental Justice in the Postmodern World." In *Environmental Justice And Market Mechanisms. Key Challenges For Environmental Law And Policy*, edited by K. Bosselman and B.J. Richardson, 21–29. The Hague, London and Boston: Kluwer, 1999.

Shum, P.K. and S. L. Yam. "Ethics and law: Guiding the invisible hand to correct corporate social responsibility externalities." *Journal of Business Ethics* 98 (2011), 549–571.

Simakova, E., and D. Neyland. "Marketing Mobile Futures: Assembling Constituencies and Creating Compelling Stories for an Emerging Technology." *Marketing Theory* 8, no. 1 (2008): 91–116.

Simmons, A. John. *Political Philosophy*. New York: Oxford University Press, 2008.

Singh, A. and A. Zammitt. Labour Standards and the 'Race to the Bottom': Rethinking Globalisation and Workers Rights from Developmental and Solidaristic Perspectives. ESRC Centre for Business Research, University of Cambridge, Working Paper 279, 2004.

Sklair, Leslie. The Transnational Capitalist Class. Malden, Blackwell, 2001.

Slinger, G. "Spanning the Gap: The Theoretical Principles That Connect Stakeholder Policies to Business Performance." *Corporate Governance: An International Review* 7, no. 2 (1999): 136–51.

Smart, J. J. C., and Bernard Arthur Owen Williams. *Utilitarianism; For and Against*. Cambridge: Cambridge University Press, 1973.

Smith, Adam. "An Inquiry into the Nature and Causes of the Wealth of Nations." In *The Glasgow Edition of the Works and Correspondence of Adam Smith*, edited by R.H. Campbell. Oxford: Clarendon Press, 1976.

Smith, N. C. "Corporate Social Responsibility: Not Whether, but How?" London Business School Centre for Marketing Working Paper No. 03–701 (2003):1–35.

Smith, Roy C., and Ingo Walter. *Governing the Modern Corporation: Capital Markets, Corporate Control, and Economic Performance.* New York: Oxford University Press, 2006.

Snyder, Francis. "Soft Law and Institutional Practice in the European Community." In *The Construction of Europe,* edited by Stephen Martin. London: Kluwer, 1993.

Spekman, R. E., P. Werhane, and D. E. Boyd. "Corporate Social Responsibility and Global Supply Chain Management: A Normative Perspective." Darden Business School Working Paper No. 04–05. 2005. http://ssrn.com/abstract=655223.

Spence, Laura. "Does Size Matter? The State of the Art in Small Business Ethics." *Business Ethics: A European Review* 8, no. 3 (1999):163–74.

Spender, Peta. "Scenes from a Wharf: Containing the Morality of Corporate Law." In *International Corporate Law,* Vol. 1, edited by Fiona Macmillan, 37–68. Portland, OR: Oxford University Press, 2000.

Starik, M. "What Is a Stakeholder?" In *Toronto Conference: Reflections on Stakeholder Theory, Business & Society* 33 (1994): 82–131, 89–95.

Starik, M. "Should Trees Have Managerial Standing? Toward Stakeholder Status for Nonhuman Nature." *Journal of Business Ethics* 14 (1995): 207–18.

Stark, A. "What's the Matter with Business Ethics?" *Harvard Business Review* 71, no. 3 (1993): 38–40, 43–44, 46–48.

Starkey, K., and Sue Tempest. "The Future of the Business School: Knowledge Challenges and Opportunities." *Human Relations* 58, no. 1 (2005): 61–82.

Stenberg, E. *Corporate Governance: Accountability in the Marketplace.* London: The Institute of Economic Affairs, 2000.

Stephens, B. "Corporate Accountability: International Human Rights Litigation Against Corporations In US Courts." In *Liability Of Multinational Enterprises Under International Law,* edited by M. T. Kamminga & S. Zia-Zarifi, 209–229. The Hague: Kluwer, 2000.

Sterba, J. P. *Justice: Alternative Political Perspectives.* Boston: Wadsworth/Thomson, 2003.

Stern, Robert N., and Stephen R. Barley. "Organizations and Social Systems: Organization Theory's Neglected Mandate." *Administrative Science Quarterly* 41 (1996): 146–62.

Stevens, Beth. "Corporate Accountability: International Human Rights Litigation against Corporations in US Courts." In *Liability of Multinational Corporations under International Law,* by Menno T. Kamminga and Saman Zia-Zarifi, 209–29. The Hague: Kluwer Law International, 2000.

Stiglitz, Joseph E. *Globalization and Its Discontents.* New York: W. W. Norton, 2002.

Stiglitz, Joseph. "Guided by an Invisible Hand.." *New Statesman,* October 16, 2008. http://www.newstatesman.com/business/2008/10/economy-world-crisis-financial.

Stiglitz, Joseph E. *Freefall: America, Free Markets, and the Sinking of the World Economy.* New York: W. W. Norton, 2010.

Stopford, John M. "The Growing Interdependence between National Corporations and Governments. *Transnational Corporations* 3, no. 1 (1994): 53–76.

Stovall, O. S., J. D. Neill and B. Reid, "Institutional Impediments to Voluntary Ethics Measurement Systems: An International Perspective." *Journal of Applied Business Research* 25, no. 2 (2009): 119–126.

Streeck, Wolfgang, and Philippe Schmitter. "Community, Market, State – and Associations? The Prospective Contribution of Interest Governance to Social Order." In *Private Interest Government: Beyond Market and State,* edited by W. Streeck and P. C. Schmitter, 1–29. London: Sage,

Sullivan, R. "Legislating for Responsible Corporate Behaviour: Domestic Law Approaches to an International Issue." In *Global Governance and the Quest for Justice. Volume II: Corporate Governance,* edited by S. MacLeod, 183–196. Oxford and Portland: Hart, 2006.

Sunstein, Cass R. *Free Markets and Social Justice.* Oxford: Oxford University Press, 1997.

Swedberg, Richard. *Principles of Economic Sociology.* Princeton, NJ: Princeton University Press, 2003.

Swift, Adam. *Political Philosophy.* Cambridge, UK: Polity Press, 2007.

Swift, Tracey. "Trust, Reputation and Corporate Accountability to Stakeholders." *Business Ethics: A European Review* 10, no. 1 (2001): 16–26.

Swyngedouw, E. "Globalisation or 'Glocalisation'? Networks, Territories and Rescaling." *Cambridge Review of International Affairs* 17, no. 1 (2004): 25–48.

Synnestvedt, T., and I. Aslaksen. "Ethical Investment and the Incentives for Corporate Environmental Protection and Social Responsibility." *Corporate Social Responsibility and Environmental Management* 10, no. 4 (2003): 212–23.

Taylor, J. R., F. Cooren, N. Giroux, and D. Robichaud. "The Communicational Basis of Organization: Between the Conversation and the Text." *Communication Theory* 6 (1996): 1–39.

Teece, David J. "Technology Transfer by Multinational Firms: The Resource Cost of Transferring Technological Know-How." *Economic Journal* 87 (1977): 242–61.

Tofalo, Ines. "Overt and Hidden Accomplices: Transnational Corporations' Range of Complicity for Human Rights Violations." In *Transnational Corporations and Human Rights,* by Olivier De. Schutter, 335–58. Oxford: Hart Publishing, 2006.

Treviño, Linda Klebe. "Moral Reasoning and Business Ethics: Implications for Research, Education, and Management." *Journal of Business Ethics* 11, no. 5–6 (1992): 445–59.

Treviño, Linda Klebe, and Katherine A. Nelson. *Managing Business Ethics: Straight Talk about How to Do It Right.* New York: J. Wiley, 1999.

United Nations Environment Programme (UNEP). "Press Releases August 2011—UNEP." August 4, 2011. http://www.unep.org/newscentre/default.aspx?DocumentID=2649.

United Nations Environment Programme Finance Initiative (UNEPFI). "The Materiality of Social, Environmental and Corporate Governance Issues to Equity Pricing." Report, 2004.

Utting, Peter, and Jose C. Marques. *Corporate Social Responsibility and Regulatory Governance: Toward Inclusive Development?* New York: Palgrave Macmillan, 2009.

Vagts, Detlev F. "The Multinational Enterprise: A New Challenge for Transnational Law." *Harvard Law Review* 83, no. 4 (1970): 739–92.

Vagts, Detlev. "And the Multinational Enterprise: The Costs of Illumination." In *Legal Problems of Codes of Conduct for Multinational Enterprises,* edited by Norbert Horn. Antwerp: Kluwer-Deventer, 1980.

Van Der Bly, M.C.E. "Globalization and the Rise of One Heterogeneous World Culture: A Microperspective of a Global Village." *International Journal of Comparative Sociology* 48, nos. 2–3 (2007): 234–56.

Van Marrewijk, Marcel. "Concepts and Definitions of CSR and Corporate Sustainability: Between Agency and Communion." *Journal of Business Ethics* 44 (2003): 95–105.

Vernon, Raymond. "Transnational Corporations. Where Are They Coming From, Where Are They Headed?" *Transnational Corporations* 1, no. 2 (1992): 7–35.

Vidal, John. "Nigeria on Alert as Shell Announces Worst Oil Spill in a Decade." *Guardian,* December 22, 2011. http://www.guardian.co.uk/environment/2011/dec/22/nigerian-shell-oil-spill? intcmp=239.

Visser, Wayne. "Meaning in the Life and Work of Corporate Sustainability Managers." PhD dissertation (Business and Management), University of Nottingham Business School, UK, 2007.

Vitols, S. "Varieties of Corporate Governance: Comparing Germany and the UK." In *Varieties of Capitalism: The Institutional Foundations of Comparative*

Advantage, edited by P. A. Hall and D. Soskice, 337–60. Oxford: Oxford University Press, 2001.

Vogel, David. *The Market for Virtue. The Potential and Limits of Corporate Social Responsibility*. Washington, DC: Brookings Institution Press, 2005.

Vogel, David. "Private Global Business Regulation." *Annual Review of Political Science* 11, no. 1 (2008): 261–82.

Vogel, Kenneth. "2010 Complete Election Coverage: Court Decision Opens Floodgates for Corporate Cash." Politico.com, January 21, 2010. http://www.politico.com/news/stories/0110/31786.html.

Vogelaar, T. W. "The OECD Guidelines: Their Philosophy, History, Negotiation, Form, Legal Nature, Follow-Up Procedures And Review." In *Legal Problems Of Codes Of Conduct For International Enterprises*, edited by N. Horn, 127–139. London: Kluwer-Deventer, 1980.

Voiculescu, A. "Towards an acquisition of human rights by way of business practices." In *Global Governance and the Quest for Justice. Volume II: Corporate Governance*, edited by S. MacLeod, 239–262. Oxford: Hart, 2007.

Warhurst, A. "Corporate Citizenship as Corporate Social Investment." *Journal of Corporate Citizenship* 1 (2001): 57–73.

Wartick, S.L., and P.L. Cochran. "The Evolution of the Corporate Social Performance Model." *Academy of Management Review* 10 (1985): 758–69.

Weissbrodt, David, and Muria Kruger. "Norms on the Responsibilities of Transnational Corporations and Other Business Enterprises with Regard to Human Rights." *American Journal of International Law* 97 (2003): 901.

Welford, R. "Globalization, Corporate Social Responsibility and Human Rights." *Corporate Social Responsibility and Environmental Management* 9, no. 1 (2002): 1–7.

WestLB. "What Really Counts: The Materiality of Extra-Financial Factors." Report, 2007.

Wettstein, Florian. *Multinational Corporations and Global Justice: Human Rights Obligations of a Quasi-Governmental Institution*. Stanford, CA: Stanford University Press, 2009.

Whitley, Richard. "Internationalization and Varieties of Capitalism: The Limited Effects of Cross-National Coordination of Economic Activities on the Nature of Business Systems." *Review of International Political Economy* 5, no. 3 (1998): 445–81.

Whitley, Richard. *Divergent Capitalisms: The Social Structuring and Change of Business Systems*. Oxford: Oxford University Press, 1999.

Wiig, Arne, and Ivar Kolstad. "Multinational Corporations and Host Country Institutions: A Case Study of CSR Activities in Angola." *International Business Review* 19, no. 2 (2010): 178–90.

Williams, Paul F. "The Legitimate Concern with Fairness. *Accounting, Organizations and Society* 12, no. 2 (1987): 169–89.

Williams, Simon. "How Principles Benefit the Bottom-Line: The Experience of the Co-Operative Bank." In *Human Rights Standards and the Responsibility of Transnational Corporations*, by Michael K. Addo, 63–68. The Hague: Kluwer Law International, 1999.

Williamson, Oliver E. *The Economics of Discretionary Behaviour*. New York: Prentice Hall, 1964.

Williamson, Oliver E. *The Mechanisms of Governance*. New York: Oxford, 1996.

Windsor, Duane. "The Future of Corporate Social Responsibility." *International Journal of Organizational Analysis* 9, no. 3 (2001): 225–56.

Windsor, Duane. "Corporate Social Responsibility: Three Key Approaches." *Journal of Management Studies* 43, no. 1 (2006): 93–114.

Wood, Geoffrey. "The Institutional Basis of Economic Failure: Anatomy of the Segmented Business System." *Socio-Economic Review* 4, no. 2 (2006): 239–77.

Wood, Geoffrey, and George J. Frynas. "The Institutional Basis of Economic Failure: Anatomy of the Segmented Business System." *Socio-Economic Review* 4, no. 2 (2006): 239–77.

Wood, Graham. "Ethical Issues in Purchasing." In *The Ethical Organization*, 21–38. Basingstoke: MacMillan, 1996.

Worthington, I., M. Ram, and T. Jones. "Exploring Corporate Social Responsibility in the U.K. Asian Small Business Community." *Journal of Business Ethics* 67 (2006): 201–17.

Yeung, Karen. *Securing Compliance: A Principled Approach.* Oxford, UK: Hart Publishing, 2004.

Yosifon, David G. "The Public Choice Problem in Corporate Law: Corporate Social Responsibility after Citizens United." *North Carolina Law Review* 89 (2011): 1197–247.

Zadek, Simon. "The Path to Corporate Responsibility." *Harvard Business Review* 82, no. 12 (2004): 125–32.

Zadek, Simon. "Responsible Competitiveness: Reshaping Global Markets through Responsible Business Practices." *Corporate Governance* 6, no. 4 (2006): 334–48.

Zadek, Simon. *The Civil Corporation. The New Economy Of Corporate Citizenship.* London: Earth Scan, 2007.

Zairi, M., and J. Peters. "The Impact of Social Responsibility on Business Performance." *Managerial Auditing Journal* 17, no. 4 (2002): 174–78.

Zerk, Jennifer A. *Multinationals and Corporate Social Responsibility, Limitations and Opportunities in International Law.* Cambridge: Cambridge University Press, 2006.

Zia-Zarifi, S. "Suing MNEs in the U.S. for Violating International Law." *UCLA Journal of International Law and Foreign Affairs* 4 (1999): 81–147.

Zyglidopoulos, Stelios. "The Social and Environmental Responsibilities of Multinationals: Evidence from the Brent Spar Case." *Journal of Business Ethics* 36, no. 1–2 (2002): 141–51.

CASES

The Albazero [1977] A.C. 774.

Amoco Cadiz [1984] 2 Lloys Rep. 304.

Atlas Maritime Co. v. Avalon Maritime Ltd (No 1) [1991] 4 All ER 769 (Staughton LJ).

Bosal Holding BV [2003] STC 1483.

Bowoto v. Chevron No. C99–2506 CAL (ND Calif.).

Cape Industries v. Adams [1990] Ch 433.

Dartmouth College v. Woodward [1819] 4 Wheaton (U.S.) 518, 4 L.Ed. 629 at p. 636.

DHN Food Distributors Ltd v. London Borough of Tower Hamlets [1976] 1 WLR 852 (Lord Denning).

First National Bank v. Belotti [1978] 435 U.S. 765.

ICI v. Colmer [1998] STC 874.

Littlewoods Mail Order Stores v. Inland Revenue Commissioners [1969] 1 W.L.R. 1241 at 1254; [1969] 3 All ER 855 at 860 (Lord Denning).

Maritime Union of Australia v. Patrick Stevedores Operations No. 1 Pty Ltd [1998] 153 ALR 602 (North J.).

Patrick Stevedores Operations No 2 Pty Ltd v. Maritime Union of Australia [1998] 153 ALR 643.

Re Union Carbide Gas Plant Disaster at Bhopal India 634 F.Supp. 842 [SYDY 1986], 25 ILM 771 [1986]; affirmed as modified 809 F.2nd 195 [2nd Cir. 1987], 26 ILM 1008 [1987]; Cert.den. 108 S.Ct. 199 [1987].

Salomon v. Salomon & Co. [1897] A.C. 22.

Santa Clara County v. Southern P.R. Co. [1886] 188 U.S. 394.

WEBSITES

http://www.derrickfarnell.org/articles/Responsibility_without_Answerability.htm

http://www3.baylor.edu/American_Jewish/resources/jphil_articles/Levinas-violence.pdf

http://www3.baylor.edu/American_Jewish/resources/jphil_articles/levinas.htm

http://www.lamp.ac.uk/philosophy/Part%20Two%20Courses/modules/far.html

http://www.derrickfarnell.org/articles/Responsibility_without_Answerability.htm

http://www.cleanclothes.org/codes/ccccode.htm

http://www.opsi.gov.uk/acts/acts1996/96018-ah.htm#231

http://www.via3.net/pooled/articles/BF_DOCART/view.asp?Q=BF_DOCART_110951

http://www.businesshumanrights.org/Categories/Lawlawsuits/Lawsuitsregulatory action/Lawsui

About the Authors

KENNETH AMAESHI is the director of the Sustainable Business Initiative at the University of Edinburgh Business School, United Kingdom, where he is also an associate professor (reader) in strategy and international business. He is a visiting faculty at Cranfield School of Management, UK, and the Lagos Business School, Nigeria. He consults for multinational corporations, NGOs, and governments in the broad areas of strategic corporate responsibility and governance, sustainability strategy and sustainable investing, and stakeholder strategy and reputation management.

PAUL NNODIM is an associate professor and the chair of the Department of Philosophy, Interdisciplinary Studies, and Modern Languages at Massachusetts College of Liberal Arts (Massachusetts State University System), Massachusetts, United States.

ONYEKA OSUJI is a senior lecturer in law at the University of Exeter, United Kingdom. His research interests include corporate social responsibility, corporate governance, nonfinancial reporting, globalization, multinational enterprises, and regulation. He is qualified as a barrister and solicitor of Nigeria and a solicitor of England and Wales and has advised individuals, corporations, and national and international governmental and nongovernmental organizations.

Index